THE NEW COMPLETE
BRITTANY

Ch. Auten's Max-A-Millon on point, owned
by Carol Auten.

Ch. Shannon Creek Sir Blu (Ch. Shannon Creek Jacques ex Ch. Shannon Creek Star O'Edwards), shown winning Best of Breed at the American Brittany Club Specialty, Ravenna, Ohio, 1985. Yoko O'Shell handled the dog under judge Mrs. Elaine E. Mathis for owners Mark S. Schneck and Fukue M. O'Shell. *Alverson photo.*

The NEW Complete

BRITTANY

by Maxwell Riddle

SECOND EDITION

Macmillan General Reference
A Simon & Schuster Macmillan Company
1633 Broadway
New York, NY 10019-6785

Library of Congress Cataloging-in-Publication Data

Riddle, Maxwell.
    The new complete Brittany.

      Rev. ed. of: The complete Brittany spaniel.   1974.
      1. Brittany spaniel. I. Riddle, Maxwell.
Complete Brittany spaniel. II. Title.
SF429.B78R52   1987   636.7′52   87-3891
ISBN 0-87605-090-9

10 9 8

Printed in the United States of America

Contents

Foreword

N O MAN WALKS ALONE. A book is never the work of one man alone, whether it is a technical book such as this one or a novel. The author is indebted to many people, living and dead, for their help. The following are only a few of the acknowledgements that could be made.

In preparing this book, I have had the use of three great libraries: those of the American Kennel Club and the Cleveland Public Library, and the private library of Herm David. I have had the use of the American, Canadian and French Kennel Club stud books. A. Hamilton Rowan Jr., secretary of the American Kennel Club, gave personal help. The Canadian Kennel Club permitted me to check through the records of every Brittany Spaniel registered in Canada up to July, 1971.

I gratefully acknowledge the help given to me by Jacques R. Joubert, brother of René; Mrs. Gertrude L. Thebaud, widow of Louis A. Thebaud; and by Mme Monica Choulot, daughter of Juan Pugibet. Mrs. René Joubert and Mrs. Walter B. Kleeman also supplied valuable information and pictures. Mme Genie Rundle also helped in supplying information on the modern Brittany Spaniel in France.

Jack L. Whitworth and Donald L. Benjamin supplied valuable early information. John G. and Ellyn Lee, and Mr. and Mrs. James Cohen also helped. So did Bill Brown and his staff at the *American Field.* I am indebted, too, to Mrs. Nicky Bissell, brilliant editor of the *American Brittany Magazine,* and to Mrs. LaReine Pittman, secretary of the Missouri regional club.

In Canada, Jack Mayer of Moncton, N.B., Bill McClure of Manotic, Ontario, and Mrs. Pat Ristau of Regina, Sask. helped.

The magazine *Brittany Field and Bench,* which has become the *American Brittany Magazine,* has been a treasure chest of information. Jack Whitworth and the Lees supplied most of the past issues for reference.

The people who made the magazine, and who have kept its high quality, deserve both credit and thanks. They are Jack Whitworth, Dr. David Ruskin, Hugo Blasberg, Mrs. Evelyn Monte Van Horn, Dr. Allen Truex, Dr. Fred Z. White, Mrs. Nicky Bissell and others. In addition, Dr. White was the author of the *Brittany Spaniel In America.*

A special thanks goes to Señora Thelma von Thaden of the Mexican Kennel Club for her help. To others whom I may have overlooked, though not intentionally, my grateful thanks.

Maxwell Riddle

Dual Ch. Faulkner's Reddy, owned by Ejner and Gilda Lund.

Foreword to the
New Edition

IT IS NEARLY 15 years since I completed work on the first edition of *The Complete Brittany Spaniel.* At first I thought of scrapping the foreword to the first edition and writing a new one. But somehow I couldn't do it. I owed too much to too many people, and I might have to cut out some of them and, among other things, cause confusion. They gave freely of their time and memories. It was the same with the pictures. A new edition will have to have new pictures, which might require deleting older ones. That would mean scrapping the pictures of some of the great pioneers, and some who had been very dear personal friends. Of course, a writer does not always have free say in this. The publisher has a budget and a page limit, and this affects his judgment as to what pictures should be taken out.

Over the past fifty years, I have had dealings with several dozen national "parent clubs" of various breeds. For the most part, this has been frustrating. In trying to establish a sum total of the dual champions in the world, I have had little success. For the most part, club factions interfere. Often I get the answer "We have no idea." So I can be truthful in saying that The American Brittany Club is the finest national club in America, and so far as I can determine, one of the finest in the world. I am not bragging about the breed I admire so much, but am simply telling the truth as I have found it to be.

For this revised edition I have used every source available, and always people have responded enthusiastically. LaReine Pittman is gone. This book is dedicted to Nicky Bissell, an incomparable statistician, a breeder and

11

trainer, and above all, an enthusiastic helper to all who wanted to get information on the Brittany. Some of the editors who have kept the *American Brittany Magazine* the best in America have been Evelyn Monte Van Horn, Joy Watkins, Linda Young, Rheta Cartmell, and now, Ella Conable, whose many-faceted talents have brought her into the Life Members group, and thus, never to be forgotten.

I have used the staff of the American Kennel Club, and particularly Roberta Vesley, the AKC librarian. I never cease to be astonished when I call Velma Tiedeman and find her always there, willing to help, supplying even more information than I had asked for. Bill Brown is gone from the *American Field*, but Bernie Matthys is there, willing to help wherever he can. And Barbara Wade is also willing and competent. Finally, Rheta Cartmell, the new club statistician, is a worthy successor to those who have gone before her.

Always the story of Alan Stuyvesant has fascinated me. He did so much for the breed, and yet so little was known about him, even by those of his day. So I have devoted a chapter to him using material from France, *The New York Times,* and libraries in the Allamuchy, New Jersey area. Since my French has deteriorated, I am indebted to Professor George Gautier of Hiram College for making translations for me; to M. Pouchain, so great a world figure in the breed, for allowing me to quote from his great book, *L'Epagneul Breton;* and to his friend and publisher, M. Robert Thenlot who, beside granting permission, sent me the records of some of the best dogs, bench and field, in France.

I should perhaps correct one error in the first foreword. Mrs. Pat Ristau does not live in Regina, but in Saskatoon, Saskatchewan. She and Ed Dixon, Vice President of the Canadian Kennel Club, as well as Mrs. Michele McIntyre, have helped me. There are others, I am sure, and I beg their pardon for leaving them out. Lastly I thank my wife, Lenora, for her assistance in typing and sorting out the new material.

Maxwell Riddle

The Brittany Spaniel
Becomes the Brittany

WHEN THE AMERICAN BRITTANY Club was given final recognition by the American Kennel Club on July 14, 1944, the newly formed club asked to have the name of the breed changed from Brittany Spaniel to Brittany. The feeling was that the Brittany Spaniel was a true pointing dog, and thus should not be lumped in with the spaniels, which are flushing dogs. The request was denied. The American Kennel Club was not prepared to change a breed name from other than that of its country of origin.

However, in the following years, the Brittany proved to be an outstanding pointing dog, an intense hunter of upland game, and one with the greatest record of producing dual champions in the world. It was evident also that the dog ranged in greater patterns than is required of spaniels. So, after considering the request again, the American Kennel Club agreed to drop the "spaniel."

The name change was voted upon at the April, 1982 meeting of the AKC Board of Directors, was then published in *Pure-bred Dogs—American Kennel Gazette,* and became effective on September 1, 1982. However, the Brittany remains the Brittany Spaniel in all other countries, including Canada, Mexico, the F.C.I. (Federation Cynologique Internationale), and the country of the Brittany's origin, France.

This has presented problems for the author. Should he go through the entire book, eliminating the word "spaniel" wherever it appeared? Or should he eliminate the word only in chapters dealing with the present? Which would create the least confusion? Can one legitimately change a breed name of a dog that won its championship under that name? Records live and in the records the dog is a Brittany Spaniel. Moreover, in the first sentence of the official standard the Brittany is called a leggy "spaniel" and is again called a spaniel in the section on feet. The author cannot change the official standard by eliminating the two "spaniels." If he could, what words could replace it— "leggy dog"?

While no answer will be totally satisfactory, the author has felt that he should leave the early history as it was when made. In one sense, this has been made easier by the practice of the national and regional clubs of always listing their events under "Brittany," as for instance American Brittany Futurity.

Ch. Suzabob's Bobo, C.D. on point and being backed by his liver and white son Suzabob's Five O'Clock Shadow. Both dogs are owned by R. E. Young.

A Note on Brittany
Names and Spellings

THE NAMES GIVEN TO dogs are often complicated. Owners may misspell them in their registration applications. Importers may misspell them. Confusion sometimes results. In this book, the author has used the actual names registered, even though the dogs have been customarily known by a slightly different name.

There are two examples that may be used. The first American champion was an imported dog. In both the French and American stud books, the dog is listed as Hasbask Guid de Charvogue. But the dog was usually known as Habask Guid de Charvogue.

Louis A. Thebaud imported Franche du Cosquerou. The dog was sent to Eudore Chevrier's kennels at Winnipeg to be used at stud. Chevrier returned him to Thebaud, who then sent him to René Joubert at Detroit. This dog became, under Joubert's handling, one of the most famous of all time. He impressed the entire Midwest sporting world. Everyone—Thebaud, Joubert, and all sportsmen—knew the dog as Fanche. But he was registered in the French, American, and Canadian stud books as Franche.

Many of the early dogs were registered first in the *Field Dog Stud Book*. Dr. R. C. Busteed registered a dog in that stud book as Broad Arrow of Richmont. The dog was later registered in the American Kennel Club as Broad Archer of Richmont. As such, he became a dual champion.

In general, French breeders have used "de," which means "of," without capitalizing. Most Americans, and some Canadians, have capitalized it.

However, this has not always been the case, so no generalization can be made.

Typists may further confuse the matter by using the lower case once and the upper case the next time. Thus, Mae de Cornean is the French name and spelling. But it sometimes appears as Mae De Cornean.

"Cornouaille" is the Breton name for Cornwall. Dr. Chester Keough named his kennel MacEochaidh. It is said to be the Gaelic for Keough. The "Mac" makes it "son of."

The Michigan State Dog

In 1957, the Gaines Dog Research Center suggested that states should have official state dogs. Harry Miller, then director of the Research Center, argued that states had official state flowers and, many of them, official state birds. Why not a state dog? Harvey Barcus, of the *Detroit News,* thought this was a great idea. Barcus talked to state officials, and then convinced *The News* to conduct a statewide poll. The breed that got the most votes would then be declared the official Michigan State Dog.

Ballots were sent out over the state and Barcus, who was dog editor, also published one in *The News.* When balloting had ended, 29,245 people had thought enough of the project to vote. Of these, 6,407 voted for the Brittany. The breed led all the others by a wide margin. This was adequate testimony on the popularity of the Brittany in Michigan and the place it had won in the hearts of sportsmen in less than 25 years.

Detroit City Historian, George W. Stark, was also interested in the project. "There is definite evidence," he reported, "that the Brittany was brought here by Cadillac when he founded Detroit in 1701, and began to colonize the Detroit Shore." We do not know the source of his evidence. But those wishing to believe it can claim that the Brittany arrived in Canada and what would later become the United States with some of the first white settlers.

1

The Development of Bird Dogs

THE ARTS OF THE pointing dog and the flushing spaniel were developed more than 300 years ago. These were dogs with highly developed aptitudes for using wind-borne scents in locating upland game birds. There are no names in this period. We do not know how the training and hunting procedures were developed. But we can speculate upon why they arose.

During the 16th century—the great age of discovery—a landed gentry came into being. World discovery was followed by world conquest. The treasuries of the explorer nations—England, France, Spain, and Portugal— were filled with gold. So were the pockets of the merchants and artisans. From these two groups there came the landed gentry. They were not nobles. They were gentlemen. They had the leisure time for field sports, for hunting and fishing. This was particularly so in England.

By 1650, a wealthy middle class had sprung up. This was particularly so in England. More and more men found more and more time to fish for trout or to hunt for upland game. The passion these men had for hunting and fishing led to a demand for authoritative texts on the subjects.

Izaak Walton is one of the most famous of all the world's authors. He wrote excellent biographies. But he lives for most of us because of *The Compleat Angler*. The first edition was published in 1653 and had 13 chapters. The fifth edition, published in 1676, had 21.

In 1674, Nicholas Cox wrote *The Gentleman's Recreation*. Cox had a remarkable understanding of dogs, and of their uses in the field. In his own time, and for a century later, Cox was as famous as Walton. The sixth edition of his book was published in 1721.

Cox included a section on partridge hunting with dogs. We quote it here because it is a classic description of the use of dogs:

There is no Art to taking Partridges so excellent and pleasant as by the help of a Setting Dog; wherefore before we proceed to the Sport we shall give you an Account of what this Setting Dog is.

You are to understand then, that a Setting Dog is a certain lusty Land Spaniel, taught by nature to hunt the Partridge more than any chace whatever, running the fields over with such Alacrity and Nimbleness as if there was no Limit to his Fury and Desire;

And yet by Art under such excellent Command, that in the very height of his Career by a Hem or Sound of his Master's voice, he shall stand, or gaze about him, look in his Master's Face and observe his Directions, whether to proceed, stand still or retire:

Nay, when he is even just upon his prey, that he may even take it up in his Mouth, yet his Obedience is so framed by Art, that presently he shall either stand still, or fall down flat on his Belly, without daring either to make any Noise or Motion till his Master comes to him, and then he will proceed in all Things to follow his Directions.

Having a Dog thus qualified by Art and Nature, take him with you where Partridges do haunt, there cast off your Dog, and by some Word of Encouragement with which he is acquainted, engage him to range, but never too far from you.

And see that he beat his Ground justly and even, without casting about, or flying now here, now there, which the mettle of some will do, if not corrected and reproved. And therefore when you perceive this Fault, you must presently call him in with a Hem, and so check him that he dare not do the like again for that Day, so he will range afterwards with more Temperance, ever and anon looking in his Master's face, as if he would gather from thence whether he did well or ill.

If in your Dog's ranging you perceive him to flop on the sudden, or stand still, you must then make in to him (for without doubt he has set the partridge) and as soon as you come to him, command him to go nearer him, but if he goes not, but either lies still or stands shaking of his tail, as who would say Here they are under my nose, and withal now and then looks back, then cease from urging him further and take your circumference, walking fast with a careless Eye, looking straight before the Nose of the Dog, and thereby see how the Covey lie, whether close or straggling.

Then commanding your dog to lie still, draw forth your Net and prick one End to the Ground and spread your net all open, and so cover as many of the Partridges as you can, which done, make in with a Noise, and spring up the Partridges, which shall no sooner rise but they will be entangled in the Net. And if you shall let go the old Cock and Hen it will not only be an act like a Gentleman, but a means to increase your pastime.

Thus, almost 300 years ago, the art of the setting spaniel was defined. Might we not almost say, the art of the Brittany Spaniel?

By implication, Cox tells us how the setters got their name. They kept game "setting" until the hunter could come up. Cox links "setting" and "spaniel," and this is important. But he does not explain the origin of "spaniel." He is not interested in specific breeds, only in performance.

In his day, there were no stud books. The passionate interest in breed type had not yet developed. Yet even in 1670, a family of Land Spaniels existed. They probably differed greatly in type.

They were alike in having excellent scenting powers, and in using body scents carried to them by air currents. From these Land Spaniels came the setters. And from some of them, and from other spaniels elsewhere, there arose the Brittany Spaniel.

2

Origin of the Spaniel

M OST WRITERS HAVE GIVEN the origin of the name "spaniel" to a family of dogs that came from Spain. In this group are the English Pointer, the setters, many of the pointing breeds of France and Italy, and those dogs we now call spaniels. It is supposed that though these breeds developed in other countries, they are still descendants of dogs that came from Spain. Yet the problem is puzzling.

The Greeks called the Spanish Peninsula Iberia, and its people Iberians. After the Celtic invasions of Northern Spain in the 7th and 6th centuries B.C., the Greeks called the people Celtiberians.

The Greeks were interested in both dogs and hunting. They do not mention hunting dogs in Iberia. Had they found such dogs there, it seems certain that they would have called them Iberian dogs. The Celts had moved across the Pyrenees, and had settled in northern and central Spain. They are believed to have brought several types of dogs with them. But there is no record of a Celtic dog of spaniel type.

In the 4th century B.C., the Carthaginians conquered most of the coastal areas of southern Spain. The Romans drove out the Carthaginians in 206 B.C., during the second Punic War. The Romans, too, were interested in hunting. But they do not mention a Carthaginian dog of spaniel type.

The two provinces seized from Carthage were *Hispania Citerior* and *Hispania Ulterior*. Hispania was the ancient Latin name for Spain. Spaniards call their country *España,* pronounced Es-pan-ya. The relationship between Hispania and España is obvious.

Reproduction of an 18th Century painting by Jean Baptiste Oudry, showing an early type of spaniel found in France and The Netherlands.

Questions immediately arise. Did the Carthaginians develop the spaniel family? Did the Romans, finding the dogs in their new provinces of Hispania, name them after the provinces? If not, who did? And did the Romans take the dogs into France, and later to Britain? If so, why didn't they take the dogs home to Rome?

The *Velasquez Spanish Dictionary* suggests that the word spaniel is derived from the French, *espagneul*. *Webster's Third International Dictionary* also states that spaniel is derived from the Middle French word for Spaniard, *espaignol*. This would indicate that spaniels were taken into France, and later into Britain. If so, then there is meaning to the modern French, *epagneul*, and the various English terms, *spainell, spanyell, spanyol*, and finally *spaniel*.

The answer is not so simply reached. The earliest known reference to the spaniel is in a Welsh manuscript, dated about 300 A.D. It mentions a "native spaniel." The next reference also is from Wales. It appears in the laws of King Howell Dda, who ruled from 943 to 950. These laws list the Greyhound, Tracker, Buckhound, and Spaniel. The latter was said to be of equal value to the king's Buckhound, or to a stallion.

It is not until 1387 that spaniel appears in French. In that year, Gaston de Foix, or Gaston Phoebus, wrote his *Livre de Chasse*. Gaston de Foix lived near the Spanish border. At times he had as many as one thousand dogs. Some of them were spaniels, and Gaston said they came from Spain.

Edward C. Ash studied the paintings that illuminated the famous Gaston Phoebus manuscript. One picture showed spaniels fairly close to modern Springer Spaniel type. In another, the spaniel was clipped in Poodle fashion.

Edward, second Duke of York, based his *The Master of Game* on the *Livre de Chasse*. It was written between 1406 and 1413. He wrote that "hounds for the hawk and spaniels, for their kind, cometh from Spain, notwithstanding that there are many in other countries."

It will be seen later that some authorities have suggested that the Brittany Spaniel and the Welsh Springer Spaniel are closely related. The latter is a red-and-white dog.

To summarize, the preponderance of the evidence is that the spaniel family gets its name from the Roman provinces of Hispania on the southern coast of the Iberian Peninsula. They were known in Wales before they were found in England, Scotland or France. It is possible that the name has no connection with Spain, and that the original spaniels were taken from Wales to Spain. There they prospered. From Spain, they then spread into France, England and Scotland.

3

Origin of the Brittany Spaniel

DOG SHOWS BECAME POPULAR about one hundred years ago. Most dog breeds, as we know them today, do not date before that time. The years after 1870 were of great change. The Industrial Revolution was destroying the largely rural order. Isolated areas were being connected and opened up by railroads. The need for cattle, drover and sheep dogs was disappearing. Isolated, and even less isolated areas, had their own locally developed breeds, or strains of breeds. Suddenly, the dog fanciers of the day realized that the breeds they admired so much were disappearing. Dog shows helped to save these breeds. Fanciers gathered together. They studied the various strains they had developed. The best points of each strain were selected. Breed standards were set up. Stud books were established. The era of the purebred dog had begun.

The Breton peasant was not wealthy. In Brittany, as in the rest of rural France, local varieties of hunting dogs, principally setters and spaniels, had been developed. There were also the pointing breeds known as *Braques*. These local dogs were excellent workmen. But the fancy of the day was the English dog.

Wealthy English sportsmen brought their own beautifully trained dogs with them for the shooting season. These were sometimes Pointers, but more often English Setters and Irish Setters. A few spaniels, probably the red-and-white Welsh Springers, were brought in. Some of these sportsmen left their dogs with local people to await the next shooting season.

To show what happened, let us quote from John Kemp, whose *Shooting And Fishing In Lower Brittany* was published in 1859. Kemp spent years in hunting and fishing, so he was one of the great authorities of his day.

> If, however, I had to select the brace of dogs best adapted for every kind of shooting throughout the season, I should, without hesitation, prefer a brace of well-broken spaniels; but as no dogs are more difficult to obtain, and I have just a sneaking affection for an animal with a little more dash than the aforesaid breed, I have tried the following cross with success.
>
> I have put a spaniel to a well-bred setter bitch, and been lucky enough to combine the ranging qualities of the latter and the hunting perseverance of the former. The French have tried this cross frequently. I lately purchased one of the produce; and I can say that few dogs perform better in the field than this one. My reason for discarding Pointers is, that they are too thin skinned for the work required in Landes for partridge shooting, and are of little use, as every one knows for cover shooting.

Kemp writes of the shooting at Callac and Mael Carhaiz in the Côtes du Nord, and at Huelgoat and Carhaix in the Finistere. But he hunted and fished in other areas as well. At the time he wrote, it had been announced that a railroad would be built from Nantes to Brest. It would make a "grand detour" around the north coast. Of Callac—a most important district in Brittany Spaniel history—he wrote:

> It is a capital district for shooting that quite rivals the preserves near Cairhaix . . . I knew most of the people in the country, and consequently had no difficulties thrown in my way by farmers and others. Strangers who have dropped in have found it the contrary, because they have managed to excite the jealousy of the natives by exhibitions of much slaughtered game, and by their general behaviour. A mild and inoffensive individual would get on well with the "men of Callac," jealous and sensitive though they are respecting field sports.

Kemp supplies clear and irrefutable evidence that as early as 1850, local French sportsmen were crossing their spaniels with English Setters. They were doing so to get a dog superior to either—the dog that eventually would be the Brittany Spaniel.

About 1910, M. Le Comte Le Conteux de Canteleu drew up a chart of current French breeds. He lists one of them as the *Chien de Bretagne,* the dog of Brittany. For reasons not known today, he did not call it the *Epagneul Bretagne*—the Brittany Spaniel.

Louis De Lajarrige, who wrote the *Manuel Pratique de L'Amateur De Chiens,* followed the Comté Le Conteux de Canteleu's chart. But De Lajarrige relied upon the research of Ronan de Kermadec and others. And by their day, the breed had become known officially as the Brittany Spaniel.

In 1906, Major P. Grand-Chavin, a cavalry officer and veterinarian, was assigned to the garrison at Pontivy. His job was to classify the cavalry horses, and to order discarded those he considered unfit. He was also to search the provinces of Morbihan, Finistere, and Côtes du Nord for suitable horses that might be purchased.

Everywhere he went, he noticed small spaniels with short tails or no tails. They had rather short ears for a spaniel. Their colors were white-orange, white-liver, and white-black. Some were tri-colors. The major reported that they had what he called a "short gait."

It is sometimes difficult to translate words representing colors. Moreover, words for color often change in meaning from time to time. Thus, early writers on the Brittany Spaniel used the word *marron*. This has been translated as "maroon." To us, this is a shade of very dark red. Modern French dictionaries translate *marron* as dark chestnut or mahogany. The latter is a very dark reddish brown or liver color. Since liver and mahogany are more familiar terms to Americans, we use these terms, instead of maroon or chestnut.

Now while the major's job was to classify horses, he seems to have done so in a leisurely manner. This allowed him many full days of hunting, a sport in which he was both enthusiastic and proficient. Also, since he was both a horseman and a veterinarian, he had an excellent knowledge of animal conformation and field performance.

Major Grand-Chavin found the dogs of the area to have remarkable scenting powers. They braved the most tangled thickets in their search for woodcock. They were utterly fearless in crossing rivers and canals. And they could chase a hare for at least three quarters of an hour over rough country.

Señor Juan Pugibet of Villa Obregon, near Vera Cruz, Mexico, was the first to bring Brittany Spaniels to North America. Señor Pugibet began a book on the history of the Brittany Spaniel. Unfortunately, he died before it could be completed. His daughter, Monique, has made available to the author that part he had written.

Señor Pugibet, of whom more later, translated and quoted from an article by Ronan de Kermadec. The latter was a pioneer Brittany fancier. He was a judge of all breeds in France, and he was at one time vice president of the Brittany Spaniel Club of France. The article appeared in *La Vie à la Campagne* in September, 1923. At the time, at least, de Kermadec was convinced that the Brittany Spaniel was closely related to the Welsh Springer Spaniel. Here is Señor Pugibet's translation:

> It was very tempting to suppose that the Brittany Spaniel was only a variety of the French Spaniel. But it would be very difficult for those who thought so, to explain how a long-headed and long-lined dog could have been able to produce a short-headed and short-lined dog. The character is more different yet: The French Spaniel is a very quiet dog, the Brittany full of life, activity, and as a good Welsh must be, single minded.
>
> The study of this dog with its swarming animation and the examination of his skull and anatomy, suggested to M. Paul Pegnin and to myself, that the Brittany Spaniel and the Welsh Spaniel were only two branches of the same origin.

Juan Pugibet, a pioneer
fancier, is believed to
have been the first
sportsman to bring the
Brittany Spaniel to
America. His home was
Villa Obregon, Vera
Cruz, Mexico. He died
there in 1945.

French Dual Ch. and 1966 national field Ch. Laskar de Saint Tugen, owned
By Madame Marchand. *Dim photo.*

Knowing the ethnical affinities of those two countries: Wales and French Brittany, and that both have the same kind of rough coated hounds, the hypothesis built on the study of the skeleton becomes a certainty. And that resemblance is evident because an English gentleman residing in French Brittany, used to tell me: "One day I will bring from my country a short tail Brittany Spaniel"; and [he] was always establishing a parallel between both breeds.

It is a fact that most of the typical subjects are found among the white and orange families and the white and mahogany, sure evidence they are from French Spaniel blood, and the best among those have signs of that cross: cephalic profile and the shape of the ears. Is that the reason buyers prefer light colored dogs? Maybe it is also because mahogany and roan colored dogs are not easily distinguished in the woods for quick shooters.

It is not only what we have said above, which connects the Brittany Spaniel with the Welsh Springer. When the woodcock hunters were so pleased with him, his setting aptitudes were weak and always [he] was ready to flush the bird when ordered, and sometimes before. He did that, barking like a spaniel.

He flushed so much that, before sportsmen began to breed the pure Brittany Spaniels, some hunters, to make him more staunch, conceived the idea to cross him with well chosen setters. A long time ago that cross was useful and beneficial, improving the staunchness and the power of scent and contributing to make him a more useful dog in the field. But that cross should not be continued without danger of seriously modifying the character, aptitudes, and originality of the breed, which has the special qualities of both spaniels and setters.

To prevent the effect of new crosses, the breeders are keeping away from mating even typical dogs not born short-tailed and the Judges did not reward in shows dogs not born short-tailed, this character being the base in selecting the breeding dogs from the beginning.

Some comments on this early article need to be made. Modern readers will consider the Welsh Springer Spaniel as it is today. Breeding to such a dog would be disastrous for Brittany Spaniels. The modern Welsh Springer is not very fast afield. And it is purely a flushing dog. R. de Kermadec was more knowledgeable about bench dogs than field performance. Certainly long before his time, the dogs that were to become Brittany Spaniels were staunch pointing dogs. A decade later, French breeders were to eliminate the requirement that dogs born with tails were not to be used for breeding.

On the other hand, the Welsh Springer Spaniel of today is much different than was the Welsh Springer of 1900. In those days, in England, a litter of spaniels would be born. Some might be small, and would be called Cocker Spaniels. Some would compete first as Cockers, then would exceed 25 to 28 pounds in weight and compete as Springers. Those Springers born liver-and-white or black-and-white would compete as English Springers. Those born orange or red-and-white would compete as Welsh Springers. Yet both might have come from the same litter.

Pictures extant of the Brittany Spaniels of the 1900 period show them to look very much like the modern English Springer Spaniel field type. There is, in this breed, a wide divergence in type between bench Springers and field Springers. One could say that, at least in type, the Brittany Spaniel has vastly improved since 1900, while the field Springers have equally deteriorated. Each reader must decide for himself how de Kermadec's theory fits into the story of the Brittany.

There are several versions of the following story. It is taken from the *annuaire* (yearbook) of the Brittany Spaniel Club of France for 1933. The author was M. Mège, the well-known breeder. While the story, in any form, is supposed to be only a legend, it is interesting to compare it, in both time and substance, with the quotations given earlier from the Kemp book. Again, the translation is by Señor Pugibet.

> About a century ago, there were two Englishmen who came to Brittany to shoot woodcock. They settled down at Pontou, a little town situated in the valley of Bouron, bordering on the National Road, Paris to Brest, fifteen kilometers from Morlaix.
>
> These Englishmen brought with them several small dogs, white and lemon, long tails, in height about 17½ to 19 inches, cobby built, with small ears. They were perfect in the woods.
>
> An old hunter of this region, who accompanied these Englishmen, had a bitch, white and mahogany, looking very much like the English dogs. This bitch, coming in season, the old hunter bred her to one of the English dogs. The resulting litter consisted of a mixture of black and white, white and orange with long tails, and also two curiosities. One had no tail and "pattes de grenouille" (a free translation might mean "frog footed"). A second one was considered a curiosity as he also had no tail. This dog proved himself to be wonderful in the field and was therefore largely used for stud purposes. In all his get there were many without tails, frequently little stubs. The original were much lighter in build and in appearance, very nervous, small boned and very cobby. For a long time they were small and runty. This was undoubtedly due to the feeding which consisted largely of milk, potatoes, and pan cakes.
>
> From all time, this breed has been known as a dog good on all game. He hunted on a gallop with high head marking his point, very fond of brush. When hunting a hare or a rabbit he gave tongue. He was noted as being extra good in the swamps and woods, and a natural retriever. The Brittany of today is not the same in bone, head and line of back, due to careful breeding.

In his book, *Le Chien,* the renowned French veterinarian and dog authority, Dr. Fernand Mèry, has a short account of the origin of the Brittany Spaniel. As will be seen, it differs somewhat from other accounts. Dr. Mèry has very kindly given me permission to quote from it:

> It was in 1906 that the veterinarian, Major P. Grand-Chavin, gave an official description of them. He described them as "little spaniels almost all with a short tail, a nearly homogeneous breed, and with a white-mahogany, white-orange, or white-black coat. These little animals are appealing because of the wide-awake

appearance, a wide-awake bearing, a good expression in the eye, and (they) appear intelligent."

Since 1896, one has seen French spaniels of the Breton breed in shows. But the true Breton Spaniel will not make an appearance in the great Paris Exposition until 1904. This first (one) "Max de Callac" was the son of a little bird dog from Monts d'Arrhee, named "Cora": she herself an issue of a black and flame setter, and of a French Spaniel of the light breed, and of a white-mahogany color. Descendants of "Max" were in their turn crossed with these little spaniels, a more or less cross-breed of Braque [French Pointer] which were quite numerous in the north of Finisterre, and on the coasts of the North. Forewarned, breeders managed to save and to better these families of white-liver which were for a long time the predominant strain.

The white-orange would have as origin, Scottish setters brought to Brittany by M. de Moll. The offspring were then crossed with Welsh Springers. One knows from a sure source that there was introduced Irish Setter blood and English spaniel to favor the trips of more and more numerous English hunters, who came to Brittany with their dogs to hunt woodcock; which explains the persistance in the interior countryside of the old type white-liver, while the new white-orange breed progressed on the northern shores.

We suppose that when Dr. Mèry refers to "black and flame" setters, and to "Scottish setters," he means the Gordon Setter.

The passion of the Brittany Spaniel for woodcock, and of those sportsmen who considered woodcock hunting the supreme sport, is illustrated in a story told by Ronan de Kermadec. He had the pleasure of hunting with His Royal Highness, Prince Albert of Monaco, one of the great ornithologists of his day. Their hunting companion was a Brittany Spaniel named Sam, and they hunted in the Forest of Rambouillet. So specialized was Sam that when he came on point, he was almost certainly pinning a woodcock.

De Kermadec tells the story of the crossing of the English Setter with the French Spaniel belonging to the Breton hunter Lulzac. But he has Lulzac being the gamekeeper for M. de Pontavice, a pioneer Brittany breeder close to the end of the 19th century.

Perhaps in summary, a reasonable statement of the origin of the Brittany Spaniel is this: The Brittany Spaniel is the result of the crossing of English Setters with small French Land Spaniels. This process began as early as 1850, and possibly earlier. The English Setter was itself developed from some of the swifter Land Spaniels of England, and possibly Wales. In the interior of Brittany, liver-and-white dogs predominated. In the coastal areas, orange-and-white colors were prominent. By 1904, the Brittany Spaniel had evolved into a distinct breed.

4

The Tailless Brittany

ALL ACCOUNTS AGREE THAT at some point in French Spaniel history, a dog was born without a tail. Most accounts believe that this occurred during a French Spaniel-English Setter cross. At first, this was seized upon as a distinctive feature of the new breed. After many arguments, it was decided that dogs born with tails could be registered. But the tails were to be docked close to the body. Later, a further relaxation was made. A short, stubby tail was to be allowed.

One is forced to wonder why sportsmen docked the tails of their hunting dogs. Some of the answers are supplied in an entry in *The Sportsman's Dictionary* by Henry James Pye, Esquire. We quote here from the fifth edition, published in 1807. The entry is entitled: The Benefit Of Cutting The Tip Of The Spaniel's Tail Or Stern.

> It is necessary that this be done when he is a whelp, for several reasons: First, by doing so, worms are prevented from breeding there; and in the next place, if it be not cut he will be less forward in pressing hastily into the coverts after his game, and besides it will make the dog appear more beautiful.

One can analyze this in the following way. The tails of sheep are always docked. If they are not, flies lay their eggs in the hair about the rectum and set-on of the tail. The eggs hatch into maggots, and these invade the rectum. Infection and death are likely to follow.

Spaniels crossbred with setters seem to inherit the long tail of the setters. That is, on the English Setter, the tail tip will reach the hock joint. The same tail, upon a spaniel, will reach the ground. Such a tail will pick up burrs. And these spaniels were being used in the copses and brushwood. They had to press into briars. Among the English Setters of today, there are those known as "tail beaters." They hunt merrily, waving or beating their tails back and forth. Such dogs invariably slash their tails into bloody ribbons when in briar country. The scar tissue that forms will not permit hair to grow, and it bleeds easily. The author of the above quotation is implying that such dogs may not willingly enter heavy cover, whether it contains briars or not.

And then he adds: "and besides it will make the dog appear more beautiful." Perhaps Pye meant by this that the dog would not have a bloody, hairless, scar-tissue tail. And he may have meant that an abnormally long tail would drag behind the dog and make it appear both clumsy and slow.

In the early days of the Brittany in America, the fanciers included converts from the Pointer and setter ranks. They felt that there was nothing so beautiful as the sky-pointing, stiffly held tail of a bird dog on point. So some sportsmen did not dock the tails of their Brittanys. Great discussions followed. But eventually, all agreed that the Brittany should have no tail, or one docked very short.

There have been other reasons why people have docked the tails of their dogs. They must be mentioned at our point in time because we cannot know what influence they had upon the custom. For a time, men believed that docking the tail prevented rabies. And the tails of fighting dogs were taken off at the body. They were a serious impediment, and they offered an easy hold for the adversary. And they bled easily. Docking neatly eliminated the problems as it did the tail.

A group of breed immortals performing the breed's work: (l. to r.) Dual Ch. Angelique De Bretagne, Fld. Ch. Broad Archer of Richmont, Fld. Ch. Allamuchy Valley Addie and Dual Ch. Avono Happy.

5

Why the Brittany
Became Popular

TWO OF THE MOST common questions asked of dog fanciers are these: "How did you happen to get into the dog game?" and "How did you happen to pick this breed?" As far as the first question is concerned, the answer is quite simple. Sportsmen need dogs to help them to locate game. Declining game populations have made the use of a dog mandatory, not only to locate game, but to find and to retrieve the cripples brought down.

The second question is less simply answered. First, sportsmen who want hunting dogs fall into many categories. The passion of one may be the trailing dog. He may be a rabbit hunter, and the voice of a Beagle stirs him as does that of no other dog. So he gets a Beagle. Another may be stirred by the sight of a pointing dog frozen on a solid point. Still another may get his greatest thrills from seeing a flushing dog outwit a running and dodging pheasant.

Cynical observers have sometimes explained the choice of breed in this way. The sportsman cannot control the dog he has. Or it is a quitter, or it has a poor nose. He then equates all the other dogs of this breed with his own. A new breed comes along. Perhaps the propaganda for it is intense. He is ready to switch, and he does. Breeders of bench dogs may find the competition too great for them. But they are hobbyists and animal lovers. They cannot defeat the established breeders, or more likely, believe that they can't. So they switch to a new breed. Our interest is the Brittany. To some extent all the reasons given have been responsible for the steady rise in popularity of the breed.

People have come to the Brittany from other breeds. Some have tried Brittanys and then have moved to other breeds.

The Brittany was never either the beneficiary or the victim of a heavy barrage of publicity. As noted in other chapters, Louis A. Thebaud was the American pioneer. Stewart J. Walpole was then the publisher of the *American Field.* It was—and is—a magazine devoted primarily to pointing dogs. Pointers and English Setters got the bulk of attention. But Walpole was one of the first to own a Brittany in the United States. His articles in the *American Field* brought the Brittany to the attention of thousands of bird-dog lovers.

An American pioneer in English Springer Spaniels was Dr. A. C. Gifford of Oshkosh, Wisconsin. His Winnebago Kennels were already well established when the Brittany first came to America. Dr. Gifford decided to try the breed. He liked the dogs. But he was first of all a lover of flushing dogs, and secondly, his interests lay with Springer bench dogs. So he did not persevere with the Brittany.

Dr. Samuel Milbank, a prominent breeder of Wire Fox Terriers, and for years head of the Westminster Kennel Club in New York City, decided to get into field trials. He, too, tried Brittanys. But, as with Dr. Gifford, Dr. Milbank found his interests to be with the flushing dogs and retrievers. So he moved into the ranks of the Labrador Retriever and English Springer Spaniel field trialers.

The reverse was also true. Edward Borger was an early competitor in English Springer Spaniel field trials in northwestern Pennsylvania and northern Ohio. But Borger's true interest was in the pointing dog. He switched to Brittanys and has remained with the breed.

Charles Frank, whose sporting-dog act was for years an attraction at winter sportsmen's shows, was another who began with Springer Spaniels. His dogs first distinguished themselves in the conformation ring and in obedience. When he developed his act, Frank added Golden Retrievers. Then he became interested in Brittanys. His "Duckerbird" dogs then became prominent in the ranks of the Brittanys.

The author has asked some of the pioneers who are still with us why they decided to go with Brittanys. Speaking for her deceased husband, Mrs. Walter B. Kleeman said simply: "Walt wanted a pointing dog with which he could hunt on foot." He was one who learned of the breed through Walpole's articles in the *American Field.*

Louis A. Thebaud introduced the Brittany to the United States. What is less well known is that he also introduced to America the breed then known as the Korthals Griffon. We now know it as the Wirehaired Pointing Griffon. Thebaud tested both breeds. The Griffon failed to meet the test of American hunting conditions and game birds. The Brittany succeeded.

Henry Briggs, M.D., lived at West Orange, New Jersey. He met Louis

Thebaud and became interested in the breed. His brother-in-law, Edgar W. Averill, Ph.D., came to visit. Dr. Briggs had a lovely Brittany bitch in the house. She jumped into Dr. Averill's lap, and cuddled up there. Dr. Averill was entranced. The bitch was Yvonne de Sharvogue. On Sept. 13, 1936, Yvonne whelped a litter by Gwennec de L'Argoat. That Christmas, Dr. Averill received a male puppy. The puppy was to become Ch. Patrice of Sharvogue. Dr. Averill—Bill to everyone still—had been hooked by Yvonne. Patrice made him forever a Brittany fancier.

"All those dogs could hunt," Bill said later. "Those of us in Michigan set out to improve their looks, while keeping their hunting abilities." This the Brittany breeders have done with remarkable success—a record of success achieved by no other breed in world history. But that story belongs in the chapter of dual—bench and field—champions. Dr. Averill hunted Ch. Patrice of Sharvogue until the dog was past 14 years old.

René Joubert, another early pioneer, lived at this time in the Detroit area. He is often listed as having been the nephew of Louis A. Thebaud. But in fact, Louis Thebaud was a first cousin of René Joubert's mother. Before her marriage to Emmanuel Joubert, she was Isabelle Thebaud. The families were of French descent, but they lived in the New York-New Jersey area.

Isabelle Thebaud's father, Dr. Jules Thebaud, was killed by an explosion of cartridges as he prepared for a hunting trip. His widow took her numerous children back to France. She never returned. Isabelle married Emmanuel Joubert in Paris. They had two sons, Jacques and René.

René inherited the passion for the outdoors and the game fields from the Thebauds. He always referred affectionately to Louis Thebaud as "Uncle Louis." René served in the French Army in World War I and won the *Croix de Guerre* and the *Medaille Militaire.* He came to New York to work for the *Compagnie Générale Transatlantique,* and then was transferred to Houston, where he married his wife, Margaret. In 1932, he was transferred to Detroit, where he remained until the French Line office was closed in 1940. With this background, his relationship to Louis Thebaud, his knowledge of France, and with the rapidly burgeoning interest in Michigan and Ohio in the Brittany, it was natural that he should take up the breed. René Joubert returned to Texas in 1940, but not until the Brittany had won its acceptance as a great American sporting dog.

In France, the Brittany and its ancestors had demonstrated a remarkable passion for woodcock hunting for roughly one hundred years. In America, the dog had to prove itself upon ruffed grouse, prairie chicken, quail and pheasant, as well as woodcock. In addition, Michigan and northwestern Ohio had the chukar, or Indian rock partridge. Juan Pugibet had brought the Brittany to Mexico. There game birds were often scarce, the hunting was difficult, and the valley quail was an entirely different sporting proposition than the bobwhite quail. The Brittany was tested on all these game birds, and it passed the tests brilliantly.

But not even all this will explain how and why the Brittany caught on and became so popular. Remember that it had to survive the Great Depression, World War II and the Korean War. Yet during the next 25 years it moved into the first 20 of all American breeds registered by the American Kennel Club. In 1985, it was in 24th place with 15,048 registrations. In one recent year, 2,380 Brittanys competed in field trials under American Field procedures. All this the breed had to accomplish without the fantastic, and often unfair, publicity that has been dreamed up for the promotion of other breeds.

To understand what happened, we have to go back to Mrs. Kleeman's simple statement: "Walt wanted a hunting dog he could use on foot." American game areas have become steadily more restricted. In only a few areas can men follow wide-ranging pointers and setters, as they once did, on horseback, or in wagons or trucks. Usually the remaining such areas are privately owned and are denied to most sportsmen. The passing of these great game areas somewhat lessened the need for big, fast, wide-ranging dogs. More and more highways cut through the game areas. Traffic became an increasing hazard for the dogs. Sportsmen began to think in terms of smaller, less-wide-ranging dogs. The German Shorthaired Pointer and the English Springer Spaniel were already well established. The latter is a flushing dog, the former a pointing dog that adapts well to all the above requirements. As does the Brittany, the German Shorthair lacks sufficient tail to get torn by briars. Both the German Shorthair and the Brittany make excellent house dogs, and this has become an increasingly important requirement for a sporting dog. But the latter has an additional advantage. It is small enough to be easily transported in the family car.

To sum it up: The Brittany has passed the test upon every type of game for which pointing dogs are used. It has the disposition of the best house pets and companions, and yet a remarkable passion for hunting. It can face any kind of weather. It can be kept within the range of modern hunting conditions. It is small, yet can do a big job. And it makes an ideal dual purpose—bench and field—dog.

6

Early Brittany Spaniel History in France

IN EARLIER CHAPTERS WE have tried to indicate how and why bird dogs developed. Moreover, we have pointed out that the great period in the development of specific dog breeds came during the last half of the 19th century, and during the first decade or two of the 20th. The true history of the Brittany Spaniel, as a breed, falls into two decades—from 1890 to 1910.

F. Rothschild published his book, *Notre Ami Le Chien,* in 1897. He does not mention the Brittany Spaniel specifically. But he does list the known French hunting breeds, and he devotes some space to the French spaniels. His descriptions of some of them fit the Brittany. They were white-and-chestnut, white-and-orange, often speckled. They were 19½ to 20½ inches tall at the withers. Their hair lay flat, and some of them had short tails or no tails.

The year before, a dog of this type was shown at the Paris Exposition. He was whelped in 1892, by Printemps out of Fauville, and his name was Pincon Royal. The owner was the Viscount de Cambourg. Pincon Royal was listed as a Brittany Spaniel. In 1902, another Brittany was shown. This was Das de Magenta, whelped January 20, 1898 by Kim out of Eda. He was owned by M. Laveissiere. These two dogs had to be shown in a miscellaneous class for French spaniels. Neither impressed the judges of the time. And it seems likely that neither impressed the sophisticated sportsmen of Paris who came to see the show.

But during that same year, a Brittany Spaniel competed in a field trial for continental dogs. This means that it was a trial for pointing dogs that were required to be steady to point and flush, to be steady to shot, to mark the fall and then to make the retrieve. Myrrha d'Amorique was the dog. She was owned and had been trained by M. Treuttel. The trial was at Cany, and Myrrha won. Today we would call Myrrha a very poor type. She was white-and-liver, and she looked very much like a present-day English Springer Spaniel field type. But Myrrha won, and her victory turned attention to the hitherto ignored spaniels of Brittany.

Two years later, in 1904, M. Patin showed Max de Callac at the Paris Exposition. In the preceding chapter, we have quoted from John Kemp's *Shooting And Fishing In Lower Brittany.* He mentions the dogs and the shooting at Callac. So the appearance of Max de Callac—a dog from a great woodcock territory—did bring both attention and credit to the new breed. Max became the breed's first champion in 1909.

Then, in 1907, dogs owned by M. de Pontavice, M. de Fougeres and Dr. Gastel were shown at the Paris Exposition. They won the acclaim of sportsmen, and particularly that of men who had hunted in lower Brittany. Stories about the breed appeared in the sporting journals for that year. Brittany Spaniels were given separate classification at Toulouse that year.

John Kemp had mentioned that a railroad was to be built from Brest to Nantes, that is, along the coast. Kemp wrote in 1859. By 1907, the railroad was a reality. And major highways had also been built across and around the Brittany Peninsula. The once isolated hunting areas were now opened up to an increasing number of sportsmen. Parisian and Northern French sportsmen were now learning about a hunting area and its dogs already long familiar to the English. For example, a highway had been built from Quiberon, on the Bay of Biscay, through Pontivy, and on to St. Brieuc on the English Channel. North of Pontivy this road split, and one section went east through Fougeres. And there was also an excellent highway from Nantes to Rennes. One could also travel from Nantes to Carhaix. These are all important names in the history of the breed.

In 1907, Arthur Enaud, Dr. Gastel and M. de Fougeres met with others at Loudeac. This town is some 85 miles west of Rennes, 22 miles north of Pontivy, and 68 miles east of Carhaix. It is therefore in the heartland of the Brittany Spaniel. The purpose of the meeting was to found a breed club and to draw up a standard. This was done. The Brittany Spaniel Club was formed. The standard called for a dog about 19⅝ inches tall at the shoulder. The head was to be broad, with a rounded skull. The ears were to be rather short—a departure from the traditional long spaniel ear—and only slightly fringed with hair. Body hair was to be flat, and in no sense curly. The body was to be short—"cob"—and the tail was to be "naturally short."

A second general meeting of Breton sportsmen was held at Pontivy on June 7, 1908. A more definitive standard was drawn up. And this was again modified at another meeting at Pontivy on June 16, 1912. Field trials for continental dogs and for French spaniels were already being held. Dogs belonging to M. Patin and others were winning, and were demonstrating remarkable scenting powers, as well as both searching ability and stamina. These dogs, by proving themselves in the field, brought true recognition to the breed.

The greatest dog of the pre-World War I period was Bac du Kerlossac. Ronan de Kermadec says he was "of the blood of Fougeres." He was bred by M. de Fougeres, and he was predominantly of the strains bred in the Fougeres section of Brittany. Bac du Kerlossac did not become a champion. World War I probably prevented him from becoming one. De Kermadec wrote that although he conformed to the standard of 1908, he was of a "strengthened model" with a good Breton head on a cob body.

The Great War seriously impeded French breeding. Yet the best dogs were somehow kept. Gistr, bred by M. Le Denmat, and owned by M. Patin, was born November 25, 1916. He won third prize at Paris in 1919. Gistr was by Klask IV de Callac, who had been a first-prize winner at Nantes in 1913. His dam was Miss, by Dick. Klask IV was by Klask de Callac. Gistr became one of the great dogs of the postwar period, and serves as an example of the conservation of their best breeding stock by the Bretons.

Names fabled throughout Brittany history now began to appear. Duck de Callac, bred by M. Patin, was whelped April 12, 1920. He was by Rac II de Callac out of Noz de Callac. The Cosquerou Kennels also appeared. M. Mège registered Miss du Cosquerou, whelped July 15, 1920, by Frileux de Cosquerou, out of Souris II de Cosquerou. Shimmy du Cosquerou was whelped March 29, 1921, by Franchic out of Kiss de Cosquerou, by Pen Bas de Kerbrug.

Perhaps it should be pointed out here that, because of the war, registration activities ceased for some years. But breeders did not stop breeding, though they continued on a small scale. They kept careful records, and these were placed in the stud book years later.

Another kennel that has played a major role in Brittany Spaniel history since its founding was the Pradalan Kennel of M. Quemener. One of his first great dogs was Perlic de Pradalan, a winner at the Rennes shows of 1922 and 1923. During this period, M. Chech bred Mousse, born in April 1919, and heavily inbred to Gistr.

The greatest dog of the 1920s, and one who has been a major stud factor in both French and American dogs, was the immortal Aotrou de Cornouaille. He was bred by Emile Bourdon, and was whelped November 15, 1926. Perlic de Pradalan later came to Mexico. Aotrou remained in France where he won one hundred first and honor prizes in shows, won at several field trials, and took first in the International Brittany Spaniel Club trials in 1929. Gistr, mentioned earlier, appears in Aotrou's pedigree.

French Ch. Aotrou de Cornouaille was one of the great foundation sires of American Brittany Spaniels. (Photo, courtesy of L. Bourdon, Cornouaille Kennels).

Gaston Pouchain has dedicated this picture of his famed field trial champion and immortal sire to his late friend, Alan Stuyvesant. The dog, Poilu de Droulet, had a strong influence on American Britts through dogs sent by Pouchain to Stuyvesant.

Earlier in this chapter, we pointed out that F. Rothschild did not mention the Brittany Spaniel in his list of French hunting dogs when he wrote his book, *Notre Ami Le Chien* (Our Friend the Dog). Less than 30 years later, Aotrou was to come on the scene, and the Brittany Spaniel was to become world famous. The other breeds of French spaniels either died out or have remained relatively unknown outside their local areas of France. It is time now to place the Brittany Spaniel in North America.

7

The Brittany Spaniel
Comes to North America

TWO MEN ARE RESPONSIBLE for introducing the Brittany Spaniel to North America. Both had French antecedents. They were Juan Pugibet of Villa Obregon, near Vera Cruz, Mexico, and Louis André Thebaud of Morristown, New Jersey. Of these two, Juan Pugibet comes first.

Juan Pugibet was an engineer. His father was French and his mother Mexican. He was a lover of field sports, especially of hunting upland game birds. He was a close friend of J. A. Sanchez Antuñano, the great Mexican authority on bird dogs. Sanchez Antuñano's *Practical Education of the Bird Dog* was for years the standard American guide to bird-dog training.

Sanchez Antuñano was at home with bird dogs under all the varying conditions to be found in North and Central America. Juan Pugibet was nearly as well versed. Neither appears to have known anything about the Brittany Spaniel. But Juan Pugibet went to France in the winter of 1924 and he learned about the breed. He was sufficiently impressed to want to test the breed in southern Mexico. That September he bought the Brittany Spaniel bitch Perlic de Pradalan. She arrived at Vera Cruz in December. Perlic was very well bred, and she adapted well to hunting conditions in Mexico. She stood intense heat, tropical humidity and upland dryness equally well. Yet it was four years before Pugibet decided to breed Brittany Spaniels.

In 1928, he imported Djinn des Veaux. Djinn was a grandson of one of the great dogs of his time, Rac II de Callac. Rac II de Callac appears in many of the pedigrees of dogs imported to North America. He has therefore been a stud force in Mexico, the United States and Canada. Djinn des Veaux arrived at Vera Cruz in time to be bred to Perlic de Pradalan during her early-fall heat period. Her litter—the first ever recorded in North America—arrived in December, 1928.

Pugibet imported many more Brittany Spaniels. His Casa Blanca Kennels became famous in Mexico, the United States and Canada. Dogs bred at Casa Blanca became the foundation stock in all three countries.

One of Pugibet's imports was the famous bitch Histr de Cornouaille. Pugibet and his daughter, Monica, took Histr to a field trial at the King Ranch in Texas. There she performed brilliantly, though competing against both pointers and setters.

Most of the early Brittany Spaniels to come to America were registered with the *Field Dog Stud Book* of the American Field. In addition, it was at that time possible to register Mexican dogs with the American Kennel Club. Thus, until about the time of his death in 1946, Pugibet registered all of his dogs with the American Kennel Club. In many cases, he also registered them with the *Field Dog Stud Book*. To explain this further, Pugibet would import dogs from France. These would be registered by the American Kennel Club. Litters born in Mexico of parents registered with the American Kennel Club would then be registered by that organization. But in about 1946 the American Kennel Club began to refuse such registrations. In some cases, it would register imported dogs for new owners living within the United States. But this was so only if the stud books of the country of origin were recognized by the American Kennel Club. For example, a dog owned in France could not be registered by the American Kennel Club. Neither could a dog owned in Mexico. At this time, the American Kennel Club recognizes the stud books of England, France, Germany, Canada, Australia and South Africa. If an American imports a registered dog from one of these countries, the AKC will, in most cases, transfer ownership to an American owner. But it will not do so if the dog is owned in Mexico. Moreover, the American Kennel Club does not currently recognize the stud books of the Latin American countries, including Mexico.

This accounts for the odd fact that dogs from Pugibet's Casa Blanca Kennels were not registered by the Mexican Kennel Club until after his death. Had the American Kennel Club policy of from 1946 to the present existed when Pugibet began importing and breeding, the Brittany Spaniel could not have got the start it did in the United States and Canada. The Casa Blanca influence in Canada is shown in the chapter dealing with the Brittany Spaniel in Canada.

Louis André Thebaud is a legend in America, and legends are sometimes hard to pin down. Legend tends to obscure facts, but many people have aided the writer in working out the history that follows. Among these is Vice Admiral Leo H. Thebaud, U.S. Navy retired. He collaborated with Robert L.

Louis A. Thebaud is considered a legend among American Brittany fanciers. He was one of the first to bring the breed to North America and played a major role in the breed's rise to prominence in the field and on the show bench.

One of the great names among the first Brittanies in the United States was that of Franche du Cosquerou (above)—Louis Thebaud's favorite hunting dog. The famous dog portrait photographer Rudolph Tauskey took this picture of Franche at the request of the American Kennel Club to represent the breed in the 1936 Edition of *The Complete Dog Book*. Franche subsequently became the property of Réne Joubert.

Réne Joubert, celebrated sportsman and breed pioneer, with two early greats; Fanche due Cosquerou (left) and Gwennec de L'Argoat.

de Larosiere, a retired French naval captain, in writing a history of the Thebaud family in both France and the United States. Admiral Thebaud has very kindly supplied me with this history, plus other information.

Louis André Thebaud and his twin brother, Edward Paul, were born October 24, 1859 at Orange, New Jersey. They were the sons of Paul Louis Thebaud, a member of the Thebaud Brothers firm in the import-export business. This firm closed its doors in 1907. Paul Louis Thebaud was a director and officer in many New York firms, including the Atlantic Mutual Insurance Company.

It has been said that Paul Louis Thebaud was for some years a banker in Yucatan, a state in southern Mexico. It is further said that his son, Louis, spent his younger years in Yucatan, where he became a passionate devotee of both hunting and fishing. We have not been able to verify any part of this story. In a personal letter to the author, Admiral Thebaud writes: "Neither Louis A. Thebaud, nor his father, ever lived in Yucatan. Louis Thebaud was a highly successful insurance man with Mutual Life in New York. His father was a member of the firm of Thebaud Brothers. All Thebauds have roots in Morristown, New Jersey, where the family has been well known for over a century. I was born next door at Madison, New Jersey. No Thebaud ever known to me ever met or heard of Juan Pugibet." Yet as stated elsewhere in this book, Juan Pugibet had planned to dedicate the book he was writing to Louis Thebaud.

Louis A. Thebaud went almost annually to France where he divided his time between an apartment in the Rue Spontini, Paris, and a seacoast home at St. Briac in Brittany. He is described as being "handsome, charming, and courtly" and "also a great sportsman; hunting, shooting, fishing, and sailing." He financed the building of the famous Gloucester schooner, *Gertrude L. Thebaud,* which was named after his wife. This schooner, under the command of Capt. Ben Pine, enhanced the prestige of New England fishermen at sea in the international fishermen's races against the Nova Scotia schooner *Bluenose.*

It is generally supposed that Louis Thebaud annually attended French field trials, and particularly those for Brittany Spaniels. But this seems not to have been true. He appears to have spent most of this time at St. Briac in sailing and fishing.

Earlier, we have pointed out the close personal relationship between the Joubert family and the Thebauds. The Jouberts had an apartment very close to the Thebaud apartment in the Rue Spontini. The two families went together to St. Briac, and the Joubert brothers always called Louis Thebaud "Uncle Louis." In a personal letter to the author, J. R. Joubert writes:

> My uncle, Louis A. Thebaud, except during the First World War years, came over to France every year from 1900 to 1939, the year of his death. He and his wife, Gertrude, usually arrived in March. Then in July and August we all went to St. Briac. My uncle was fond of fishing, but he often went on shooting parties.

During the time between 1905 and 1920, he bought two or three dogs in France and brought them back to the United States, but none of them was a Brittany Spaniel. [Author's note: They were Korthals Griffons, later to be known as Wirehaired Pointing Griffons.]

It is only between 1930 and 1939 that my uncle talked to me for the first time about Brittany Spaniels. The main reason, I think, is that my uncle thought that the breed would be very efficient for quail hunting, which he did on horseback in Florida. . . He asked me to find five. . . Brittany Spaniels for him, which I did with the greatest pleasure. My uncle never attended field trials in France, but I did it for him, with the aim of finding the finest dogs possible.

The result was that I bought four or five dogs for him, among which were Edir (very nervous, turned mad a few times) and Clap de Callac. (Callac is the name of the Brittany village where the first Brittany Spaniel was born) As far as I remember, this latter dog was famous.

I went to the U.S.A. with two of the dogs, and accompanied my uncle to New York to have the breed recognized and the dogs registered on the American Kennel Club's Stud Book. Sometime later, the second World War broke out, and I was separated from my brother, to whom my uncle had given some of the dogs before his death.

One of the dogs J. R. Joubert sent to his uncle in 1933 was the bitch Genette du Mesnil. She was carrying a litter sired by Gredin du Mesnil. After her arrival in the United States, Thebaud shipped her to Winnipeg, to Eudore Chevrier's Avandale Kennels. There she whelped. Thus, to Canada belongs the honor of producing her litter. It is a strange story: bred in France, imported with her puppies "in utero," and then sent to Canada.

8

Early History of the Brittany Spaniel in America

AMONG THE DOGS SELECTED in France by Jacques Joubert for Louis A. Thebaud were Edir du Mesnil, Genette du Mesnil, Franche du Cosquerou, Hai du Cosquerou and Fenntus. As stated earlier, Genette was in whelp to Gredin du Mesnil. She was sent to Winnipeg, Manitoba, to Eudore Chevrier's Avandale Kennels. After producing her litter, she was returned to Thebaud.

Franche du Cosquerou arrived in this country with the reputation of being France's finest field Brittany Spaniel. He appears not to have been brought over by René Joubert, as stated by some authors. René Joubert did not return to France during that period, according to the recollections of his brother. Franche was mated to Genette du Mesnil, and was then sent to Winnipeg to be used on Genette's daughters. Then he was returned to Thebaud.

Meanwhile, Jacques Joubert and Louis Thebaud went to the American Kennel Club to try to get the breed recognized and admitted to the stud book. They took with them two dogs—Edir du Mesnil and Genette du Mesnil. As a result, the board of directors of the AKC formally recognized the Brittany Spaniel in August, 1934.

The French Kennel Club had sent the "Standard of Perfection" for the breed at Thebaud's request in July, 1934. But oddly enough, the AKC did not approve the standard until Miss Clara G. Perry had made an acceptable translation of it. Approval came on March 12, 1935. Franche, described as "Mr. Thebaud's favorite hunting dog," was photographed by famed dog photographer Rudolph Tauskey. His picture was used to illustrate the history and breed standard in the official AKC book, *Pure-bred Dogs*. Arthur Frederick Jones, of the AKC staff, wrote the breed history. That particular edition of the book was published late in 1935, or early in 1936.

It should be pointed out here that it was much easier to gain breed recognition in the mid-1930s than it is today. Then, Jacques Joubert and Louis Thebaud could take two dogs of the breed to the American Kennel Club, present their certified French pedigrees and import certificates, and get the breed recognized immediately.

Today that would be impossible. First, the AKC would require proof that a certain number of dogs—perhaps 600—were in the country, and well spread from coast to coast. Then they would admit the breed to "miscellaneous class" status. A strong national breed club would have to be set up. And that club would have to establish an accurate stud book under AKC supervision. If then some 600 dogs were registered in this stud book, and if the AKC considered their pedigrees to be accurate, the breed might be elevated to full breed status. In the years since, it has taken some breeds a decade or more to achieve what Joubert and Thebaud accomplished in one day with two dogs.

Miss Clara G. Perry was also a true pioneer of the breed. She had maintained a home in France, and there she had owned Brittany Spaniels. Finding that there was an interest in the breed in the United States, she joined Thebaud in importing dogs. So did Louis de la Fleche, a Breton Frenchman, who was then living in the New York-New Jersey area. David Barbieri and Dr. Henry Briggs also began importations. Later, Louis de la Fleche returned to France and remained there.

Miss Perry brought over Gilda des Causses and Douglas de l'Odet. The year was 1935. The following winter the dogs were shown at Westminster, in Madison Square Garden, and at Boston. They were the first to appear at a U.S. show. That same year, Thebaud imported Hai du Cosquerou. Juan Pugibet brought over Histr de Cornouaille, bred to Gwennec de l'Argoat. La Fleche imported Keryvon de Basgard, and Keryvette du Roselier. At about the same time, Laurence Richardson imported Meg, Barbieri and Tango.

Fenntus was sired by the immortal French dog, Aotrou de Cornouaille, out of Plahic by Potic II. She was closely inbred to the latter dog, since Aotrou was himself sired by Potic II. An orange-and-white, she was bred by M. Le Coz and whelped March 6, 1931.

Hai du Cosquerou was bred by M. F. Mège, and was whelped March 1, 1933. He was orange-and-white. He was by Esop du Cosquerou out of a bitch by Aotrou de Cornouaille.

Histr de Cornouaille was bred by Emile Bourdon, and she was born May

French Ch. Potic II, an influential sire during the early history of the Brittany in North America. His name appears three times in the pedigree of Histr de Cornouaille (below).

French Ch. Dingo de Monts Noir, an early Brittany whose name appears in the pedigrees of many American dogs.

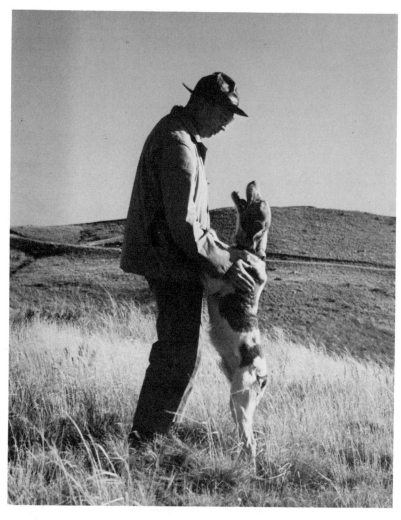

Pioneer fancier Walter B. Kleeman enjoying a personal moment with the celebrated Gwennec de L'Argoat.

18, 1933. She was white-and-orange and was by Flist III de Cornouaille, out of Diwal de Cornouaille, by Potic II. Flist III de Cornouaille was inbred to Aotrou de Cornouaille.

Keryvon de Basgard was bred by M. Poilbout. He was born August 1, 1932 by Cren de Callac out of Eyra de Basgard, by Aotrou de Cornouaille. These dogs show the powerful influence of Aotrou de Cornouaille upon Brittany history in the United States. But there were other powerful lines to cross with that of Aotrou.

Douglas de l'Odet was by Cyrano de Ler Leo out of Coant, by Yan du Cosquerou. He was whelped September 25, 1929, and was thus six years old when brought to the United States. Gilda des Causes was sired by Ali de la Marphee out of Biscotte de Callac, by Yoko de la Marphee, out of Cora V de Callac. Rac II of Callac appears twice in her pedigree.

Meg was bred in France by Miss Clara Perry. She was whelped April 8, 1934 by Sam out of Gilda des Causses. Djinn des Veaux was whelped February 22, 1926, a white-and-orange dog bred by B. Benoist. He was by Ramus des Veaux out of Monne I des Veaux by Lac II d'Armorique. Rac II de Callac appears twice in his pedigree.

The first litter born in the United States was from the mating of Douglas de l'Odet to Gilda des Causses. That litter was born June 28, 1935. From this litter, Laurence Richardson bought Bragoubras, D. G. Mann bought Pembas, Louis de la Fleche bought Daoulas, and Mrs. Ruth B. Perry bought Bigotin. Lassie went to George E. Benson.

Louis A. Thebaud imported the great Gwennec de l'Argoat at this time. Gwennec was whelped April 6, 1932. He was a white-and-orange dog by Aotrou de Cornouaille out of Coantic de Cornouaille, by Potic II. Gwennec became a major stud force in the U.S., and in Mexico by puppies taken "in utero" by Histr de Cornouaille.

Brittany Spaniels now began to appear in the United States in surprisingly large numbers. For example, 11 were registered in November, 1936. Ten of these were bred by Juan Pugibet's Casa Blanca Kennels in Mexico. But American-bred dogs were also beginning to appear.

It was in 1936 that the Brittany Spaniel Club of North America was founded. It received official membership in the American Kennel Club on September 15, 1936. Louis A. Thebaud was the first president. Aldo Balsam of Bridgehampton, New York was vice president. Louis de la Fleche of Farmingdale, New York was elected secretary-treasurer and delegate to the American Kennel Club. Among the members in the club's first years were Walter B. Kleeman of Springfield, Ohio; Laurence E. Richardson of Concord, Massachusetts; Dr. Chester Keogh of Chicago, Illinois; Howard P. Clements of Chicago; H. B. Conover of Chicago; René Joubert, then of Detroit, Michigan; Juan Pugibet of Villa Obregon, Mexico; George B. Perry of Boston, Massachusetts; Miss Clara Perry of Boston; and Western Higbie of Lynmour, British Columbia.

On August 12, 1940, Alan Rutherford Stuyvesant of Allamuchy, New Jersey became president. He succeeded Louis A. Thebaud, who had died at the venerable age of 80. Frederick S. Wildman of Bellows & Company became secretary. By then World War II was in progress and it was virtually to destroy the club.

Alan R. Stuyvesant, who had become a great importer of Brittany Spaniels, had joined his brother in organizing an ambulance corps. This was sent to North Africa. The Stuyvesant brothers were captured. Alan returned at the end of the war; his brother was never heard from again.

René Joubert had been the head of the French Line office in Detroit. Louis Thebaud had sent him some of his great dogs. Outdoor sports were a passion with René Joubert. And he did much to promote the breed in the Midwest. But the war brought the closing of the French Line office. Joubert moved to Houston, Texas. Louis de la Fleche would return to France at the end of the war. War duties forced other members to become inactive. But Brittany Spaniel interest was seething. And this was particularly so in the Midwest, which was clamoring for licensed championship Brittany Spaniel field trials. Thus, the stage was set for the formation of the American Brittany Club.

9

First Official American History of the Breed

WHEN THE BRITTANY SPANIEL was first recognized by the American Kennel Club, Arthur Frederick Jones was assigned to write the official history of the breed. Jones was on the staff of *Pure-Bred Dogs— American Kennel Gazette,* and he would later become its editor. His history of the breed differs in some respects from others. And so we feel that it should not be entirely ignored.

Jones obtained his material from several sources. These included Louis Thebaud and Jacques and René Joubert. Louis de la Fleche, a native of Brittany, was then living in the New York-New Jersey area. He, also, may have contributed to this history.

As respects the first Brittany Spaniels to reach America, there is a notable difference from Jones' account and those of others. It is generally accepted as a fact that the first Britts to appear at bench shows were Gilda des Causses and Douglas de l'Odet. They were shown at Boston and Westminster by their importer, Clara G. Perry, in 1935. Westminster is a mid-February show, and Boston was, at that time, an early March show. The American Kennel Club's *The Complete Dog Book,* published early in 1935, contains the first official history of the breed. And in it, Jones says: "The first specimens of the Brittany Spaniel were imported to America in 1931, and they have been exhibited at many of our shows since that time." Jones neither names the dogs nor the shows at which they may have been exhibited. Yet he has always been an accurate reporter. So the possibility does exist that Brittany Spaniels did

Dual Ch. Amos of Edough, a famous early winner and the first Dual Ch. Brittany to win a Sporting group. *Worwick photo.*

Ch. Retta of Avono was an early specialty winner. She was handled by Lee S. Wade.

appear in the Miscellaneous Class at U.S. dog shows before 1935. The following is the complete text of the Jones history as it appeared in 1935.

SPANIELS (BRITTANY)

During the past few years American sportsmen have begun to realize the qualities of a French breed that has been known on the Continent for many centuries. This dog is officially known in the United States as the Brittany Spaniel, but from his size and the manner of his working he might, properly, be called a setter. He stands 18 to 20 inches at the shoulder, is liver and white or, preferably, orange and white, and is either without a tail or has one of only a few inches.

The basic stock for all the spaniels, pointers, and setters came originally from Spain, but the migration of these dogs took place so long ago that it is impossible for anyone to say with certainty just when it occurred. The greatest development of these breeds took place in England, Ireland, and Scotland, but many of them spread through various parts of the Continent, and today there are many varieties—particularly in France—that trace back to the old Spanish strains.

The Brittany Spaniel is one of the oldest of them all, and he was bred up from the original spaniel size in much the same manner as the British, using similar stock, produced the setters. In fact, there is reason to believe that he had attained his present size long before his cousins across the channel had attained to recognizable type.

It is believed by some that the Brittany Spaniel was related to the red and white setter which preceded the golden red setter in Ireland. There is a strong possibility that some of the Irish chieftains, who invaded Gaul—or what is now France—during the first third of the Fifth Century A.D., carried their hunting dogs with them. These dogs, left in France may have contributed something to the development of the Brittany Spaniel. The Irish influence also is seen in the orange and white *Epagneul Ecossais,* or Scotch spaniel—especially if it is remembered that at the time of these invasions the Irish were known as Scoti.

The first tailless ancestor of the modern Brittany Spaniel was bred, about a century ago, at Pontou, a little town situated in the Valley of Douron. It was the result of a cross between a white and mahogany bitch, owned by an old hunter of the region, and a lemon and white dog brought to Brittany by an English sportsman for woodcock shooting. Of the two tailless specimens produced in this litter, only one was considered worth keeping. He grew into a splendid dog. His work in the field has been described as wonderful, and because of this he became a popular stud. All his litters contained puppies either without tails or with short stubs.

The modern history of the Brittany Spaniel dates back only to the beginning of the present century. At that time, the breed had degenerated badly, principally because it had been closely inbred, but also because it had not been regarded as a show specimen. Eventually it caught the attention of Arthur Enaud, a French sportsman with a biological turn of mind. He admired the all-around working qualities of the breed so highly that he undertook to improve its appearance.

M. Enaud went about his work very thoroughly, and he did not try to accomplish too much in too short a time. He was forced to use certain crosses, but

In this photo of Parisienne de Klemanor one can observe correct shoulder angulation in the long extension of the left front leg.

Int. Ch. Wanda de L'Argoat pointing pheasant.

56

after each cross he returned immediately to the old breed. Unfortunately, like many breeders who have done the same thing with other breeds, he left no clear record of the different dogs that entered into this restoration. In fact, it is only through a study of the other breeds available that it is possible to follow this period in the history of the Brittany Spaniel.

The intensification of the desired orange and white color was one of the chief aims of M. Enaud, and for this he found two breeds that had not only the colors but keen scenting ability. One was the *Italian Bracco,* or pointer, and the other was the *Braque de Bourbonnais,* also a pointer. This second breed was the more suitable for his purposes, for besides its other points it was possessed of a very short tail.

The only drawback to the use of pointers was that the coat of the Brittany Spaniel might be affected, but as sparing use was made of crosses and the rest was a matter of selective breeding after improving the blood lines, the modern dog was still the counterpart of his ancient Breton ancestors. By 1907 the breed had been restored to all its former glory.

The first specimens of the Brittany Spaniel were imported to America in 1931, and they have been exhibited at many of our shows since that time. The breed has proved a capable gun dog, and like most of the Continental-bred setters and pointers it can be trained very easily as a retriever. The original use of the breed in France was for woodcock hunting, but it is far from a specialist. And it has proved already that it can hold its own in field trials, for, the first time in competition in America, a Brittany Spaniel carried off a prize against a field of more experienced dogs from other breeds.

Thus ends the first official American history of the Brittany Spaniel. As is so often the case in breed histories, it leaves a lot of questions unanswered. We know that Franche du Cosquerou placed third in the Jockey Hollow shooting-dog stake on April 20, 1935. This is the first officially recorded placing of a Brittany in an American field trial. Yet the last sentence in the official history would indicate that a Brittany Spaniel had placed in, or won, some trial earlier. For the Jockey Hollow trial came too late for Franche's placing to be mentioned in that history. But the dog and the trial elude us.

This photo shows (l. to r.) Walter B. Kleeman with Ch. Buckeye De Klemanor, Hilmer Peterson with Duffy of Chippewa and Tommy Cox with Fld. Ch. Allamuchy Valley Addie.

The judges and winners at an early field trial assemble for the camera. Judges are James Tallmadge (left) and R. L. Sutton. The dogs and their handlers (l. to r.) are Fld. Ch. Georges of Leeway, with owner John W. Lee; Ch. Avono Jake, with Buck Bissell; Burt's Buddy Fentress, with Bill Kull; and Luke's Allamuchy Valley Fury, with Lee Holman.

10

Organization of the American Brittany Club

For MANY YEARS, THE American Kennel Club has had a recognition policy for parent breed clubs. The first club to be organized would be considered as the parent club for that breed. This was occasionally harmful to the breed, since the club might be entirely local in scope, and might be dedicated to only one facet of the sport of dog breeding. For instance, the club might be interested only in conformation and shows, or in field trials.

In recent years, the AKC policy has been more rigid. Before recognition, the breed would require 600 or more dogs, spread over the country, and registered in a breed stud book. But such was not the case when the Brittany Spaniel Club of North America was founded. World War II had hurt the club. Some officers and members could not be located, or were in no position to work for the club or for the breed. Meanwhile, some of the best of the Thebaud dogs had gone to René Joubert in Michigan. Walter B. Kleeman had bought Parisienne from her breeder, Andre Vaudoyer of Winnipeg, Manitoba. She was, you will remember, by Franche du Cosquerou out of Genette de Mesnil.

Dr. Chester H. Keogh of Chicago had established his famed Mac-Eochaidh Kennels, and had bought a son of Gwennec de l'Argoat, named Mirabile Dictu. He had also imported Leltic de Pradalan, and the great Idoc de Cornouaille. He also bought dogs from Juan Pugibet.

Kleeman had produced a litter from Parisienne sired by Gwennec de l'Argoat. The famed all-breed judge, George S. Thomas, had bought Louis Quatorze of Tintagel from Juan Pugibet. Dr. Samuel Milbank, later to be a power in English Springer Spaniels and Labrador Retrievers, and for some years an officer of the Westminster Kennel Club, bought Marie Therese of Tintagel from Pugibet. Alan Stuyvesant's great imports had included Kaer de Cornouaille, a son of Idoc of Cornouaille out of Hem'za de Cornouaille, by Flist III de Cournouaille.

Eugene D. Britton of Fort Worth, Texas had established a kennel under his own name. Dr. Edgar W. Averill, a brother-in-law of Dr. Henry Briggs, had received Patrice of Sharvogue from Dr. Briggs. Patrice, whelped September 13, 1936, was by Gwennec de l'Argoat out of Yvonne de Sharvogue. J. G. White of Walla Walla, Washington, had bought Kelov of Casa Blanca, by Jalov of Casa Blanca out of Jenoff of Casa Blanca.

Thus, Brittany Spaniels had spread across America. But the great importer-breeder Alan Stuyvesant was a prisoner of war. Louis A. Thebaud was gone. And the Midwest was seething with Brittany Spaniel activity. The time had come to found a new parent club, one that would be national in scope.

What follows is taken from the first issue of *The Brittany Field and Bench,* dated October, 1942. Dr. D. B. Ruskin of Karomish Kennels, Caro State Hospital, Caro, Michigan, was editor. Jack L. Whitworth of Avon, Ohio, was business manager. Until his retirement in August, 1971, Whitworth operated the print shop at Hotel Cleveland, later the Sheraton-Cleveland. Dr. Ruskin wrote the following text:

> The American Brittany Club was founded on May 16, 1942, in the Lafayette room of the Hotel Fort Shelby in Detroit. With the Honorable Judge Homer Ferguson, presiding, the meeting was called to order. Those present were Dr. and Mrs. Chester Keogh of Chicago, Mr. and Mrs. H. P. Cline of Rocky River, Ohio, Mr. and Mrs. A. H. Ady of Detroit, Mich., Mrs. Kathryn Adams of Detroit, Mich., Mr. Edgar W. Averill of Birmingham, Mich., Mr. Jack L. Whitworth of Cleveland, Ohio, Mr. Thomas C. Fitzpatrick of Pontiac, Mich., Mr. William K. Martin of Detroit, Mich., Dr. Charles C. Lynch of Detroit, Mich., Mr. Don Waller of Farwell, Mich., Mr. Ralph E. Hughes of Lansing, Mich., Mr. R. B. McCurdy of Detroit, Mich., and Dr. D. B. Ruskin of Caro, Mich.
>
> The meeting opened with a discussion on the advisability and purpose of organizing a club of Brittany Spaniel owners on a national scale, such a club to further the interests of Brittany Spaniels, obtain recognition of the FDSB and the AKC, and to further develop the breed for field and bench.
>
> Formal action was then taken to form a club, national in scope, of Brittany Spaniel owners, to be called the American Brittany Club. It was then necessary to elect officers and it was decided that there should be a three man Board of Directors who, in turn, would be the officers of the Club. The members elected to the Board are: Mr. A. H. Ady, Mr. E. W. Averill, and Dr. D. B. Ruskin, and by

Dr. Chester H. Keogh and four of his early Brittanies. Dr. Keogh was extremely active with Brittanies and played a large part in their early progress. The dogs with him are (l. to r.) Mirabile Dictu, Leltic de Pradalan, Idoc de Cornouaille and Banba MacEochaidh.

action of the Board, Dr. Ruskin was elected as secretary of the Board and the Club.

All owners of registered Brittany Spaniels are eligible to membership and any member of their immediate family is eligible to associate membership. More information on membership can be found elsewhere in this publication.

The members present at the meeting of May 16th also showed their appreciation for the work done and the services rendered the Brittany Spaniel Club by voting honorary memberships to Dr. Chester H. Keogh and to Mr. René Joubert. This is a life sentence, folks.

At a later date, the Board of Directors met and drew up a constitution and by-laws which was subjected to the criticism of the members, and when all the smoke cleared a final draft was drawn up. We include it in this issue for your pleasure and ask you to keep it for future reference.

A membership campaign was then started, and we already are getting results. This is truly becoming a national club. Memberships from all parts of the country. To those who live too far away to be active in the parent organization, we say that in the near future we will be able to assign regions for local chapters. You will then be a member of both the local chapter and the parent organization, and will profit from the activities of both.

This was the beginning. But the road was to be difficult. The American Kennel Club had recognized the older club. The new one could not hold licensed field trials or specialty shows without permission from the Brittany Spaniel Club of North America. Partly because of the inability to communicate with many of the officers and members of the latter club, such permission could not be obtained.

The services of two people were enlisted. One was the author. The other was Frank L. Grant. The author was a dog columnist for the *Cleveland Press,* and was the president of a Springer Spaniel field-trial club. Grant was then the show chairman of the Western Reserve Kennel Club. He was a Doberman Pinscher breeder, and an original obedience trainer before the American Kennel Club established obedience trials. He was also delegate to the American Kennel Club and as such had represented several show-giving clubs.

Both the author and Grant made several trips to New York to plead the cause of the American Brittany Club. Henry D. Bixby was then vice president. It was his policy to defend member and parent clubs even when they had not entirely lived by the American Kennel Club's rules. He also thought it would be unfair to kick out the Brittany Spaniel Club of North America just because it had been so badly crippled by the war. Bixby also had reservations about the new club's name. He felt that "Brittany" should not stand alone, and that the name should be American Brittany Spaniel Club. But many in the new club objected. A spaniel, they felt, was a flushing dog, the Brittany a pointing dog, and therefore not a true spaniel.

A compromise was finally worked out. This was mainly brought about by Grant with the advice of Judge Homer Ferguson. The compromise consisted of merging the two clubs. The name would be the American Brittany Club. Members of the Brittany Spaniel Club of North America would, if they wished, automatically become members of the new club. All the members of both clubs would be permitted to vote on the merger. In the meantime, with a sort of tacit approval by the older, and still parent, club, the American Brittany Club was to be allowed to have licensed, or championship, field trials and shows.

All of this was not accomplished within a couple of weeks or months. It was slightly more than two years after its founding that the American Brittany Club became what its letterhead already stated: Sponsor of the Brittany Spaniel. That letterhead listed A. H. Ady, president; E. W. Averill, vice president; W. B. Kleeman, second vice president; R. B. McCurdy, vice president at large; and Jack L. Whitworth, secretary-treasurer.

Because of its historic importance, we are reprinting in full the official merger letter sent to Henry D. Bixby:

June 6, 1944

Dear Mr. Bixby:

We are happy to inform you that the American Brittany Club and the Brittany Spaniel Club of North America have merged. As you were one of the first to recommend this merger, we feel certain the American Kennel Club will approve it.

The attached joint resolution was agreed upon by the officers of the Brittany Spaniel Club of North America, namely Mr. Louis de la Fleche, Mr. Laurence E. Richardson, and Mr. René Joubert, nephew of the late Mr. Louis Thebaud, former president and organizer of that club; and by Mr. A. H. Ady, Mr. E. W. Averill, Mr. W. B. Kleeman, Lt. Robert B. McCurdy, and J. L. Whitworth, officers of the American Brittany Club. Mr. Alan Stuyvesant, acting president of the Brittany Spaniel Club of North America, and also an active member of the American Brittany Club, is out of the country and cannot be reached, but his manager, Mr. Arthur Danks, assures us he will be in favor of any move that will help the breed.

A copy of this resolution was mailed along with a ballot to the active and voting members of both clubs. List of members of the Brittany Spaniel Club of North America furnished by its secretary, Mr. de la Fleche. List of members of the American Brittany Club furnished by its secretary, Mr. Whitworth. Both lists were given to Mr. Frank L. Grant, Euclid, Ohio, who was selected to mail, check, and receive the returned ballots.

Under the terms of the Merger, as outlined in the joint resolution, fourteen days were allowed for the return of the ballots. A majority was to mean a majority of the actual ballots returned.

112 ballots were mailed to the members of the American Brittany Club, and 20 ballots were mailed to the members of the Brittany Spaniel Club of North America. Two letters addressed to members of the American Brittany Club were returned by the Post Office marked "incorrect address," and three addressed to members of the Brittany Spaniel Club of North America were returned. Two

were marked "addressee deceased," and one was marked "addressee returned to France."

A total of sixty-one (61) ballots were returned to Mr. Grant, fifty nine of them [an apparent discrepancy] were from members of the American Brittany Club and all of them voted "YES" for the merger. There were eleven (11) ballots returned from members of the Brittany Spaniel Club of North America, and all of them voted "YES" for the merger. There was not a single vote against the merger.

Therefore, subject to A.K.C. approval, the merger will take effect immediately. The name of the club will be changed from the Brittany Spaniel Club of North America to the American Brittany Club.

The constitution and a list of members are enclosed.

The officers of the club until the next election in November are as follows: A. H. Ady, president. E. W. Averill, vice president. W. B. Kleeman, 2nd vice president. R. B. McCurdy, vice president at large. Jack L. Whitworth, secretary-treasurer. Delegate to the A.K.C., Louis N. de la Fleche.

The Board of Directors are: Alan Stuyvesant, Laurence E. Richardson, Louis N. de la Fleche, René Joubert, A. H. Ady, E. W. Averill, W. B. Kleeman, R. B. McCurdy, and J. L. Whitworth.

We sincerely hope the above meets the full approval of the American Kennel Club, and ask an early acknowledgment, so that future plans may be made for the advancement of the breed.

Very truly yours,

American Brittany Club	Brittany Spaniel Club of North America
Jack L. Whitworth, Secretary	Laurence E. Richardson, Vice President

Immediate approval was given, and the parent club of the breed became the American Brittany Club. In the ensuing years it has expanded, and its officers and members have worked tirelessly for the breed. It is worth pointing out here that, in the very beginning, the club meant to give each member a voice in the club's operation by establishing regional clubs. This policy, difficult and never easy to administer, has paid in great dividends to the breed, and to clubs and individuals within it.

Ch. Auten's Misty Morning. Owned by Auten's Brittanies. *Booth photo.*

11

The Brittany Spaniel in Canada

THE HISTORY OF THE Brittany Spaniel in Canada is intimately tied into that of the United States and Mexico. The breed gained its initial impetus from Louis A. Thebaud of the United States and Juan Pugibet of Mexico. In Canada there was a third pioneer—Eudore Chevrier, a Frenchman by extraction.

Chevrier operated a breeding and sales kennel, which he registered. It seems probable that he named the kennel Avandale in order to link it to the then-famous Avendale Kennels of England. Avendale bred English Springer Spaniels, and Chevrier bought, bred, imported, and sold hundreds of this breed.

Chevrier had a remarkable ability to sense well in advance the rising popularity of a given breed. He was essentially interested in sporting dogs. He imported hundreds of dogs in the sporting breeds, used them for breeding, and often then resold them. His puppy sales mounted into the thousands.

The connection between Eudore Chevrier and Louis A. Thebaud is not entirely clear. But this much is known. Thebaud imported Genette du Mesnil from France. She was born January 6, 1932, a white-and-orange bitch bred by G. Metayer from Escault du Mesnil out of Crevette de Hirondelle. Before shipping her, Metayer bred her to Gredin du Mesnil, a grandson of the immortal Aotrou de Cornouaille, through his son, Emir du Cosquerou. Earlier accounts state that Genette du Mesnil arrived in the United States on August 6, 1933. But this would appear to be an error. If one allows at least six days for travel, Genette could not have been mated before August 1. Yet, as will be shown, the mating must have taken place much later.

Upon her arrival in the United States, Thebaud shipped her to Eudore Chevrier at Winnipeg. There she produced a litter of six living puppies on October 12, 1933. This is the whelping date, as certified by the Canadian National Livestock Records and the Canadian Kennel Club Stud Book. If Genette arrived on August 6, then her puppies would have had a gestation period of 73 days or more, or at least 10 days longer than normal, which seems improbable.

The Brittany Spaniel was not recognized by the Canadian Kennel Club until 1935, when the breed was given official stud book admission by both the Canadian and American Kennel Clubs. Thus, Chevrier did not register Genette du Mesnil until after the breed's recognition in 1935.

The first of Genette's litter to be registered was Yvette of Avandale, in 1935. Although she was "whelped the property of Chevrier," and was given his Avandale kennel name, Yvette was registered by her second owner, Andre Vaudoyer of Winnipeg. In 1936, Chevrier registered one of the litter that he had kept, Agincourt of Avandale.

In the meantime, Thebaud had imported Franche du Cosquerou from France. He sent Franche to Winnipeg. Andre Vaudoyer bred Yvette of Avandale to Franche. Her litter, born October 31, 1934, included the famous Parisienne. Chevrier bought Parisienne from Vaudoyer, and later sold the dog to Walter B. Kleeman of Springfield, Ohio. Parisienne was entered in the Greater Winnipeg Kennel Club show in 1936 to become the first Brittany Spaniel ever entered in a Canadian dog show.

After using Agincourt of Avandale at stud, Chevrier sold the dog to A. Miller McKay, who showed him at the Picton, Ontario, show in 1937 and got Best of Breed.

But Brittany Spaniel activity in Canada remained weak until 1940. Chevrier seemed to have lost most of his interest in Brittanys. In 1940, five Brittany Spaniels were registered in the Canadian Kennel Club Stud Book. These were Iva de Sainte-Yveline, Izel, Langoat of Casa Blanca, Loquirec of Casa Blanca and Lossac of Casa Blanca.

The Casa Blanca dogs all came from the kennels of Juan Pugibet of Villa Obregon, Mexico. Iva de Sainte-Yveline was whelped in France on July 25, 1934. She was bred by Louis Pigassou. Alan Stuyvesant imported her to the United States, then sent her to Canada. Her sire was Frileux, a son of Cassis du Cosquerou, and her dam was Era de l'Etat by Vite 2nd de l'Etat.

Izel was bred in France by Emil Le Jannick, and was imported by Samuel B. Wells. He sold the dog to Alan Stuyvesant. The latter sold her to F. H. Hatheway of Fredericton, New Brunswick. Izel was white-and-orange-roan in color.

Langoat and Lossac of Casa Blanca were both by Jilgrim of Casa Blanca,

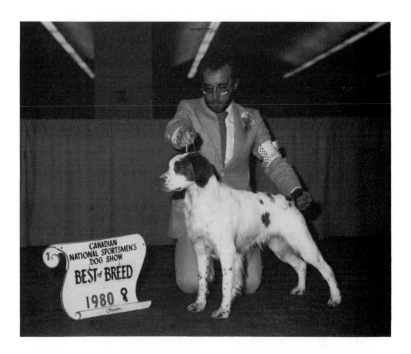

Can., Am. Ch. Torbec Red Hot Prospect going Best of Breed at the Canadian National Sportsmen's Show. Owned by T. G. and Michelle McIntyre, Torbec Kennels and handled by Garrett Lambert. *Streeter photo.*

Can., Am. Ch. Torbec Red Hot Prospect (Can., Am. Ch. Gilkey's Jamboree ex Torbec Red Letter Day), owned by T. G. and Michelle McIntyre, Torbec Kennels. "Boyd" is shown here in the field at a pointing breed Specialty.

The first dual champion of the breed was Britt of Bellows Falls owned by Lucien Ufford.

Canadian Dual Ch. Kipewa's Breton Belle, owned by William McClure, is a Brittany with accomplishments in field, bench and as a producer. She won the ABC 1966 Grouse Classic and has 32 field wins. She is also the dam of two show champions and two field winners. *McNeill photo.*

out of the famous Histr de Cornouaille. Pugibet sold them both to J. Harold McMurray of Fredericton, N.B. They were whelped August 19, 1937. Loquiric of Casa Blanca, a white-and-orange dog whelped October 9, 1937, was by Kobold of Casa Blanca out of Jaiet of Casa Blanca. His Canadian owner was H. G. Chestnut, also from New Brunswick.

In 1941, only four dogs were registered in Canada. Hatheway registered Gunner of Lincoln, by Loquirec of Casa Blanca out of Izel. Frank Shute of Fredericton registered three puppies under his Sunstead name—Jacques, Jalna, and Jeanette of Sunstead. They were whelped September 3, 1939 by Langoat of Casa Blanca out of Iva de Sainte-Yveline.

There were eight registrations in 1942. Two of the more important ones are mentioned here. C. Leslie Laing of Vancouver, British Columbia, bought Allamuchy Valley Pierre, later a champion, from Alan Stuyvesant. Pierre was by Allamuchy Valley Mike out of Iane de Cornouaille. A. J. Pocock of Beebe, Quebec, bought Allen's Tex from R. C. Ward of Missoula, Montana. Tex was by Ace of Brittany, a son of Gwennec de l'Argoat, out of Pride of Brittany. Tex was whelped September 19, 1940, and was described as being brown-and-white.

Brittanys now began to appear at dog shows. Bob Along of Langoat, owned by R. E. Healy of Moncton, N.B., was Best of Breed at the Moncton show in 1942. Mae De Cornean, owned by W. R. Willgrass of Burnaby, B.C., was Best of Breed at the International Kennel Club of Vancouver show in the same year.

In 1943, Lucien Ufford of Bellows Falls, Vermont, took Loufel Daisy to Moncton where she won Best of Breed. Mae De Cornean was Best of Breed at the International Kennel Club of Vancouver show of 1943, and at the Taunton House School Kennel Club. Pierre De Basgard was Best of Breed at London, Ontario, and Voyageur MacEochaidh was Best of Breed at the second Vancouver Island K.C. show.

There were only seven dogs shown in 1944, but the sudden surge of interest in the breed in the Pacific Northwest resulted in the crowning of the first three Brittany Spaniel champions in Canadian history. All three were owned in the area of Vancouver and Western British Columbia. In all, 33 dogs competed at shows that year. The three champions were: Nan of Chippewa, bred by Hilmer Peterson of Brandon, Minnesota, and owned by Western Higbie of Lynmour, B.C.; Pierre de Cornean and Voyageur Mac Eochaidh, both owned by W. R. Willigress of New Westminster, B.C.

Pierre de Cornean, or Pierre of Cornean, as he was also known, was unregistered at the time he became a champion. There was a technical defect in his registration application, so registration was refused. He was whelped on February 4, 1944, by Jotek Jr. out of Mae de Cornean. In October of 1947 the Canadian National Livestock Records granted him registration under Article 33, Section 7, of the rules. This rule permits the registration of a champion when there is only a technical error in the pedigree. Pierre won his championship while still a puppy.

Interest in the breed now grew rapidly. There were 120 registrations in 1946, and four dogs completed championships. These were Allamuchy Valley Pierre, Mae de Cornean, Cecile of Westhaven and Pride of Westhaven.

Perhaps the greatest name in the Canadian field-trial history of the Brittany Spaniel is that of Jack T. Mayer. Even before 1940 Mayer was training field dogs. His headquarters were in the great woodcock and grouse area around Moncton, N.B., near Gunningsville and Coles Island. Mayer began training Pointers and English Setters. But these breeds are—ideally—wide-ranging dogs. In the thick wooded cover of New Brunswick they were apt to get out of sight and hearing, and therefore out of control. Thus, unless trained to work rather closely, they were not ideal for New Brunswick hunting. Mayer later developed a method of "range training" the wide-going dogs, but in the early days this was extremely difficult.

Mayer was a close reader of the *American Field.* And in early Brittany Spaniel history, both the American and Canadian Brittanys were registered with the American Field's *Field Dog Stud Book.* It was in the *American Field* that Mayer first read about the close-working French pointing spaniels. They appeared to be perfect for New Brunswick woodcock and grouse hunting.

One day he showed an *American Field* article to a Massachusetts client. Then he asked: "What is the use of getting our arms pulled off trying to bring the big dogs back into range? Why don't we try one of these Brittany Spaniels?"

Along with the article there was an advertisement for Brittany Spaniel puppies owned in Kansas. The Massachusetts man immediately sent off a telegram to purchase one. Later, he sent the pup to Mayer for training. She was only six months old, and when Mayer first took her into the field he was amazed to see her point and retrieve without training. She was named Coverdale Mitzie. Coverdale is Mayer's kennel name. She was by Duke of Windsor out of Wallie Warfield.

Mayer believes that Iva de Sainte-Yveline was the first Brittany to arrive in New Brunswick. And he recounts that Alan Stuyvesant had a policy of placing Britts where they would bring the most attention. Thus, Iva went to his New Brunswick hunting companion, Frank Shute, of Fredericton. Later, he placed Izel with Hatheway.

In the fall of 1940, Lucien Ufford of Bellows Falls, Vermont, was experimenting with Gordon Setters. These were slower and closer-ranging dogs than Pointers and English Setters. Ufford took his dogs to the Moncton area for the woodcock shooting season. On the first morning, Jack Mayer hunted with Ufford and the Gordons. Not a single grouse or woodcock was brought down. That afternoon, the Gordons were kenneled, and Mayer brought out his bitch, Coverdale Mitzie. The men got their game limits.

This is Jack
Mayer, a pioneer
trainer of Brittany
Spaniels in
Canada.

Coverdale Mitzie, owned by Jack Mayer, was a famous
Canadian field trial performer in the earlier days of the
breed. She is shown here on point.

Ufford said later that Mitzie's work had been nothing short of fantastic. He was instantly converted to the breed. Within weeks, he had bought the famous Mollie de Ver Der Mont. She was by Puchyan Britt out of Leostic of Casa Blanca.

The success of the New Brunswick Brittany Spaniels brought about the organization of the Maritime Brittany Club. On October 26–27, 1946, Ufford and Alan Stuyvesant judged the first trial given by this club. A. D. Gray and Grover Torrens, both of Moncton, were in charge.

Of this trial we know only that Gray's Brittanys were major winners. The following year, there was a trial at Charlottetown, Prince Edward Island. In it, the Brittany Spaniels had to compete against Pointers and English Setters. Alan Stuyvesant's Allamuchy Valley Addie, though still young enough to compete as a puppy, won the open all-age stake.

The following year, the Maritime Brittany Club gave its second trial. It stands out as one of the greatest of all the early trials. The dates were October 27–28, 1947, and the courses were over the famous Rampasture Covers near Elgin. There were 44 dogs entered, of which 36 were American, and 8 were from New Brunswick and Prince Edward Island.

The judges were Raymond Hoyer and Robert Farnsworth, both from Andover, Massachusetts. A report of the trial said: "The judges placed the winners solely on merit and ability to find birds." Tommy Cox and Bill Kull had strings of dogs with them. Cox had four puppies entered and placed all four in the puppy stake. Yves Besnier, a Mexican fancier and a representative of the Mexican Kennel Club, attended. The trial was held under the rules of the American Brittany Club.

Broad Archer of Richmont, owned by Dr. R. C. Busteed, then of Savannah, Georgia, won the open all-age stake, with Cox handling. Avono Jill of Karomish, owned by Jack L. Whitworth of Avon, Ohio, and handled by Kull, was second. Iza Mac Eochaidh, owned by Dr. H. E. Longsdorf of Mt. Holly, New Jersey, and handled by Jack Mayer, was third. Aotrou's Jacques, owned and handled by J. T. Sprague of Honeoye Falls, New York, was fourth.

Bill Kull handled the first and second dogs in the Derby. They were Georges of Leeway, owned by John W. Lee of Indianapolis, Indiana, first, and Calatin Mac Eochaidh Sam, owned by Dr. T. J. Talbott of Lima, Ohio, second. Third went to Rouge Kaer de Klemanor, owned and handled by Walter Kleeman, then president of the American Brittany Club. A. J. Hicks of Gunningsville, handled his Meil du Shepodie to fourth.

The open shooting-dog stake was won by Buckeye de Klemanor, owned and handled by Kleeman, who also handled his Brittany House Abner into second. Parky's Joan, owned by Eral Larsen of Minneapolis, Minnesota, was third. And Brittany House Ann, owned by Dr. Talbott, was fourth.

Ray Goland handled his Pepper of Loufel to first in the shooting-dog stake. An odd feature of the trials was that Allamuchy Valley Addie, winner of

Can., Am. Ch. Ketch's Redwing Freckles (Can., Am. Ch. Jacques Prince Valiant ex Ch. Gilkey's Spring Time, C.D.), bred by Tobi and Greg McNeal. Owner-handled by Ronald W. Ketcham of Ketch's Brittanies, Montville, Ohio. He is shown completing his Canadian championship under judge John Lawreck. *Alex Smith photo.*

Can., Am., Bermuda Ch. Torbec First Dawn (Ch. Torbec Filibuster ex Francesca of Torbec) was the personal gun dog of T. G. McIntyre until her death at 11 years of age.

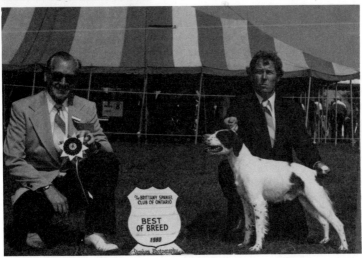

Ch. Torbec Coronation finished his championship undefeated in the breed. Corky is a litter brother of Ch. Torbec Red Hot Prospect. Co-owners: Ted Palmer (handling) and T. G. and Michelle McIntyre. *Stonham photo.*

the open all-age stake the week before on Prince Edward Island, got only a second in the puppy stake, and was otherwise unplaced.

The Maritime Brittany Club had actually originated field trials in New Brunswick. In 1948 its affiliate, the Moncton Brittany, Pointer & Setter Club, held trials at Turtle Creek. Jack T. Mayer served as field marshall. His son, Jack T. Mayer Jr., made his debut as a trainer-handler. The Coverdale affix was now making a name for itself all over Canada. Three of the four first-place winners were bred by Mayer and carried the Coverdale name.

Jack Mayer Jr. handled Coverdale Eva, owned by Alan Stuyvesant, to victory in the puppy stake, and to second in the derby. First place went to a Pointer. Coverdale Slug, owned and handled by G. B. Wetmore of Hillsboro, N. B. won the open all-age. Mayer had also bred Luke's Allamuchy Chesta, owned and handled by Alan Stuyvesant, which won the shooting dog stake. He had also bred the Pointer, Shawinigan Brown-Eyed Susan, winner of the derby.

Allamuchy Kaergirl of Loufel, handled by Cox for Mrs. Rene Espourteil of Angle Point, Oregon, was second in the all-age. The Pointer was third. Alan Stuyvesant handled Rumba de L'Argoat to fourth. All told, Americans captured 10 of 16 placements. But the work of the outnumbered Canadian dogs proved that they were the equal to any in North America.

Ever since the early days, Brittany Spaniels have competed against each other on both sides of the border. Perhaps three American dogs should be mentioned here. The first was Dr. Edgar W. Averill's American Ch. Diane de Beauch, U.D. Diane won her bench championship in Canada, and also completed a C.D.X. title there.

American Dual Ch. Way-Kan Jeff also won a Canadian dual championship. He is the first dog of any breed ever to do this. Way-Kan Jeff died in the summer of 1971 at the age of 12. During that same month Bernie's Butch, owned by Bernus Turner of Kent, Washington, joined Way-Kan Jeff by winning his Canadian and American dual championships. Other Brittany Spaniels have starred on both sides of the border. Their records appear in the Canadian statistics given below.

Up to 1974, Canada had produced five dual champions—show and field. It had crowned 73 show champions and 10 field champions. Nineteen Brittany Spaniels have won Companion Dog (C.D.) titles only. Five have won Companion Dog Excellent (C.D.X.) titles. And two have won Utility Dog (U.D.) degrees. In addition, one Brittany Spaniel has won a Tracking Dog (T.D.) title.

Besides American Ch. Diane De Beauch, U.D., American Ch. Sun Tan's Happy Hi Tone, C.D., also won both a Canadian show title and a Canadian C.D. Canadian Ch. Jocko's Tic Toc Spice also won a C.D.X. title. Canadian Field Ch. Corky De Leigh and Can. Ch. Poplar Hill Riptide also won C.D. degrees.

The foregoing was written for the first edition of this book, published in 1974. Since that time, two Britts have won dual championships—show and field—a number have won field trial championships, and numerous dogs have won in obedience. The American Best in Show winner, Ch. Ffynant's Happy Time won a Best in Show at Lionsgate, the only Britt to take this high honor in Canada. Also, American Champion Diane de Beauch, U.D., repeated her titles in Canada.

Listed below are the official Canadian Kennel Club statistics with, in most cases, the dates they received their awards.

SHOW CHAMPIONSHIPS

Alimont's Bushwack'R of Aluvia	7/10/80
Aluvia Auten's Misty	9/23/81
Aluvia Can-Dee	4/8/76
Aluvia Jacques Peter	10/2/79
Aluvia Long Shot	6/18/76
Aluvia Rustic Prince (USA)	6/20/75
Aluvia Pepi La Tigre	3/11/76
Aluvia Rusty Bell Of Snowdon	7/26/77
Aluvia Spring Sadie	3/28/31
Donnyweir Western Boy	2/23/83
Doubledees Way-Kan Gus	10/1/79
Evergrays Tick Tock Basil	12/14/81
Exploits Sparkle	4/19/73
Faison's Loudmouth Lime	11/29/85
Fanny-Lynns	7/30/79
Foothills Rustic Prince	4/29/81
Fosters Pride Benji	10/16/80
Frech Farah Star Light	5/22/51
Gilkey's Apricot Brandy	3/27/79
Gilkey's Jamboree	10/15/75
Greenlane's Majestic Lady	4/12/79
Halina's Cheyenne Samantha	5/5/83
Harris Parklake Lil Bit	11/17/81
Hob Nobbin Holly Hobbie	10/8/82
Hunterlane Yankee Storm	1/23/79
Hunterlane's Copper Tigre	5/24/79
Hunterlane's Duc D'Argyll	9/30/81
J W Woodstock	3/23/81
Jacques Prince Valiant	5/29/74
Jeff's Tic Toc Brandy	4/4/78
Jock O'Rion	2/13/79
Jogus' Freya	7/12/79

K Star Cheyenne Macdevil	8/2/85
K Star Cheyenne Nickette	1/13/86
Kathy's Cheyenne Starlina	7/18/84
Kathy's Maverick Starlet	8/2/85
Kathy's Star Buck IL	7/18/84
Killy's Danny Boy	11/16/78
Kathy's Star Double Dribble	7/18/84
Kinwashkly Bambi Sue	4/13/82
Kinwashkly B an-Dee Max	5/7/83
Kinwashkly Boomerang	10/16/80
Kinwashkly Brown Sugar	12/6/80
Kinwashkly Commandin Bandit	9/30/76
Kinwashkly Country Rambler	4/9/81
Kinwashkly Flying Fox	4/12/82
Kinwashkly Love At First Bite	1/19/83
Kinwashkly Magnum Rider	10/16/80
Kinwashkly Princess Sioux	9/30/76
Kinwashkly Ran-Dee	9/30/76
Kinwashkly Regal Blue	9/28/84
Kinwashkly Sugarpatch Tina	6/7/63
Kipewa's Le Roux	6/19/79
Kipewa's Siandra	10/2/73
Kipewa's St. Ives	2/2/78
Lady Samantha's Tippy	9/17/73
Lady's Sir Charles Of Geridon	12/11/73
M and M's Magic Muffin	11/13/81
Maggie Muggen Of Aluvia	7/26/77
Mar-J's Happy Daze	12/11/78
Mirbel	5/9/80
Mitzys Blu Ridge River Cholly	5/28/80
Moore's Brandy Cork	6/17/81
Mousse	10/25/78
Nojo's Gusto	4/7/82
P-Jay Of Aluvia	4/7/83
Plainsman's Special Lady	9/22/82
Plainsman's Trailblazer	10/19/84
Prince Mercer	4/6/86
Prince Valiant's J and J	2/8/82
Princess Brittina Et Sue	9/18/51
Ramblin Chocolate Dandy	4/18/84
Rebecca of Aluvia	2/28/79
Red Alder Jen's Anna	10/29/75
Renwoods Nicodemus	10/1/75

Fld. Ch., Amateur Fld. Ch. Windagail's Belle Prince F.D., (Kipewa's Kington ex Kipewa's Encore Belle), owned and handled by Pete Dolynski, Beamsville, Ontario, was one of the few Brittanies on the CKC field-trial circuit in the early 1970s. He was campaigned extensively in the AKC all-age events and in Canada against Pointers in addition to regular CKC stakes. His competitive career continued until he was thirteen.

The sun is sinking on a good day in the field for these Canadian hunters.

Rockview's Buck	6/7/82
Rockview's Queen Of Layn	2/23/79
Rustic Hills Devon Canadian	10/8/82
Sequani's Jody of Aluvia	4/17/78
Shannon Creek Star O'Edwards	10/16/80
Span-Dor's Ruffed Duff	10/13/75
Sparky's Little Dan	12/17/79
Summertime Glory	7/12/84
Suzabob's Hun Harrasser	8/9/79
Sweet Seasons Call Me Oats	2/10/83
Tande's Cisco Kid	8/24/77
Tande's Midnight Lady	2/8/78
Tande's Rambling Shandy	1/17/80
Tande's Midnight Susie	2/8/78
Dandy's Royal Dusty	3/14/79
Tierra Buena's Baron De Tigre	3/9/78
Torbec Brain Wave	7/27/76
Torbec Coronation	9/12/79
Torbec Country Fair	3/15/83
Torbec Dexterity	4/3/73
Torbec Field Day	9/12/79
Torbec Northwind Thor	5/4/82
Torbec Pay Day	5/14/75
Torbec Priority	1/22/75
Torbec Re-Gal Alicia	7/10/78
Torbec Ed-Gal Lila	12/2/75
Torbec Re-Gal Mist	7/15/77
Torbec Red Hot Prospect	9/11/79
Torbec Regal Wave	6/27/73
Torbec Samson	1/8/80
Torbec Tag Day	9/25/73
Tous Amor Anjou	10/20/81
Vashti Of Rondy	12/20/76
Victory Banner	7/15/80
Whispering Tick	1/7/82
Wincrest Number One Son	5/18/82
Windagail's Sunshine Belle	3/11/74

OBEDIENCE AND FIELD TRIALS

Bo Brandy Of Scipio, C.D.	4/15/81
Brittspan's Sharptail Sheila, Field Trial Ch.	11/14/72
Buffy's Cinnamon Triscuit, C.D.	9/1/77

Kaychuck's Brutus, C.D., F.T.Ch., F.D.X.   3/30/79
Lea's Candy, F.T.Ch.   5/10/73
Sharptail Lady, F.T.Ch.   2/2/76

OBEDIENCE TRIAL CHAMPIONS

Rita White Shadow   1/11/84
Taffy Dethorsen   8/22/74

Judges of the New Brunswick trial Dr. John Likely (left) and Charles Bennett (center) with Bill McClure, columnist for *Dogs in Canada* and noted field trialer on both sides of the border.

Canadian Ch. Kipewa's Paradise Rex, owned by William McClure, has placed in the Sporting group and is the sire of two field winners.

Coquette of Bonnechere, owned by William McClure, is the dam of two field winners.

12

The First Field Trial Tests

THE FIRST BRITTANY SPANIELS to come to North America came to hunt. Their reputation had been made in France principally as superb woodcock and grouse dogs. But Louis Thebaud thought they might be ideal for quail hunting. Others thought they might be suitable for use in rather restricted hunting areas where men wanted a pointing dog that could be used by a man on foot. Others were eager to try the new breed on pheasants. So it was that the first Brittany Spaniels were eagerly tried under American shooting conditions. They quickly proved their merit. Yet for most sportsmen a big question remained. How would these dogs compare to Pointers and English Setters? So sportsmen tended to reserve judgment until the dogs had proven themselves on American game birds in field trials. There were plenty of these in most sections of the U.S. and Canada, and there were also trials in Mexico. Almost all of them were run under the procedures set up by the American Field and the Amateur Field Trial Clubs of America. These trials had become virtually "breed specific." That is, Pointers and English Setters dominated them to so great an extent that few dogs of other pointing breeds competed against them. For most of the sportsmen who competed, the Brittany, a spaniel, seemed a ridiculous possibility for their trials.

Trial procedures in some countries, and in various areas of those countries, differed. In England, and in some areas of continental Europe, a dog was required to point. Then, upon command, it went in to flush. Some trials required that the flushed bird be shot. The dog might be sent in to flush, or the handler might flush it. The handler or a professional gunner might do the shooting. The dog would have to be steady to flush, mark the fall, and then make the retrieve. A somewhat similar situation exists today in the United States at trials for Gordon Setters. Eastern clubs normally require the owner or handler to flush the bird. The handler fires a blank pistol. At Pacific Coast trials, the handler flushes the birds. Professional gunners then bring them down. The dogs must mark the birds and retrieve to hand. But at pointing dog trials under the procedures of the American Field, the handler flushes the bird, then fires a blank cartridge. For the new Brittany Spaniel owners, this was a change from European procedures. So some slight retraining of the dogs was necessary. Still, these sportsmen were anxious to test their dogs against the well established and highly competent Pointers and English Setters.

We do not know when the first Brittany Spaniel appeared in an American field trial. There are hundreds of informal events that go unreported. But the Jockey Hollow Field Trial Club in New Jersey was already an old, well-established club, and one hallowed by long tradition. At its event on April 20, 1935, Franche du Cosquerou, owned by Louis A. Thebaud, placed third. Shortly thereafter, Brittany Spaniels began to appear in trials in Mexico, in many areas of the United States and in British Columbia. Histr de Cornouaille ran creditably in Mexico and Texas. Meanwhile, Alan Stuyvesant, a member of Jockey Hollow, had seen the Thebaud dogs. He imported Iane de Cornouaille in 1936. Iane had been whelped in France before Histr went to Mexico. Iane placed in American events, as did Ebob's Jannick Kay, a son of Hart de la Casa Blanca, and a fully bred Mexican dog.

It must be remembered that Louis Thebaud began importing Brittany Spaniels at an age when most men have retired to the fireside. He was 76 years old when Franche du Cosquerou placed third in the Jockey Hollow trials. Now Thebaud sent his three finest dogs to his near-nephew, René Joubert, at Detroit. The three were Franche du Cosquerou, Fenntus, and Hai du Cosquerou. René Joubert has said that hunting and field sports were a way of life for him. Consequently, he spent as much time as he could with the three dogs. Under his handling, Fenntus placed second in the members' shooting-dog stake at the Royal Oak Club trials. The next spring, in April 1937, she won the stake.

In the years that followed, Michigan, Ohio and the Chicago area became a great triangle in which Brittany Spaniel activity increased greatly. In the fall of 1939, the first all-Brittany trial was held in the Detroit area. The winner was Fanche's French Line (usually called Napoleon). Since René Joubert represented the French Line shipping company, the relationship to René Joubert's dogs is obvious. Fanche's French Line was owned and handled by Judge Homer Ferguson. The dog defeated Franche du Cosquerou and Gwennec de l'Argoat. The following year, Kaer de Cornouaille won with Fanche's French Line second. It is of note that Judge Ferguson did most of the legal work in the founding of the American Brittany Club. But his work with Brittany Spaniels ended shortly after the club's organization when he became

Ch. Avono Jake (left) and Ch. Kaerson of Loufel at the breakaway of the American Brittany Club Trials of 1948.

Allamuchy Valley Luke, owned by Walter Clements, was a trailblazer that brought fame to himself and his breed. A French-bred, he competed successfully against pointers and setters at American field trials.

the United States Senator from Michigan.

At these early Michigan trials, the birds were shot. Consequently, most of the dogs had to run under entirely different conditions at different trials. We have mentioned the victory of Kaer de Cornouaille. He is one of the great dogs in American Brittany Spaniel history. He competed in trials against Pointers and English Setters in this country and Mexico, and the brilliance of his performances did much to give the Brittany Spaniel its place in the American bird-dog field.

Kaer was whelped on August 1, 1936. He was bred by the great Frenchman, Emile Bourdon, at his Cornouaille Kennels. A short pedigree of him reads like this: By Idoc de Cornouaille out of Hem'za de Cornouaille, by Flist III de Cornouaille out of Diwal de Cornouaille, by Potic II out of Ayout. Idoc was a son of Huch de Bleun Brug, out of Gaud de Guilben by Dag de Basgard, out of Dora de Carigne, by Bath de Callac out of Yotte de Basgard. Idoc de Cornouaille was brought to America by Dr. Chester H. Keogh of Chicago.

Alan Stuyvesant imported Kaer de Cornouaille in September 1938. Some two months later, Kaer ran in the trials of the Jockey Hollow Field Trial Club. He placed third in the shooting-dog stake. The *American Field* report says that "Kaer ran the course with good judgment and with considerably better pace and range than most of the pointers and setters running against him. A nice find, followed by a good retrieve, climaxed his race."

Kaer took a second the following month in the members' shooting-dog stake at Jockey Hollow. He then placed second at trials near Vera Cruz, Mexico. Kaer won first place in finals of the Jockey Hollow gun-dog competition for 1941. Jockey Hollow had a series of trials, with the winners of each to compete in a final event. Having won a preliminary, Kaer now won the finals. The victory made him the best shooting dog to be owned by a member.

Howard Clements had bought Allamuchy Valley Luke from Alan Stuyvesant. In 1940, Luke took a second in the all-age stake at the Chicagoland trials. And he was voted the second best all around shooting dog in the trials. Walter Kleeman's Parisienne also was placing in trials, in competition with Pointers and English Setters.

Then a critical time came for the Brittany Spaniel in America. Louis Thebaud had died in 1939. Alan Stuyvesant, who had seen Thebaud's dogs at Jockey Hollow, had begun an astonishing import program. But Europe was involved in World War II. Alan Stuyvesant and his brother had entered the war on the side of France. They had organized and equipped an ambulance corps. Alan was now a prisoner of war, his brother was to be forever "missing in action." The Brittany Spaniel Club of North America had virtually ceased to exist. The American Brittany Club was organized, in part, because Brittany Spaniel owners could not make contact with the parent club. In part, also, the center of Brittany activity had moved into the Michigan-Ohio-Illinois

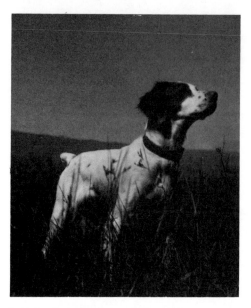

Dual Ch., Canadian Ch., AFC Sirius Sashay, owned by
Nancy and John Hultquist.

Dual Ch. Sequani's Kwail Kall Jud, owned by Manuel
J. Vagos, is the second Field champion and the first
Dual from the Brookmont Kennels.

triangle. At its October, 1942 meeting, the club could report that 59 per cent of its members came from these three states. But the club had members in 17 states, and Juan Pugibet in Mexico.

At that meeting, Dr. D. B. Ruskin reported that, for more than a year, mail sent to the Brittany Spaniel Club of North America had been returned unclaimed. Meanwhile, there had been seven trials for Brittany Spaniels alone in the Michigan area. Dr. Ruskin had been named correspondent and official columnist on the breed for the official AKC magazine, *Pure-Bred Dogs—The American Kennel Gazette.*

Cries were being heard all over America for an official trial. But ideas as to procedure differed. Some wanted to follow the procedure at American Field trials, in which the pointed game was flushed but not shot. Others wanted the birds flushed, marked, and retrieved—the procedure that had been used in the trials for Brittany Spaniels alone. And Allamuchy Valley Luke had won the last.

The American Brittany Club now sponsored a formal national amateur shooting-dog stake. It was held at the Outland Riding Club, 14 miles from downtown Detroit, on October 11, 1942. R. B. McCurdy was field trial chairman. The judges were Hunter Gaines of Lansing, Michigan, and Robert Herndon of Detroit. In addition to the shooting-dog stake, there was a derby and a puppy stake. In the national amateur shooting-dog stake, two pheasants were planted in the bird field for each brace. In some cases, the birds had flushed before the dogs entered the bird field.

In its second issue, December, 1942, *The Brittany Field & Bench* gives an official report of the trial:

FIRST PLACE went to Suzette of Chippewa, owned and handled by Hilmer Peterson of Brandon, Minn. Suzette broke fast and ran a beautiful field. She made her find in the bird field, but the bird flew low and towards the gallery, and there was no kill. She was later called back to work in the bird cover. She made her find. Peterson killed the bird and the dog made a perfect retrieve.

SECOND AWARD was won by Reliew Rene, owned and handled by C. L. Williams of Birmingham, Mich. Reliew Rene was in the fifth brace and by that time the day was getting quite warm. Reliew Rene made her find and Williams got the bird. The dog retrieved nicely.

THIRD was taken by Marron Glace, owned by Dr. Keogh of Chicago, and handled by Mr. Thomas W. Cox of South Dakota. She broke fast, made her find and point. Mr. Cox dropped the bird with a wing shot. Marron Glace was unable to make the find or retrieve. Marron Glace was called back to work in bird cover, being braced with Suzette of Chippewa, and made a sight back while Suzette made her find.

Other entries in the all age stake were:

Sorcha Mac Eochaidh, owned and handled by Mr. Peterson. Sorcha made her find, the bird flushed wild, but Sorcha was steady to wing.

Potainne de Sharvogue, owned and handled by E. W. Averill of Birmingham, Mich.

Patrice de Sharvogue, owned and handled by E. W. Averill. The bird flushed wild, but was brought down by Mr. Averill. But Patrice refused to retrieve.

Betsy de Bonaventure, owned and handled by R. B. McCurdy of Detroit, made the retrieve of the bird brought down by Mr. Averill.

Tutti Frutti Mac Eochaidh, owned by Dr. Keogh and handled by Mr. Cox, was paired with Suzette of Chippewa, and backed her nicely.

Kiki Mac Eochaidh, owned and handled by C. L. Williams.

Beau de Bonaventure, owned and handled by R. B. McCurdy, made his find. The bird flushed wild and out of shooting range, Beau was called back to cover the bird field, but no find resulted.

Gwennec's Pascey, owned and handled by Mrs. Mildred Ady and handled by Al H. Ady, Detroit, Mich., was paired with Reliew Rene. One bird flushed when planted and Reliew Rene made the find on the other bird.

Gwennec D'Etoile, owned and handled by Mrs. Kathryn Adams. Etoile broke fast and ran a nice field. Her bird ran, following a hedge row across the field and flushed wild. Etoile was steady to flush.

Aotrou Mac Eochaidh was a by-dog, owned and handled by Mr. Ady. The bird ran and the dog bumped him and then chased him out of sight.

SUMMARY

First—Suzette of Chippewa, bitch, by Morris de l'Argoat Basgard ex Sorcha Mac Eochaidh. Hilmer Peterson, owner and handler.

Second—Reliew Rene, dog, by Gwennec de l'Argoat ex Franche's Smarty. C. L. Williams, owner-handler.

Third— Marron Glace Mac Eochaidh, bitch, by Idoc de Cornouaille ex Leltic de Pradalan.

DERBY

The derby was run over the same field and one bird was staked out in the field for the dogs to work on. There were 13 entries.

First place went to Brit of Bellows Falls, owned by Mr. Lucien H. Ufford of Bellows Falls, Vermont, and handled by Mr. Cox.

Second place went to Chipps Brit of Chippewa, owned and handled by Mr. Peterson.

Third place went to Chartreux Mac Eochaidh, owned by Dr. Keogh, and handled by Mr. Cox.

Other entries in the Derby were:

Ogma Mac Eochaidh, owned by Dr. Yant of Cleveland and handled by Mr. Cox.

Andre Phillipe de Bonaventure, owned and handled by E. B. Galloway, Grosse Pointe, Mich.

Andre de Carnac, owned and handled by Mr. J. Whitworth of Avon, Ohio.

Brit Les Chien, owned and handled by Dr. Batson of Mt. Pleasant, Mich.

Brehon Mac Eochaidh, owned by E. Wood of Wisconsin, and handled by Mr. Cox.

Suzette of Chippewa, owned and handled by Mr. Peterson.

Zuk de Beauchamps, owned and handled by Mr. Gayek of St. Clair Shores, Mich.

Bonne de Beauchamps, owned by Mr. Whitworth and handled by Mr. Averill.

Benedictine Mac Eochaidh, owned by Mr. Cline of Cleveland, Ohio, and handled by Mr. Cox.

Macaron Mac Eochaidh, owned by Dr. Keogh and handled by Mr. Cox.

SUMMARY

First—Brit of Bellows Falls, dog, by Kaer de Cornouaille ex Oged de la Casa Blanca, owned by Mr. Ufford and handled by Mr. Cox.

Second—Chipps Brit of Chippewa, dog, by Morris de l'Argoat Basgard ex Sorcha Mac Eochaidh, owned and handled by Mr. Peterson.

Third—Chartreux Mac Eochaidh, dog, by Idoc de Cornouaille ex Leltic de Pradalan. Dr. Keogh owner, Mr. Cox handler.

PUPPY STAKE

The puppies were run on a shorter course. There were five entries.

First place went to Chiquo of Chippewa, dog, by Morris de l'Argoat Basgard ex Sorcha Mac Eochaidh, owned by Mr. H. Wassau of Minnesota and handled by Mr. Peterson.

Second place went to Brit Les Chien, dog, by Calatin Mac Eochaidh ex Bakers Flirt, owned and handled by Dr. Batson.

Third place went to Jacques de Bonaventure, dog, by Beau de Bonaventure ex Betsy de Bonaventure, owned by Mr. Fitzpatrick of Pontiac and handled by Mr. Scully of Pontiac.

Others entered were Jojo of Chippewa, owned by Mr. Dell of Minnesota, and handled by Mr. Peterson, and Biddy of Briarcliff, owned by Mr. MacMichaels (handler not known).

Notably this trial brought out two dogs who were to be among the first dual champions of their breed—Brit of Bellows Falls, and Aotrou Mac Eochaidh. A system of trial points was worked out, with five for a win, three for a second, and one for a third. Walter B. Kleeman, who had to miss the trial, gave a special silver trophy for the person who won the most points. The trophy, given to stimulate multiple entries, was won by Hilmer Peterson.

Some of the officials at the National Trials in 1944. They are the author (mounted at left), Edward Dana Knight (mounted at right). The bird planter is Jack Murphy and field marshall, Lee French, stands before Mr. Knight. The horseman in the center is unidentified.

Ch. Buccaneer de Klemanor (Ch. Buck of Chippewa ex Ch. Jule of Loufel), owned by Walter B. Kleeman.

13

The First Licensed Trial and Show

BOTH MEMBERS AND NONMEMBERS of the American Brittany Club were now clamoring for a championship field trial and a licensed bench show, or specialty show as it is usually called. Under American Kennel Club rules, the Brittany Spaniel Club of North America was the parent club of the breed and would have to give permission. But its president, Alan Stuyvesant, was a prisoner of war, and its secretary could not be reached. The American Kennel Club at last agreed to license both a field trial and a bench show without parent club permission. But it did suggest that an experienced, but non-Brittany, club act as host for both events.

The Ravenna Field Trial Club at Ravenna, Ohio, had been conducting licensed trials for English Springer and Cocker Spaniels. It had also held Pointer and English Setter trials until told by the American Kennel Club that it could no longer do so. That is, it had been told that it would have to be a spaniel or a pointing dog club. It had settled for the former, but it did have experienced personnel for both types of trials.

The American Kennel Club then agreed to allow the Ravenna club to act as host club for the Brittany field trial and bench show. The author was selected as field trial and bench show chairman. The trial and show were to be held in conjunction with a trial for English Springers and Cocker Spaniels. Today, it must appear to have been an odd arrangement, especially since the author was also field trial chairman for the flushing dog trials. Yet it worked out very well.

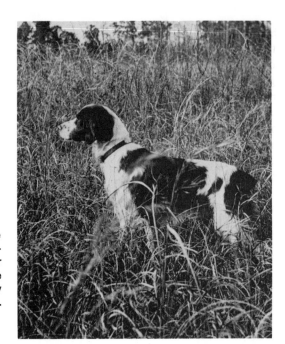

Dual Ch. Tigre de Klemanor (Ch. Buccaneer de Klemanor ex Int. Ch. Wanda de L'Argoat), owned by Walter B. Kleeman.

Ch. Andre De Carnac (left) and Ch. Avono Jake.

The situation in Ohio in 1943 was this. An attorney general had ruled that domestically raised and banded game birds became the property of the State of Ohio at the instant of release. They could not be shot, except during the hunting season, and hunting was not allowed on Sunday. So the Springer and Cocker trials had to be held during the hunting season and, in this case, on Saturday. But the American Brittany Club had decided not to permit the shooting of flushed birds. So their club's trial could be held on Sunday.

The Springer and Cocker trials were thus held on Saturday, November 27, 1943. The two clubs held a joint field trial dinner at the Masonic Temple at Ravenna. Afterward Jerome N. Halle judged the bench show. Mr. Halle helped later to revise the standard, and became an honorary lifetime member.

There were 28 dogs at the specialty show. Winners Dog and Best of Breed was Patrice of Sharvogue, owned and shown by Edgar W. Averill. Winners Bitch and Best of Opposite Sex to Best of Breed was Madame Patricia, owned by Robert M. Spangler of Massillon, Ohio. Reserve Winners Dog was Avono Jack of Karomish, owned by Dr. David Ruskin, Caro, Michigan. And Reserve Winners Bitch was Benedictine Mac Eochaidh, owned by Hal P. Cline of Rocky River, Ohio.

The following day, Sunday, November 28, 1943, the first licensed Brittany Spaniel field trial was held. The judges were William T. Windsor and James Talmadge. Windsor was a bird-dog field trial man of long experience, and he was an officer in the Ohio Department of Conservation and Natural Resources. Talmadge also was an experienced bird-dog field trial man. With his father he operated what was then one of the largest pheasant farms in the world.

Here is the official report of the trial, as written by Dr. Ruskin. It appeared in the January, 1944 issue of *Pure-Bred Dogs—The American Kennel Gazette.*

Although it had snowed on Saturday, during the American Brittany Club Specialty Show, Sunday, Nov. 28, turned out to be clear, brisk, and with a slight breeze. The trial was held on the Hohing Farm, two miles south of Ravenna, O., which was thickly covered with briars, and which provided excellent cover for both the planted pheasants and for those which had made the farm their natural home. The short, flat, wavy coat of the Brittany, and the absence of tail, or at the most, a stub of tail, proved of considerable advantage to the dog, and enabled him to work in cover which would ordinarily turn back any other pointing breed.

Under the judging of James Talmadge and Bill Windsor, the open all-age stake was run in the morning with six braces before a rest period was called, during which time the officials and others took the opportunity to warm up in a tent provided on the grounds, where sandwiches and hot coffee were enjoyed by all. It was already evident by this time that the caliber of the competition was high, and that there would be considerable difficulty in selecting the winners.

This was borne out later by the fact that several dogs were called back after the first series, among them being Allamuchy Valley Luke, Brit of Bellows Falls,

These five men were among the founders of the American Brittany Club. They are (l. to r.) A. H. Ady, Jack L. Whitworth, Walter B. Kleeman, W. E. "Bill" Averill and Dr. D. B. Ruskin.

This picture was taken in 1948 and shows four famous early field trainers. They are (l. to r.) Buck Bissell, Bill Kull, Lee Holman and Tommy Cox.

Parisienne de Klemanor, and Aotrou Mac Eochaidh. Unfortunately, Mr. Kleeman had left for home before the first series was completed, and was therefore unable to give Parisienne a chance at a second series.

After considerable weighing of the pros and cons, the judges placed the dogs as follows: First, Aotrou Mac Eochaidh, owned and handled by A. H. Ady; second, Brit of Bellows Falls, owned and handled by L. H. Ufford; third, Allamuchy Valley Luke, owned and handled by H. B. Clements; and fourth, Betsy de Bonaventure, owned and handled by R. B. McCurdy; special commendation, Parisienne de Klemanor, owned and handled by W. B. Kleeman, and Benedictine Mac Eochaidh, owned and handled by H. P. Cline.

A. H. Ady received a glass cocktail shaker, chrome tray, and six glasses for the open all-age winner. For the first time in the history of this country, a dual award was given. This too was won by Aotrou Mac Eochaidh by virtue of being the all-age winner and also qualifying by placing first in one of the classes of the bench show held the night before. This dual award was symbolized by a Handscraft Baked Bean Service Set.

The puppy stake began about 2 P.M. and included entries born after Jan. 1, 1942, thereby combining in competition puppies and derby dogs. This stake was run over the same course and three of the four ribbons went to older dogs. They finished as follows: First, Bientot Mac Eochaidh, owned and handled by E. W. Averill; second, Babette of Brookcliff, owned and handled by L. H. Ufford; third, Avono Jack of Karomish, owned and handled by Dr. D. B. Ruskin; and fourth, Geoffre de Beauchamps, owned and handled by J. F. Powers.

Special thanks are due to so many for the success of the events that a listing of the deserving people would run counter of national emergency and paper shortage. However, we would like to thank those who came from a distance to swell the entries, and those officials mentioned above, and all to give our thanks to Jack L. Whitworth, without whose industry and enthusiasm all this would have been impossible, and to Mr. Lee French who so ably helped him.—D. B. Ruskin, M.D.

It should be added here that Lee French, mentioned in Dr. Ruskin's report, had a small bird-dog training kennel not too far from the Whitworth residence. He laid out the course, and members of the Ravenna Springer Spaniel group planted the birds.

So successful was this trial and show that the American Brittany Club never again had to seek permission from another breed club to hold a licensed trial or show. And never again did it have to have a "foreign" club act as host. It was successful in another way as well. The club, when finally it became the recognized parent club of the breed, decided that, wherever possible, it would hold joint trials and shows. In this way, it would keep the concept of the dual-purpose dog before its members. As a result, and excepting German Shorthaired Pointers, the Brittany Spaniel has produced more dual champions—bench and field—than have all the other sporting breeds and hounds combined.

The caliber of the people who competed in the first field trial also is worth noting. Not a single one of the dogs who placed in either stake was handled by a professional. All were owner-handled. This means that they were thoroughly experienced bird-dog handlers. They had been schooled under fire, as it were, and they knew exactly what they wanted in the Brittany Spaniel. Their knowledge and judgment made the great history of the breed possible.

Some memorable dogs posed here at an early field trial are (l. to r.) Antonede Reservere, handler unidentified; Domino de Klemanor, handler Bill Kull; Ch. Loufel's Handsome Harry, handler Nicky Bissell and Ch. Ashurst Jerry, handler Buck Bissell.

14

The Brittany
as a Show Dog

WHEN, IN 1943 AND 1944, the American Brittany Club decided to revise the breed standard, a number of people were asked to help. This is discussed at greater length in the chapter on the history of the standard. Yet it is important to repeat part of it here.

Edward Dana Knight argued that, if the Brittany was to make any impression at dog shows, it would have to conform to the standards of beauty of show dogs. These would include close clipping of the neck and shoulders, some barbering of body coat, and heavy feathering on the legs, belly and on the rear of the thighs.

Jerome Halle was a bench-show judge. But while still in college at Cornell University, he had run Pointers in field trials. At the time of the discussions, Knight was a justly famous show judge. But he was running both English Setters and English Springer Spaniels in field trials, and he was judging Pointer, Setter, Springer and Cocker Spaniel field trials. A division between English Setter bench and field dogs had already taken place. Halle and the author argued that, to prevent such a split, the standard should be such that a Brittany could leave a field trial and compete successfully at a show. Even then the author was noting that Springer Spaniels were being split into separate breeds, bench and field. So Halle and the author argued that it was up to the American Brittany Club to teach the bench-show judges exactly what a good Brittany should be, and to understand the aims of the American Brittany Club. On their part, Brittany owners should cooperate by competing in both branches of the sport.

Dual Ch. Gringo De Britt owned by Drs. T. L. and T. E. Poling, shows the style and intensity on point that made him a field trial champion. This dog is a many faceted winner with titles in bench, field and obedience, and was the winner of the U.S. Open Championship in 1969.

Dual Ch. Gringo De Britt, C.D., is shown here making a win under judge Alvin Maurer, handler Catherine Murphy. *Shafer photo.*

This policy has, in large part, proven itself. The Brittany has more dual champions—bench and field—than any other breed. In fact, excluding the German Shorthaired Pointer, it has more than all the other breeds combined. In another way, it has been less successful. Fewer Brittanys have won groups and Best in Show than should be the case. Here let us quote from that excellent book *The Brittany in America* by Fred Z. White, M.D., second edition:

> I wish to repeat, formally and sincerely, that I mean no disrespect to the bench show judges who have done their best, with usually very little thanks for the trouble they have taken to judge our Brittanies as they saw them. The fault, if any, lies with us, the Brittany owners, breeders, and club members who may be confused about what we are trying to achieve, and for not having been able to properly instruct our judges about what we consider the most important characteristics of our breed.

This indicates his own dissatisfaction and that of many Brittany owners with the majority of bench-show judges. Yet there are several factors that must be mentioned. The American Brittany Club still needs to educate sporting-dog judges, for the roster of such judges is constantly changing. Names disappear from it, and new ones appear. A second factor needs to be discussed. E. W. "Bill" Averill once said that Midwest Brittany owners and breeders set out to improve the looks of their dogs. Alan Stuyvesant used to say that the Brittany is not a good-looking dog, but is only a superb hunting machine. Can a dog be both? The answer is: Yes, of course. But you have to apply the old proverb "Handsome is as handsome does."

Can you say that an English Bulldog is beautiful? Probably most people would roar No! But, if you are a breeder of English Bulldogs, and if the dog conforms closely to the standard, then you can say that the dog is beautiful. It follows that if breeders can teach judges to see beauty in a Bulldog, Brittany breeders should be able to teach them to recognize a good Brittany. But then, in respect to the latter, other factors must be considered.

Many of the early Brittanys, and some of those today, were flat-footed and straight in stifle, that is, with insufficient angulation at the stifle joint. Theoretically, flat feet should contribute to lameness in field work, and to some loss of stamina. Theoretically, too, straight stifles should contribute to loss of stamina. The straight-stifled dog does not drive as far forward with each step as does a better angulated dog. Thus, the same amount of energy produces more forward motion in the well-angulated dog. Or, the straight-stifled dog must use more energy to move forward the same distance and at the same speed as does the dog with better angulation. Loose elbows are universally condemned. It is supposed that they may contribute to loss of stamina and to lameness in a field dog.

Note we have used such terms as "theoretically" and "supposed." This is for several reasons, one of which we will discuss. The other is that, even in hunting, dogs are seldom driven to the point where unsoundness will become a serious factor in performance. One-hour to three-hour heats at field trials and all-day hunting would be cases where unsoundness would begin to affect performance.

Factors that might operate to mitigate the effects of unsoundness are: intensity of hunting desire, refusal to quit, stamina from other sources, wisdom, field experience, and trainability. No bench-show judge can assay these qualities. He cannot know that the straight-stifled dog has the stamina, intensity, and experience to be a great field dog. He cannot know whether the dog can face any kind of weather, the roughest terrain, briars, and heavy cover, or whether under these circumstances it will quit. The judge cannot, in short, estimate what we call "heart" or "guts."

The judge then has to base his decisions on soundness, on his conception of the standard of perfection of the breed, and upon temperament. Temperament is one attribute by which he can come close to guessing field performance. He cannot know whether a given dog will range out from the owner to search birdy cover. But he does know that most shy dogs will not. He can guess, and be close to right, that the noise-shy dog in the ring will show some degree of shyness in the field. He recognizes and usually penalizes shyness because he knows that shy dogs should never be used for breeding, that no excuses should ever be made for them. He also knows that neither viciousness nor sharpness are Brittany qualities. So if he recognizes them in any dog, he penalizes the dog for them.

Recently, a professional handler who has spent his life showing sporting dogs, said to the author: "I can't understand why this Brittany hasn't won groups. He is certainly good enough to win his share of them, and even an occasional Best in Show."

Now this comment comes from a professional who must have won several hundred Best in Show awards and countless Sporting groups during his life. So if he asks such a question, or at least complains, every Brittany owner is entitled also to ask: Why?

One reason is that, to most judges, the Brittany is not a pretty dog. It doesn't catch the eyes of either the judges or of the galleries. A second reason is that too few judges understand what a Brittany should be. And a third is that some judges are just plain afraid to give a group to a Brittany, even when they feel that it deserves to win.

A famous judge, now dead, once said to the author: "You crazy damn fools can put up those garbage breeds. I'll stick to the standard breeds." Well, it isn't the way to judge dog shows. But there are usually so many good dogs in the Sporting group that no one can prove they are simply sticking with the "standard" breeds. Another factor is that too few of the judges come from a Brittany background. So they have less sympathy for the breed than do those who are more familiar with it. Again, it is a job of education. In that respect, not enough Brittanys are being shown to educate these judges properly.

Now within its breed, the Brittany has produced its share of bench champions. Following are the records of some of the Brittanys who have won in show competition with other sporting breeds. The first Brittany to win first in the Sporting group was Ch. Queen of Paradise. She was owned by Walter S. Oberlin of DeKalb, Illinois. Queen was one of the earliest champions. Her sire was Crepe La Brilliante, a son of Kaer de l'Argoat. Her dam was Suzette de Mirabeau, a son of Tango. the circumstances of her victory are interesting.

Oddly enough, the place of her victory was Ravenna, Ohio, where the first Brittany licensed show and field trials were held. The event was the Ravenna Kennel Club's all-breed show. It was not a large one, since there were only 400 dogs in competition. The date was September 14, 1946. Mabel Pyle, one of the earliest professional handlers of her sex, showed Ch. Queen of Paradise. William L. Kendrick judged the breed and the group.

Mabel Pyle was a noted handler of pointing breeds. On this day, she won Best of Breed with the Brittany, with the Irish Setter, Ch. Janet of Aragon, with the English Setter, Ch. Bohemia of Aragon, and with a Pointer. Of course, she could not show all these dogs in the group. And Brittanys never placed anyway. So she put Queen of Paradise into a crate, and loaded her into her van along with defeated dogs. She elected to show the Irish Setter, and turned the English Setter and the Pointer over to other handlers.

When the Sporting group started, Mr. Kendrick asked about the Brittany. The author, as show chairman and chief steward, had to report that it was absent. But Mr. Kendrick refused to judge until it had been brought into the ring. The committee unloaded Miss Pyle's crates and found Ch. Queen of Paradise in the last crate to be unloaded. An exhibitor was asked to take the dog into the ring, and Mr. Kendrick sent it into first place. A parti-color Cocker Spaniel placed second, the English Setter third, and the Irish Setter was unplaced.

The second Brittany to win a Sporting group was Dual Champion Amos of Edough. Lee Holman showed him at the Lima, Ohio, show in 1950. The author was the judge. Amos was an exciting dog, both at shows and in the field. He remains the only dual champion Brittany ever to win a group.

The third dog to win a group was a California bitch, Cherie D'Oiseau. She was owned by S. Roose, and was shown by him. The show was the 29th annual Del Monte K.C. show at Pebble Beach, California, May 30, 1954. The author was also the judge at that event. Cherie had come up from the classes to go Best of Breed, and then went on to her group first. She completed her championship later. She was sired by Count Chanteur and her dam was Countess d'Oiseau Belle.

The years from 1956 to 1960 were truly great ones for the breed. In 1956, Havre Des Bois Henri completed his championship. He was bred and shown by Paul R. Vollmar of Clinton, Michigan. He was by Sonny's Mate of Cyrus out of Ch. Wild Haven Dottie. The following year, he made breed history by

Ch. Ti War Chip de Triumph, owned and handled by R. B. Edwards, shown winning fourth in the Sporting group at the Blennerhassett Kennel Club under judge Henry Stoecker. The dog was ten years old at the time of the win. *Norton of Kent photo.*

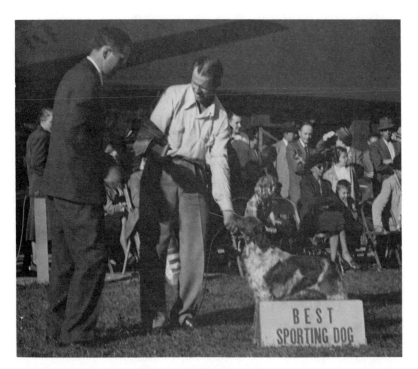

This picture shows an historic occasion. Ch. Amos of Edough is being presented with the award of best Sporting dog at the Lima Kennel Club, 1946. This is the first time a dual champion Brittany won the Sporting group in the United States. The judge was the author of this book and the handler was Lee Holman.

Ch. Havre Des Bois Henri, owned by Paul Vollmar, was the first Brittany Spaniel to win best in show at an all-breed show. He was handled by the late Horace Hollands and is shown winning a Sporting group first under judge Gordon Parham. *Norton of Kent photo.*

becoming the first Brittany Spaniel to win Best in Show at an all-breed event.

Ch. Havre Des Bois Henri was Best in Show at the Livonia Kennel Club show, September 15, 1957. There were 555 dogs competing in the show. Judge Selwyn Harris gave him first in the Sporting group, and then Best in Show. He had defeated 22 other Britts under Mrs. Marie B. Meyer. Later that year, Ch. Havre Des Bois Henri won the National Specialty show under Judge Gordon Parham. The following year Havre Des Bois Henri won the Sporting group at Canton, Ohio, and at Columbus, Ohio. He also had eight other group placements. Until 1971, he remained the only Brittany ever to win Best in Show at any American all-breed event.

Ch. Bonnie Kay's Ricki's Image now came onto the scene. He was bred by Ken Holemo, who put him in the name of his daughter Bonnie, for whom he had also named the dog. He was by Happy Hunter's Buster Brown out of Joy De Lune. Ricki's Image was Best of Breed 71 times, twice won the Sporting group, and had 18 other group placements. He was Best of Breed at the National Specialty show three times, in 1959, 1960 and 1961. Edgar W. Averill's Ch. Patrice De Sharvogue had won this show three times, in 1943, 1944 and 1945.

Two dogs now came along with truly great show records. The first was Ch. Bonnie Kay's Duke of Sequani. He is a son of Ch. Bonnie Kay's Ricki's Image, out of Alf's Queen, by Jay Jay's Rusty. He had 84 Best of Breed victories as of September 1, 1971, two group firsts, eight seconds, eight thirds, and fourteen fourths. Thus, he broke his sire's record. He was Best Puppy at the National Specialty in 1964, and was Best of Breed in the 1968 event.

Duke was now followed by his son, American and Bermuda Champion Sequani's Dana MacDuff. His dam is Dana's Jody of Kaymore, C.D., by Dual Ch. Doctor Joe of Kaymore. As of September 1, 1971, Dana MacDuff had won 70 Bests of Breed, 10 group firsts, nine group seconds, five group thirds, and five group fourths. He also had two group thirds in Bermuda. He retired in June 1973 with 14 group firsts.

Dana MacDuff had the unusual distinction of winning his championship by placing four times in the Sporting group. He was twice Best of Breed at the American Brittany Club's summer specialty shows, and he was Best of Breed at eight regional shows. Both dogs were bred at the Sequani Kennels of Mr. and Mrs. Frederick Murphy, Far Hills, New Jersey.

We now come to Ch. Beelflower Dirty Dan. He won the coveted Best in Show award at Salinas, California, in mid-August, 1971, in an entry of over 2,000 dogs. He is owned by Paul and Linda Mooney, and was shown by Mrs. Mooney. Here let us quote from the *American Brittany Magazine,* which adequately gives the dog's background.

> Dirty Dan is a winner that fulfills all the breed's specifications. He is sired by a Dual Champion, Sir Robert of Beelflower and his grandsire is a dual as well, Rusty of Beelflower. Rusty's sire was a champion and his grandsire was Ch.

Ch. Sequani's Dana MacDuff (Ch. Bonnie Kay's Duke of Sequani ex Dana's Jody of Kaymore, C.D.), owned by Mrs. F. H. Murphy and N. Rigoulot and bred by D. and N. Rigoulot.

Ch. Amie Roc de Triumph taking a group placement under judge Dr. Robert D. Smith, and handled by Jerry Vance for owners Bryan and Becky Buck. *Teri photo.*

Duckerbird's Sir Guy de Beauch, a field winner, which took best of breed from the classes at the second largest assemblage of Brittanies ever held (a Michigan specialty show).

Dan's dam (Pacolet Sam's Pierette), has produced three field winners and is a daughter of Dual Champion Pacolet Sam and Field Ch. Riviere Valley Suzette. Sam is, as students know, a son of the duals Albedo Valley Dingo and Pacolet Cheyenne. Suzette is sired by Dual Ch. Tex of Richmont and from the bench champion Ruby of Edough.

To add a little frosting to the cake, not only does Dan have a dual studded pedigree, he has placed himself in trials, twice in puppy stakes. He is OFA certified [signifies he is free of hip dysplasia]. We wonder if any other breed can boast a comparable BEST IN SHOW winner.

The author can only add that, to the best of his knowledge, the answer is no. Dirty Dan was bred by Virgil I. Davidson, and was whelped April 23, 1968.

One of the great show dogs of the 1960s was Ch. Miss Sue's Gad-A-Bout. He was owned by Richard and Anne Smith of Roswell, Georgia. In some 15 months, he won 40 Bests of Breed, 12 group placings, of which three were firsts; and a Companion Dog degree in obedience.

We single out one other dog for special mention here. Ch. Ti-War Chip de Triumph, owned by R. H. Edwards, won first in the Sporting group at Lorain, Ohio, when he was nearing 10 years old. He was shown by Daniel Sweeney, who was 17.

Our search of the records indicates that at least the following dogs, not mentioned above, have won group firsts. They are: Ch. Glenn-Pat's Rusty Shadow, Ch. Ultra-Mend Ace High, Ch. Ultra-Mend Jacques, Ch. Ffynant's Trouble, Ch. Fun Galore Chummie, Ch. Holley Haven Suzette, Ch. Lakeside Secret Joy, Ch. Havre Des Bois Seigneur, Ch. Lincoln's Skipper of Kaymore, Ch. Star Raiser and Ch. Laddie Star.

Ch. Beelflower Dirty Dan, owned and handled by
Linda Mooney, was best in show at the Salinas Kennel
Club under the author. This is only the second Brittany
to win best in show at an all-breed dog show.
Stillman photo.

Ch. Highland Redwing Bold Victor (Ch. Prince Valiant's Happy Time ex Ch. Lit'l
Egypt's Sequani Princess), bred by Frank Ettinger and Elizabeth Temple, owned
by Frank and Marjorie Ettinger.   *Alverson photo.*

15

The First American Brittany Spaniel Standard

THE FIRST AMERICAN STANDARD for the Brittany Spaniel was a translation of the French standard of 1933. Miss Clara Perry, who had raised Brittany Spaniels in France and who had been an early importer, made the translation. But the standard of 1933 had, with some alterations, existed since the first standard was drawn up in September, 1907.

In 1907, three colors were allowed. These were white with liver, white with orange and white with black. The white-and-liver dogs were preferred and white-and-orange dogs were almost barred. The reason was that the white-and-liver dogs had shown up well in field work, while some of the white-and-orange dogs had performed poorly.

French breeders were interested first in performance and second in type. Some of the white-and-orange dogs were oversized, and probably represented a late cross with English Setters. In the end, it was the white-and-black dog that was to disappear.

It will be remembered that a tailless Brittany Spaniel had been born. Many of his offspring were either tailless or had a very short tail. They were born predocked, so to speak. Early French breeders considered that the true Britt should be born either tailless or with a naturally docked tail. So the standard of 1907 said: "Always short at birth, not over six inches at the very most, sometimes a little twisted and terminating with a tuft of hair." One wonders if a screw-tailed Bulldog got somehow mixed into the breed to produce that twisted tail. A second reason for specifying a tailless or naturally docked dog was that early breeders felt this requirement would prevent crossing the Breton dogs with English Setters. By 1933, this danger had apparently disappeared. But also, breeders were beginning to understand that great field dogs could be born with long tails. It was therefore absurd, and even tragic, to bar dogs born with natural tails.

There is another point that should be mentioned here. Some of the early French fanciers feared that the Breton Spaniel might become too small. So the 1907 standard called for a dog 50 to 56 centimeters tall when measured at the highest point of the withers. This is 19½ to 22 inches. Our own early breeders feared that the dog might grow too large. The modern standard calls for a shorter dog. But some Britts do grow too tall. Thus, the problem of size has been with us since 1907. And although standards change, the problem will in all likelihood remain.

Herewith, we give the "Description and standard of points" as adopted by the American Kennel Club on March 12, 1935. It is of particular interest because of the earlier standard and later changes.

General Appearance

Height—17 inches minimum; 19¾ maximum with toleration of ¾ inch more for males, back short; head rounded; muzzle rather pointed; with lips close fitting; ears short rather than long and placed high, relatively but little fringed; hair close on body; fringes wavy; never curly, a compact cob type; tail always naturally short, about 4 inches. [See note at end]

Nose—Nostrils well open; color brown or rose according to whether the dog is white and liver; or white and orange.
 Faults—Black and shiny; tight or snipy.

Muzzle—Medium length narrowing toward nose; straight or very slightly curved.
 Faults—Too short or too long.

Lips—Fine, close fitting, the upper lip overlapping the under lip by very little.
 Faults—Thick or too overlapping.

Crown of Head—Medium length, rounded; each side of the depression well marked and rounded; well defined stop though sloping gently and not too abrupt.
 Faults—Square; narrow; apple-headed; stop too abrupt.

Ch. Ultra-Mend Ace High, owned and bred by Frank W. McHugh. He is shown making a win under the late Major B. Godsol and is being handled by his owner.

Ch. Ultra-Mend Jacques (Ch. Ultra-Mend Ace High ex Ultra-Mend Birdie Biddie), owned and bred by Frank W. McHugh, boasts a show record that places him in the front rank of show winners. He has won 86 bests of breed and ten Sporting group placings. *Norman photo.*

Eyes—Deep amber, bright and expressive.
 Faults—Too light, mean look.

Ears—Placed high, short rather than long, slightly rounded, but little fringe, though the ear should be well covered with wavy hair.
 Faults—Placed low; falling; large; curly.

Neck—Medium length, well placed on shoulders; without dewlap.
 Faults—Too long; too thin; too short, or too heavy.

Shoulders—Slightly oblique and muscular.
 Faults—Straight or too oblique.

Arm—Muscular and bony.
 Faults—Fatty or too fine.

Chest—Deep, reaching quite to level of elbow; sides rounded enough and quite large.
 Faults—Chest narrow; not deep, sides flat.

Back—Short, withers well marked; never hollow or saddle backed.
 Faults—Long or hollow.

Loin—Short and strong.
 Faults—Long; narrow or weak.

Flanks—Well tucked up but not to excess.
 Faults—Fat; falling.

Hind Quarters—Broad—strong and muscular.

Croup—Slightly sloping.
 Faults—Too narrow; too straight; too sloping.

Tail—[See note at end]—Straight and carried low; always naturally short; about 4 inches long, often screw tail ending in a mesh of hair, or *anoure*.

Front Legs—Very straight; forearm slightly oblique, fine and muscular; fringes not heavy but wavy.
 Faults—Forearm too straight or too oblique; without fringes or too heavily fringed.

Hindlegs—Thighs large, well muscled, well fringed and wavy half down

Ch. Woodstock's Lady Valentine, handled by Nancy Morabito, scoring a group placing under Joseph A. Dainty. The owners are Bill and Jane Theobald. *Ashbey photo.*

thigh, cannon well set with hock and not too angular.

    Faults—straight thighs, without fringes or too oblique.

Feet—Toes close with a little hair between them.

    Faults—Large; long, fat, too round or open.

Skin—Fine and fairly loose.

    Faults—Thick or too loose.

Coat—Hair flat on body, fine but not to excess and quite smooth or slightly wavy.

    Faults—Long, curly or too silky.

Color—Liver and white preferably with roan ticking, or orange and white preferably with roan ticking.

As a Whole—A small dog, closely knit and strong though elegant, very vigorous; energetic of movement; intelligent expression; presenting the aspect of a thoroughbred cob.

[**Note**—The question of Brittany Spaniels born with tails being admitted to the Show Ring was voted on in the General Assembly of 1933 and it was decided that a cut tail was not disqualification either in the Show Ring or the Field Trials.]

16

Modern Standard for the American Brittany

A BREED STANDARD IS often called the "standard of perfection" for that breed. Sometimes it is claimed that the standard was based upon a certain dog. This is almost never true. Often, standard writers do discuss the points of one or more dogs. But a standard is an idealization—the perfect dog. Such a dog is seldom, or never, achieved. Standard writers may use the head of one dog, the neck of another, the body of a third, and the legs and feet of still another. Thus, they achieve an ideal, but in their minds only.

One often hears an owner say: "I wish this dog had the head of that one," or "I wish that dog had the drive of this one." Again, these are only wishes, and wishes are only idealizations and not realizations. There are two reasons why this is so. First, a dog is a going unit. It has been said that the Greek nudes were idealizations, that human beings couldn't be built that way. This is to some extent true of dogs. A more important reason is that, as a working unit, a dog is the sum of its parts. You cannot say, for example, that this dog's hind legs would fit on that dog's body. Nor can it be said that this dog's head would be perfect on that dog's neck. If you could take two or three dogs apart and rearrange their parts, you would almost certainly come up with a horrible monstrosity. It would not be the sum of the good parts of all the dogs, but much more likely a badly balanced dog that could not function with half the efficiency of any of the dogs from which some of its parts came.

One must, therefore, regard the breed standard as a useful guide. But one must inevitably regard the dogs it describes as working units. Each is a whole.

Successful breeders and judges study the standard. They note the good points and faults, as listed in the standard. Then they examine the dogs as more or less successful working units.

In the previous chapter, we gave the Brittany standard as it was first approved by the American Kennel Club. Miss Clara Perry had translated it. Those who read it will recognize that it was virtually unintelligible. Yet at the time, students who wished to understand it had an advantage that is denied to most of us today. Most of the dog shows were benched, and dozens of them were two-day events. This meant that one could take the standard and go down the stall, studying each dog. Arguments or friendly discussions would take place. Owners would take their dogs off the benches and pose them for study. Perhaps more important, Brittanys could be compared to other sporting breeds. Such comparisons could often make points in the Brittany standard clearer. A good feature in another breed might be a fault in a Britt, and the student would realize why this was so.

If one reads that first American standard, one can understand why the American Brittany Club was thoroughly dissatisfied with it. So a standards committee was set up. The year was 1946. Dr. David Ruskin obtained the latest standard from France and translated it. Much of the information Dr. Ruskin obtained from France was far too technical, and therefore hardly understandable. As the author remembers it, the main committee consisted of Dr. Ruskin, Jack Whitworth, Jerome N. Halle, Edward Dana Knight and the author. He exhibited English Springer Spaniels at shows and trained them for field. He also ran English Springer Spaniels at shows and ran English Setters in American field trials. He usually had an American Foxhound or two.

Jerome Halle had run Pointers in American field trials while an undergraduate at Cornell University. He, too, was a fine sporting-dog judge. His early and long association with Brittanys is well known.

Dr. Ruskin, Mr. Halle and the author were thoroughly familiar with the tragic split of the English Setter into two breeds—bench and field. Knight and the author were watching the split of English Springer Spaniels into two breeds. Both fought against this split and lost. Halle and the author argued that the Brittany standard should be so written that no such split would be possible. One result was that the American Brittany Club began a policy of holding bench shows along with field trials. That meant that field dogs could come out of the field and compete, as they were, for bench championships. It is this factor that caused the standard writers to prescribe a dog without excessive coat and feathering. It was also argued that the Brittany could compete on equal terms with other breeds in the Sporting group at dog shows if sporting-dog judges could be properly trained. Judges had to be told that a hard, lean, field-conditioned Brittany without heavy leg feathering or fine, silky, long coat was to be desired.

This policy has, to some extent, failed. One reason is that a new generation of sporting-dog show judges has developed. And we have done nothing to educate them as we did an earlier generation. Yet in another sense, the policy has worked well. It is proven in the number of dual champions—bench and field—that the breed has produced. And it remains as an argument for conducting bench and field events at the same meeting.

The first American standard tried to explain the meaning and the reason for each point. It has survived with but a few changes since. In 1946, it was feared that the breed would grow too large. Dogs from other lands did tend to grow larger. In most cases, this was temporary, and dogs tended to return to their basic size. But in 1946, several champions were larger than the agreed-upon height. It is to the credit of the owners of those dogs that they agreed to a height that would disqualify their dogs.

It is imperative for Brittany owners to study the present standard in the light of the past. And they should understand the reasons behind each point in the standard so that a great and unspoiled breed may continue to improve, as it has in the past. Here then is the present standard as it was approved by the American Kennel Club, September 13, 1966, June 14, 1977, and slightly amended, June, 1986. It represents the thoughts and experiences of Brittany people since 1907. But it also is the result of the breeding, training, field trialing and exhibiting by Brittany owners in America since 1946.

Official Standard of the Brittany—June, 1986

General Description

A compact, closely-knit dog of medium size, a leggy dog having the appearance, as well as the agility, of a great ground coverer. Strong, vigorous, energetic and quick of movement. Not too light in bone, yet never heavy-boned and cumbersome. Ruggedness, without clumsiness, is characteristic of the breed. So leggy is he that his height at the withers is the same as the length of his body. He has no tail, or at most, not more than 4 inches.

Weight—Should weigh between 30 and 40 pounds.
Height—17½ to 20½ inches—measured from the ground at the highest point of the shoulders.
Disqualifications—Any Brittany measuring under 17½ inches or over 20½ inches shall be disqualified from bench-show competition. Any black in the coat or a nose so dark in color as to appear black shall disqualify. A tail substantially more than 4 inches in length shall disqualify.

Coat

Dense, flat or wavy, never curly. Texture neither wiry nor silky. The ears should carry little fringe. The front and hind legs should have some feathering

SKULL medium length (approx. 4¾"), width less (approx. 4⅜"); rounded, evenly-made; very slightly wedge-shaped, lateral walls well-rounded; never coarse, "apple-headed" or racy; occiput crest only apparent to touch; indistinct median line

EYES well-set; dark colors preferred; expressive; eyebrows heavy

STOP well-defined; gentle sloping; never indented

NOSE fawn, tan, light brown shades, deep pink; nostrils well-open; neither Roman nor concave curve (dish-face) desirable; (butterfly two-tone) severely penalized)

LIPS tight; dry. Upper lip overlapping lower jaw only to cover under lip. Flews penalized

TEETH well-joined; scissors bite; neither under-nor overshot

MUZZLE medium—2/3 length of skull (measuring muzzle from tip to stop, skull from occipital crest to stop); tapering gradually toward nostrils; never broad, heavy, snipy; well-chiseled under eyes

CHEST deep; reaching elbow level; neither too wide nor too rounded

FORELEGS perpendicular; not too wide apart; bones clean, graceful, not too fine; supple. Pasterns slightly bent

FEET strong; proportionately smaller than other spaniels; close-fitting, well-arched toes; thick pads

COLORS: Dark orange and white; liver and white; some ticking desirable (not enough for belton pattern). Roan patterns or factors of orange or liver (found in std. parti-color or pied) permissible; washed out or faded colors not desirable; tri-colors (liver, white with some orange markings) severely faulted

APPEARANCE: Compact; closely-knit; strong; rugged without clumsiness; energetic, vigorous, agile; leggy

EARS short, leafy; set high above eye level; reach half-length muzzle; flat, close to head; very slightly rounded tips; dense relatively short hair, little fringe

NECK medium length; strong; well-set into shoulders; not throaty

SHOULDERS sloping; muscular; blade forming nearly 90-degree angle with upper arm; perhaps 2-thumb-widths between blades

BACK short, straight; slight slope from withers to tail-set; short (3-4 finger widths) from last rib to upper thigh; slight drop from hips to tail root

TAIL high-set; tailless, natural or docked, not over 4"

HINDQUARTERS broad, strong, muscular; powerful thighs; rounded, fairly full flanks; hips well-set into short, strong loins; well-bent stifles; hocks firm, turning neither in nor out; hock to heel fairly short

COAT dense, flat, wavy; not too fine; never curly or silky; feathering moderate (excessive severely penalized). Skin fine; fairly loose

SIZE: Height, 17½"-20½", measured from ground at highest point of shoulders; weight, 30-40 lbs. Body length (point of forechest to rear of haunches): approx. same as height

RIBS well-sprung

ELBOWS turning neither in nor out; height to elbows approx. equal distance elbows to withers

DISQUALIFICATIONS: Measuring under 17½" or over 20½"; black in coat; nose so dark as to appear black; tail substantially more than 4" but too little is definitely preferable to too much. Dogs with long or profuse featherings shall be so severely penalized as to effectively eliminate them from competition.

Color

Orange and white or liver and white in either clear or roan patterns. Some ticking is desirable. The orange or liver is found in standard parti-color or piebald patterns. Washed out colors are not desirable. Tri-colors are allowable but not desired. A tri-color is a liver and white dog with classic orange markings on eyebrows, muzzle and cheeks, inside the ears and under the tail, the freckles on the lower legs are orange. Anything exceeding the limits of these markings shall be severely penalized. Black is a disqualification.

Head

Skull—Medium length (approximately 4¾ inches). Rounded, very slightly wedge-shaped, but evenly made. Width, not quite as wide as the length (about 4⅜ inches) and never so broad as to appear coarse, or so narrow as to appear racy. Well defined, but gently sloping stop effect. Median line rather indistinct. The occipital crest only apparent to the touch. Lateral walls well rounded. The Brittany should never be "apple-headed" and he should never have an indented stop. (All measurements of skull are for a 19½ inch dog).

Muzzle—Medium length, about two thirds the length of the skull, measuring the muzzle from the tip to the stop, and the skull from the occipital crest to the stop between the eyes. Muzzle should taper gradually in both horizontal and vertical dimensions as it approaches the nostrils. Neither a Roman nose nor a concave curve (dish face) is desirable. Never broad, heavy or snipy.

Nose—Nostrils well open to permit deep breathing of air and adequate scenting while at top speed. Tight nostrils should be penalized. Never shiny. Color, fawn, tan, light shades of brown or deep pink. A black nose is a disqualification. A two-tone or butterfly nose should be penalized.

Eyes—Well set in head. Well protected from briars by a heavy, expressive eyebrow. A prominent, full or pop eye should be heavily penalized. It is a serious fault in a hunting dog that must face briars. Skull well chiseled under the eyes, so that the lower lid is not pulled back to form a pocket or haw for catching seeds, dirt, and weed dust. Judges should check by forcing head down to see if lid falls away from the eye. Preference should be for darker-colored eyes, though lighter shades of amber should not be penalized. Light and mean-looking eyes to be heavily penalized.

116

Fiddle Front   Out at Elbow   Straight Front

Down in Pastern   Knuckled Over   Straight Front

Cat Foot   Hare Foot   Paper Foot   Correct
Foot

Level Back

Sloping Shoulder   Straight Shoulder

Ears—Set high, above the level of the eyes. Short and leafy, rather than pendulous, reaching about half the length of the muzzle. Should lie flat and close to the head, with the tip rounded very slightly. Ears well covered with dense, but relatively short hair, and with little fringe.

Lips—Tight to the muzzle, with the upper lip overlapping the lower jaw only sufficiently to cover under lip. Lips dry, so that feathers do not stick. Drooling to receive a heavy penalty. Flews to be penalized.

Teeth—Well joined incisors, thus giving a true scissors bite. Overshot or undershot jaw to be penalized heavily.

Body

Neck—Medium length. Not quite permitting the dog to place his nose on the ground without bending his legs. Free from throatiness, though not a serious fault unless accompanied by dewlaps. Strong, without giving the impression of being overmuscled. Well set into sloping shoulders. Never concave or ewe-necked.

Body Length—Approximately the same as the height when measured at the withers. Body length is measured from the point of the forechest to the rear of the haunches. A long body should be heavily penalized.

Withers—Shoulder blades should not protrude much. Not too widely set apart with perhaps two thumbs' width or less between the blades. At the withers, the Brittany is slightly higher than at the rump.

Shoulders—Sloping and muscular. Blade and upper arm should form nearly a 90-degree angle when measured from the posterior point of the blade at the withers to the junction of the blade and the upper arm, and thence to the point of the elbow nearest the ribs. Straight shoulders do not permit sufficient reach.

Back—Short and straight. Slight slope from highest point of withers to the root of the tail. Never hollow, saddle, sway, or roached-backed. Slight drop from hips to root of tail. Distance from last rib to upper thigh short, about three to four finger widths.

Chest—Deep, reaching the level of the elbow. Neither so wide nor so rounded as to disturb the placement of the shoulder bones and elbows, which causes a paddling movement, and often causes soreness from elbow striking ribs. Ribs well sprung, but adequate heart room provided by depth as well as width. Narrow or slab-sided chests are a fault.

Flanks—Rounded. Fairly full. Not extremely tucked up, nor yet flabby and falling. Loins short and strong. Narrow and weak loins are a fault. In motion the loin should not sway sideways, giving a zigzag motion to the back, wasting energy.

Hindquarters—Broad, strong and muscular, with powerful thighs and well-bent stifles, giving a hip set well into the loin and the marked angulation necessary for a powerful drive when in motion. Fat and falling hindquarters are a fault.

Tail—Naturally tailless, or not over four inches long. Natural or docked. Set on high, actually an extension of the spine at about the same level.

Front Legs—Viewed from the front, perpendicular, but not set too wide as in the case of a dog loaded in shoulder. Elbows and feet turning neither in nor out. Pastern slightly bent to give cushion to stride. Not so straight as in Terriers. Falling pasterns, however, are a serious fault. Leg bone clean, graceful, but not too fine. An extremely heavy bone is as much a fault as spindly legs. One must look for substance and suppleness. Height to the elbows should approximately equal distance from elbow to withers.

Hind Legs—Stifles well bent. The stifle generally is the term used for knee joint. If the angle made by the upper and lower leg bones is too straight, the dog quite generally lacks drive, since his hind legs cannot drive as far forward at each stride as is desirable. However, the stifle should not be bent as to throw the hock joint far out behind the dog. Since factors not easily seen by the eye may give the dog his proper drive, a Brittany should not be condemned for straight stifle until the judge has checked the dog in motion from the side. When at a trot, the Brittany's hind foot should step into or beyond the print left by the front foot. The stifle joint should not turn out making a cowhock. (The cowhock moves the foot out to the side, thus driving out of line and losing reach at each stride). Thighs well feathered, but not profusely, halfway to the hock. Hocks, that is, the back pasterns, should be moderately short, pointing neither in nor out; perpendicular when viewed from the side. They should be firm when shaken by the judge.

Feet—Should be strong, proportionately smaller than the spaniels, with close-fitting, well arched toes and thick pads. The Brittany is not "up on his toes." Toes not heavily feathered. Flat feet, splayed feet, paper feet, etc., are to be heavily penalized. An ideal foot is halfway between the hare- and cat-foot.

A Guide to the Judge—The points below indicate only relative values. To be also taken into consideration are type, gait, soundness, spirit, optimum height, body length and general proportions.

Scale of Points

Head	25	Running gear	40
Body	35	Total	100

Disqualifications

Any Brittany measuring under 17½ inches or over 20½ inches. Black in the coat or a nose so dark in color as to appear black. A tail substantially more than 4 inches in length.

Poor Rear
Movement

Good Rear
Movement

Cow-Hocked

Correct Front
Movement

Paddling

Weaving

Ch. Radagast Why Not shown in a double-suspension gallop, most interesting for a Britt. Owned by Dianne Kroll of Why Not Brittanies. Why Not won 63 Bests of Breed, 5 Specialties and 2 group placements before his untimely death in 1979.

National field and National Specialty show winner, Dual Ch. Pacolet Cheyenne Sam, owned by Ken and Erin Jacobson. *Roberts photo.*

17

The National Specialty Show

IN CHAPTER 13, WE have told of the first Brittany licensed specialty show and field trial. These were held at the same time for a very good reason. The organizers of the American Brittany Club clearly intended that the breed should not be split into two—bench dogs and field dogs. They had seen this happen in other breeds, and they were determined that it should not happen with the Brittany Spaniel. It was felt that this could best be prevented by holding bench shows and field trials together. In so doing, dogs could compete in both. Thus, ever since November 27–28, 1943, the national bench show has been held with the national field championship.

This policy has been slightly altered in the last couple of years to permit the holding of a separate summer bench show, held in conjunction with an all-breed show. The system has been to designate the classes at a given show as the American Brittany Club's Summer Specialty.

In the following table, we give the winners of the National Specialty alone.

Best of Breed at National Specialty

1985   Ch. Le Duc Cimmaron Storm Cloud
1984   Ch. Twin Oaks Vantage Point
1983   Ch. Dee's Picante Pepper of JB
1982   Ch. Do-Well's JB Jason

Ch. Bonnie Kay's Duke of Sequani, owned by Mr. and Mrs. Frederick H. Murphy, was sired by Ch. Bonnie Kay's Ricki's Image and is himself the sire of the breed's top winner Ch. Sequaini's Dana MacDuff. Here he is winning a strong Sporting group at the Somerset Hills Kennel Club under the author. *Gilbert photo.*

Dual Ch. Elcon's Shotgun Smoke, who won the 1967 ABC National Specialty. He is the only liver to date to win the event. He won Best of Breed from the Open class to finish his championship. He is owned by Lloyd and Ella Conable.

Eastwood of Twin Lakes photo.

1981	Ch. Do-Well's JB Jason
1980	Ch. Greenfield Le Duc De Canalle
1979	Hi Ace
1978	Ch. Jacques Prince Valiant
1977	Ch. Romar's Sweet Whiskey Man
1976	Ch. Jacques Prince Valiant
1975	Ch. Greenfield's Mister Mark
1974	Dual Ch. Suzabob's Hedgerow Happy
1973	Ch. Credence Skoshi
1972	Mechant of Breton's Lightning
1971	Ch. Sequani's Dana MacDuff
1970	Dual Ch. Pacolet Cheyenne Sam
1969	Dual Ch. Suzabob's Hedgerow Happy
1968	Ch. Bonnie Kay's Duke of Sequani
1967	Dual Ch. Elcon's Shotgun Smoke
1966	Ch. Sam's Son Buckshot, C.D.
1965	Ch. Sam's Son Buckshot, C.D.
1964	Ch. Chief of Appanoose
1963	Ch. Juchoir's Tuffy
1962	Ch. Juchoir's Tuffy
1961	Ch. Bonnie Kay's Ricki's Image
1960	Ch. Bonnie Kay's Ricki's Image
1959	Ch. Bonnie Kay's Ricki's Image
1958	Dual Ch. Dingo's Little Mike
1957	Ch. Havre des Bois Henri
1956	Ch. Avono Corky
1955	Ch. Tigre par le Tigre l'Argoat
1954	Ch. Do-Car's Flashy Showman
1953	Ch. Avono Corky
1952	Ch. Amos of Edough
1951	Ch. Buccaneer de Klemanor
1950	Ch. Buccaneer de Klemanor
1949	Tudor du Roc Hellou
1948	Ch. Avono Happy
1947	Retta of Avono
1946	Ch. Avono Happy
1945	Ch. Patrice de Sharvogue
1944	Ch. Patrice de Sharvogue
1943	Ch. Patrice de Sharvogue

Best of Breed at American Brittany Club Summer Specialty Shows

1968	Ch. Frenchman's Yankee Nickel
1969	Ch. Sequani's Dana MacDuff

Ch. Sewall's Rex, owned by Glenn
Sewall, and shown here with his
handler John G. Lee. *Klein photo.*

The main winners at the Susquehanna Brittany Club Specialty 1971. They
are (l. to r.) Ch. Ffynant's Happy Time, owned by John Mattinson and
Joan Coluccio, best of breed; Ch. Suzabob's Seminole Sadie, owned by
Robert Young, best of opposite sex; Suzabob's Freckled Miss (now a cham-
pion), owned by Edwin Jeffreys, Jr., best of winners. The judge is Clark C.
Thompson. *Shafer photo.*

126

1970   no show held
1971   Ch. Barry The Fierce
1972   Ch. Kip Tam's Little Guy
1973   Ch. Ffynant's Revelation
1974   Ch. Skyline Rambler Ross
1975   Ch. Ffynant's Revelation
1976   Can. and Am. Fld. Ch. Sequani's Dana MacDuff
1977   Ch. Mitzy's Blu Ridge River Cholly
1978   Am. and Can. Ch. Jacques Prince Valiant
1979   Ch. Sequani's Beaver Dam MacDane
1980   Ch. Stephora's Disco Ditto
1981   Ch. Starline's Pretty Boy Pete
1982   Ch. Do-Well's J.B. Jason
1983   Ch. Jen-Mar's Jolly Roger
1984   Ch. Maxwell's Kokomo Ago-Go
1985   Ch. Shannon Creek Sir Blu
1986   Ch. Woodstock's Lady Valentine

Fld. Ch. Heady's Skip Britt, owned by P. A. Pittman, has won six open stakes and is the sire of nine winners.

Dual Ch. Char-Lee O'Dee, owned by Francis Claser, was winner of the National Amateur Championships and was second in the National Open, both in 1971.

18

The National Championship Stake

NATIONAL CHAMPIONSHIP STAKES HAVE been held for Pointers and English Setters for many years under the rules of the American Field and its *Field Dog Stud Book*. But the concept of such a championship did not reach the American Kennel Club until much later. Under AKC rules, a national championship stake was first set up for retrievers. Parent bodies of other breeds then began to petition the American Kennel Club for permission to hold such stakes. Brittanys, English Springer Spaniels and others then were granted permission to hold national championship events.

It was not until 1957 that the American Kennel Club permitted the American Brittany Club to hold an actual national championship stake. The winner has ever since been officially designated as the national champion.

Yet to give a more complete history of Brittany field trials in America, it seems correct to list all the winners of the American Brittany Club's annual national trials. However, a major difference should be noted. At all the American Brittany Club national trials, the open all-age stake was, as its name indicates, open to all. And as usual, four places were given. A change was made when the first true national championship stake was held. To be eligible, dogs had to win or place at earlier regional club trials. And instead of making four placings, only the national champion was named.

As field trial interest spread across North America, the necessity for a central trial location became evident. Since the trials would be held in late

November or early December, some consideration of weather conditions had to be made.

The State of Illinois had set up an immense wildlife area called Crab Orchard. This is located in the Carbondale-Marion-Carterville area of southwestern Illinois, southeast of St. Louis, Missouri, and not far from Paducah, Kentucky. Included in the area were large, well-managed lands suitable for field trials. Both retriever and English Springer Spaniel national championships were moved to Crab Orchard. In 1950, the American Brittany Club also began to hold its trials there. Trials have been held elsewhere, for instance at Paducah, Kentucky, and Ardmore, Oklahoma. Always they have been held on well-managed areas suitable for reasonably wide-ranging pointing dogs.

The year was 1950. Until and including that year, trials were half-hour heats. But in 1951 this was changed. It was felt that a national champion should be able to carry his work over an hour period.

Famed French sculptor Jacques Fath modeled a statuette of the great French Brittany, Kaer de Cornouaille. Alan Stuyvesant had owned Kaer. He purchased the statuette and offered it to the American Brittany Club as a "traveling trophy." That is, it was to be held by the winner for one year. However, it could be won permanently if won by the same dog, or the same owner, three times.

This happened in 1959. The great Dual Champion Towsey, owned by Tom Black and handled by Delmar Smith, permanently retired the trophy. Towsey won in 1955, 1957 and 1959.

Mrs. Mary Kleeman, the widow of Walter, then replaced the trophy with an identical one. However, Mrs. Kleeman changed the conditions. The statuette cannot be permanently won. It belongs to the American Brittany Club, and it can be held for one year only. There is obvious merit to this. For each year, the names of great dogs can be inscribed on the base. And each year, tradition hallows further this memorial to a great dog, and to those who have followed.

The following are the winners from 1943 until 1985:

Winners of National Championship Stakes

1943   Aotrou MacEochaidh
1944   Tess of Chippewa
1945   Aotrou MacEochaidh
1946   Tess of Chippewa
1947   Allamuchy Valley Addie
1948   Bonaire Bob
1949   Jersey Jeff
1950   Butch's Lad
1951   Pontac's Dingo

Dual and 1967 National Fld. Ch. Colorado's Yankee Timber, owned by Lucas Ruiz. This dog was sired by the former National Fld. Ch. Hellou's Yankee Timber.

Ch. Way-Kan Fritts, a liver and white owned by Ronald Stevenson, holds the National Open Field Championship for 1969.

1952	Pontac's Dingo
1953	Tennessee Luke
1954	Miste de Klemanor
1955	Dual Ch. Towsey
1956	Jeffrey of Argard
1957	Dual Ch. Towsey
1958	Fld. Ch. Hellou's Yankee Timber
1959	Dual Ch. Towsey
1960	Fld. Ch. Holiday Britt
1961	Fld. Ch. Yankee Boy's Tommy
1962	Miller's Desert Dust
1963	Fld. Ch. Crab Orchard Duke
1964	Fld. Ch. Shenango Valley Dingo
1965	Fld. Ch. Rendezvous Skipper
1966	Bazooka's Brady
1967	Dual Ch. Colorado's Yankee Timber
1968	Fld. Ch. Goldtone's Duke
1969	Way Kan Fritts
1970	Fld. Ch. Augustus of Rivers
1971	Dual Ch. Pacolet Cheyenne Sam
1972	Kipp's Trooper Rochambeau
1973	Fld. Ch. Ban-Dee
1974	Dual Ch., AFC Ban-Dee
1975	Dual Ch. Chipp Britt Jill
1976	Fld. Ch. Senator TJ
1977	Fld. Ch. Casey's Chikamin
1978	Dual Ch., AFC Perry's Rustic Prince
1979	Way Kan Feelin' Free
1980	Dual Ch., AFC Cinnabar's Ami Roc de'Edwards
1981	Dual Ch. Tomar's Ban-Dee Sam
1982	Fld. Ch., AFC Jumpin' Jack Flash II
1983	Fld. Ch. Bean's Blaze
1984	Fld. Ch. Brought-Mar's Jazz De Campo
1985	Franklin County Bandit

19

The American
Brittany Futurities—
Bench and Field

$\mathbf{A}$ FUTURITY IS AN event in which a purse has been built up over a period of time by specific payments. In most futurities, a mated bitch is nominated at some period before she whelps. There is a cash nominating fee. After the litter is born, a second payment is made. Other payments may be required at specified times. Actual competitors then pay an entrance fee. The total purse is divided in various ways, according to the terms of the specific futurity. After expenses, some futurities divide the purse between the breeder and the owner—often the same person. More often, the purse is split to permit second, third, and fourth place winners to participate.

As a rule, part of the purse goes to the sponsoring group. This pays the cost of administration, and also adds money to the sponsoring organization's treasury. The American Brittany Field Futurity is run under *Field Dog Stud Book* and American Field rules. The conformation, or show futurity, is held under American Kennel Club rules. However, under AKC rules, a futurity's classes are nonregular and carry no championship points.

The first futurity began with an enrollment period of October 31, 1946 through July 1, 1947. Fifty-nine bitches were nominated, and forty-three were given second nominations. There were 37 actual starters. The trial was run at Inkster, Michigan, October 1, 1948.

The first of the bench show, or conformation, futurities was held in 1963. There have been far fewer nominations for this event. Yet it has become one of the most important of the parent club's activities. Both futurities are now held in conjunction with the national trials.

The American Brittany Club Futurities are established for the purpose of encouraging and benefiting the breeders and owners of the Brittany. The trials and shows were inaugurated by the American Brittany Club and are conducted under their rules:

Conditions and Rules

Litter Forfeits

Each American Brittany Club Futurity shall be open to every purebred Brittany bitch bred on or after October 30th of any year and all her progeny born on or after January 1st of the year following, the dams of which have been nominated and whose litters have been enrolled with the American Brittany Club. Bitches must be owned, co-owned or leased by a member of the American Brittany Club or by a member of his immediate family.

All dams nominated and all stud dogs used must be registered in a recognized stud book or be eligible for registration.

Nominations of dams must be made within 30 days after the bitches have been bred, at which time the sum of $8.00 must be paid. Before the litter shall have reached 30 days of age the second and final litter forfeit of $8.00 must be paid. This payment will entitle each puppy of this particular litter to be entered in the ABC Futurities (Field and/or Bench) upon fulfillment of requirements given below.

Nominations of dams must be made on or after October 30 of any year and shall close positively October 29 the following year for the American Brittany Futurity to be run the year subsequent to the closing date. Should a bitch bred in October of any year not whelp her litter until after January 1, that litter shall be considered to have been enrolled in the next succeeding futurity.

If a bitch fails to whelp or gives birth to a dead litter her nominator may substitute another, or transfer the nomination to another person in the same or next succeeding stake, subject to the approval of the American Brittany Club, provided said nominator shall give notice within 30 days after the time the bitch should have whelped. If notification is not made in accordance with this requirement the first fee shall be forfeited. Only one substitution is allowable and that must be made under the same conditions governing the original nominations.

Trial and Show

The trials and show shall be held at the time and place as may be determined by the American Brittany Club. The time and place shall be announced at least 60 days before the day set for their commencement.

Entries for each American Brittany Club Futurity shall close July 1st (except when that date falls on Sunday, then it shall be July 2nd) for the current year's Futurity. On or before July 1st those expecting to start dogs must describe their entries on entry blanks furnished free of charge by the American Brittany Club and pay on each a forfeit of $20.00 for each trial and/or $15.00 for each show in which it is planned to participate. A starting fee ($20 and $15) must be paid, in addition, before the start of the events. No dog may participate until its registration number has been received by the American Brittany Club.

Show classes shall be divided by sex. Senior classes shall be for dogs whelped January—April; Intermediate Classes shall be dogs whelped May—August; Junior Classes shall be for dogs whelped September—December.

Purse

The litter forfeits, less all expenses incurred up to the closing of entries on July 1st, will be equally divided among the regions holding Futurities. The forfeits due on July 1st will be divided by area of participation and added to the base amount above. This, after the deduction of 10% for the American Brittany Club, will constitute the purse for that region. All expenses for the preparation and running of the events will be covered by the final starting fee.

The purse will be divided in a ratio of 5 for the field to 3 for bench. Two-thirds of the purse will go to the owners of record of the winners at the time the event is held and 1/3 to the breeders of the winners, to be paid to the recipients by the National Futurity Secretary.

In the field the division of the purse will be 40% for first place, 25% for second place, 20% for third place and 15% for fourth place.

In the Show the division of the purse will be:

Best in Futurity 40%
Best of Opposite Sex 30%
2nd place male (also 2nd place female) 10%
3rd place male (also 3rd place female) 5%

Any winnings designated and not awarded shall revert to the American Brittany Club.

Dual Futurity

The Dual Futurity winner in each section will receive 5% of the gross purse for that region, divided 2/3 to the owner and 1/3 to the breeder. The owner's winnings must be paid to the registered owner. In case no Dual Futurity winner is named the 5% will revert to the American Brittany Club.

The Dual Futurity must be placed in both show and field and the winners will be determined by the point schedule on file at the ABC office.

A letter is sent from The American Brittany Club, Inc. to puppy purchasers and we quote from two paragraphs that explain quite clearly to a new Brittany owner about futurities.

"The pup you purchased, born last year, from the breeder who is mailing this to you, was from a Futurity-nominated litter. Perhaps you do not fully understand what this means so I will try to explain it to you.

"Your pup is eligible to compete in the Dog Shows and/or Field Trials to be

135

held as noted in this entry blank. Three trials in three different sections of the country will be run on native birds. Trials and shows are open only to dogs from nominated litters. You would be competing with dogs in your own dog's age group. In the field dogs are expected to hunt well and point their birds but not necessarily required to be steady to wing and shot. In the Show dogs are gaited on leash and must stand for examination for the judge."

ABC Field Futurity Winners

1948 Ch. Peg B. of Loufel. Breeder-owner-handler: Lucien Ufford.
1949 Allamuchy Valley Slim. Breeder: Mike Burnham. Owner: Alan Stuyvesant.
1950 Pontac's Hero. Breeder-owner: Coy Conwell.
1951 Allamuchy Valley Rusty. Breeder: Lee Holman. Owner: Alan Stuyvesant.
1952 Fld. Ch. Juchoir's Martin. Breeder: Dr. Thomas J. Talbott. Owner: James Williams.
1953 Hero's Master Spot. Breeder-owner: Dr. Harry E. Lee.
1954 Dingo's Little Mike. Breeder: Howard Crippen. Owner: George Wilson.
1955 Hels Oklahoma Topper. Breeder: M. F. Guest. Owner: Doyle Friel.
1956 Hels Oklahoma Rainbow. Breeder-owner: Melba Guest.
1957 Holliday Britt. Breeder: George Carver. Owner: S. Rowe Hill.
1958 Chien Fox. Breeder: Russell Cookingham. Owner: Richard Fox.
1959 Edandot Buzzer. Breeder: Edward Borger. Owner: Jerome N. Halle.
1960 Chip of LaRue. Breeder: C. P. Plyler. Owner: Louis E. Frank.
1961 Swanee Belle of LaRue. Breeder: C. P. Plyler. Owner: Glenn Eades.
1962 Skyline Banjo. Breeder: Harold Reed. Owner: Earl Chappell.
1963 Juchoir Termison Tiger. Breeder: Nicky Bissell. Owner: Dr. W. Heap.
1964 Diane of Leeway. Breeder-owner-handler: John W. Lee.
1965 Juchoir's Trooper Jill. Breeder-owner: Ted Hames.
1966 Jocko's Poker Chip. Owner: John Munson. Breeder: Gary and Rosalie Graney.
1967 Not held until the winter of 1968.
1968 (February) Highland Ginger Go Go. Breeder-owner-handler: Wendell Burdick. (November 1968) Marmalade Sarah. Breeder-owner: Clifton Boggs.
1969 Hi Spirit Bazooka's Pistol. Owner: Darrell Gaynor. Breeder: William McNutt.
1970 Jinx's Jim Dandy. Breeder-owner: Curtiss Weyer.
1971 Flint's Dust Commander. Breeder-owner: Gene Spires.
1972 Cheyenne Sam's Repeat. Owner-handler, Mrs. Marie May. Breeder: Terry Anderson.
1973 Tex's Air Man. Owner: Ken Horn. Breeder: Luther Lawrence.

136

Hereafter the field futurity was run in three sections, East, Central and West. Only winners' names are given.

1974 E   Oakenshield's Tina Champaign
     C   Way Kan Frittsie
     W   Tequila Anne
1975 E   The Real Thing
     C   The Real Thing
     W   Scipio's Foxy Lady
1976 E   Kidogo's Dixie O
     C   Sandra Dee V
     W   Del Oro's Mini Rivers
1977 E   Sweet Susie Of Franklin
     C   Pricetown Sintillating Sarge
     W   Choc Talk
1978 E   Perpetuator Of Connie
     C   Kingrow Something Special
     W   Scipio's Double Shot Of Brandy
1979 E   Home Acres Risk
     C   Highland Timber Gypsy
     W   Dajo's Spark Of Fire
1980 E   Allmac's De-Na-Dark
     C   O'Cal's Stacey's Jake
     W   Ben's Sport
1981 E   Markar's Jac's A Dand D
     C   Bay Arbor Grand Blue
     W   Bean's Blaze
1982 E   Hybrittin's Jeremiah Weed
     C   H Mar's Super Star
     W   Jessen's Lit'l Dab Of Dude
1983 E   Saint's Sawbuck Sam
     C   La-Pitt Pixie
     W   Micro Chip
1984 E   Risky Business
     C   Rimarda's Rhapsody
     W   Bi-Mar Cinnabar Cindy
1985 E   B and D's Justin Tyme Of Auten
     C   Timber's Goldtone Joker
     W   Jake's Son of a Gun Runner

The Bench Futurity

1963   Doc's Shotgun Popper. Breeder-owner: John Schuckert, D.D.S.
1964   Ch. Edandot Iane. Breeder-owner: Edward M. Borger.

Can. Ch. K Star Cheyenne MacDevil shown going BB and Best Puppy in Group at the Kingston and District KC under the author. Bred, trained, and handled by owner, Kathy Shannon. *Alex Smith photo.*

1965   Ch. Holley Haven Tam of Twin Oaks. Owners: Donald and Mary Moloney. Breeder: Henry Holleyoak.

1966   Holley Haven Brett. Breeder-owner-handler: Henry Holleyoak.

1967   Not held until February, 1968.

1968   (February) Dave O'Star Speckles. Owner: Evert Davis Jr. Breeder: Herman Bonine. (November) Trooper's Northwest Buddy. Owners: Pat and Bob Spring. Breeders: Del and Pat Foltz.

1969   Belle's Allamuchy Terry. Owner: Patrick O'Shaughnessy. Breeder: Clarence Goering.

1970   Scott's Super Trooper. Breeder-owner: Virginia Scott.

1971   Freck's Boy Pete. Breeder-owner: Louis Gombert.

1972   Ch. Sir Lancelot of Edwards. Breeder-owner-handler: R. H. Edwards.

1973   Elcia's Greenfield Quarter 'R"Horse

Starting with 1974, the show futurity was split into three divisions, East, Central and West.

Year	Div	Name
1974	E	Sequani's Holly des Collines
	C	Sequani's Beaver Dam Cinnamon
	W	Hedgerow's Cheyenne Buck
1975	E	Sequani's Beaver Dam MacDane
	C	Jance's Zeus II
	W	Delbert De Britt
1976	E	Sequani's Parklake MacTeed
	C	Pioneer Valley Gingersnap
	W	Millette's The Fire Spirit
1977	E	Sequani's Marjo Boisvert
	C	Matje's Rebel Rouser
	W	Millette's The Magician
1978	E	Sequani's Mr. MacTavish
	C	Prince Valiant's Fancy Dancer
	W	Country Cousin Sweet Sue
1979	E	Rogales Avenger
	C	Dunham's Goshawk
	W	Andino's First Try Millette
1980	E	Willow Run Go Gabrielle
	C	Hope's Perseverence
	W	Maxwell's Kokamo Rustic Spike
1981	E	Creager's Bang Bang Lulu
	C	Twin Oaks Regardless
	W	Starline's Sassy Sadie
1982	E	Woodstock's Lady Valentine
	C	Melridge Two-D Foul Play
	W	Le Duc's Tough To Touch

1983	E	Jen-Mar's Extra Trouble
	C	Cheyenne Lance
	W	Maxwell's Spike's True-Brit
1984	E	Hound's Paw Belle De Mizlu
	C	Prince Valiant's Spring A-Rival
	W	Millette's Country Sunshine
1985	E	Carosel Tropic-Ana of Jen-Mar
	C	Rolyart's Star Sapphire
	W	Maxwell's Lost River Tiga-Lily

Dual and 1985 National Amateur Field Ch. Bandee-Britt's Red Jinx, owner-handled by W. Steven Rudd, M.D.

Dual Ch. Hope's Trace of Rust owned, bred and handled by Tom and Judy Tighe. By Dual and Amateur Field Ch. Perry's Rustic Prince ex Ch. Hope's Ruffled Feathers, "Tracy" is one of four dual champions produced in a single litter. *John L. Ashbey photo.*

20

The National Amateur Championship Stake

THOSE FAMILIAR WITH THE first trials held for Brittanys know that there were hundreds of arguments as to what constituted an amateur handler. The argument was not, of course, limited to Brittanys. Eventually, the American Kennel Club defined the term as it applies to the pointing breeds. We quote the AKC definition in full.

> An amateur owner or handler is a person who, during the period of two years preceding the trial, has not accepted remuneration in any form for training or handling dogs in any form of dog activity, and who at no time in the past has for any period of two years or more operated as a professional trainer or handler of field trial dogs.

This means that, while no professional trainer can handle a dog in an amateur stake, the dog may still have been professionally trained. Thus, an owner or a friend might handle a dog in an amateur event, and then turn the dog over to its professional trainer to be handled in an open all-age stake. The dog might then win an amateur all-age stake when handled by an amateur and, at the same trial, win the open all-age stake when handled by its professional trainer-handler.

The American Kennel Club also has spelled out the basic rules for a national amateur championship stake. Herewith, we quote these rules in full.

Dual, Amateur Field and CKC Ch. Hope's Maximilien Robespierre, who has more than 50 adult AKC and American Field Trial placements, owned by Robert and Barbara Rokas, Amber Ridge Kennels.

Dual Ch. Krissy's Kaptain Kay-Cee, owned by Cliff Boggs.

The National Amateur Championship Stake for Brittanys shall be held no more than once in any calendar year, and shall be for dogs which by reason of wins previously made qualify under regulations submitted by the Parent Club and approved by the Board of Directors of The American Kennel Club. The stake shall be held by the Parent Club which shall file an application for permission to run it under procedures approved in advance by The American Kennel Club. The winner of this stake, if registered in the American Kennel Club stud book, shall be recorded an Amateur Field Champion of The American Kennel Club, and may be designated "National Amateur Brittany Field Champion for 19—."

The first National Amateur Championship stake was held at Carbondale, Illinois in 1951. There were 14 competitors. It is an important record in the history of the breed that the winner that year was American and Canadian show champion, Diane de Beauch, U.D. For she was handled by her breeder-owner, Edgar W. "Bill" Averill. Bill, who has his doctorate in mathematics, was a founding member of the American Brittany Club. Diane's record is one that may never be beaten. Besides her American and Canadian championships, she had an American Utility Dog title, and a Canadian U.D. Then, to the highest bench and obedience titles she could win, she added the National Amateur Championship. Since a dual championship with the famous Patrice of Sharvogue had so narrowly escaped him, Dr. Averill's victory with Diane must have been especially pleasing.

National Amateur Champions

1966 Fld. Ch. Towsey's Bub
1967 Fld. Ch. Little Rapa Luke
1968 Fld. Ch. Holiday Britts Ed
1969 Fld. Ch. Gringo de Britt
1970 Dual Ch., AFC Gringo de Britt
1971 Dual Ch. Char-Lee O'Dee
1972 Fld. Ch. Colorado's Jumping Gypsy
1973 Fld. Ch. Brandy's Bullet
1974 Fld. Ch. Hello Dolly Miss Kaer
1975 Dual Ch., AFC Hello Dolly Miss Kaer
1976 Dual Ch. Perry's Rustic Prince
1977 Fld. Ch. Cindy's Chief Tomahawk
1978 Dual Ch. Hi-Spirit Buck
1979 Fld. Ch. The Real Thing
1980 Fld. Ch., AFC R/J's Brandy Sniffer
1981 Dual Ch., AFC Hi-Spirit Buck
1982 Fld. Ch., AFC Gun-Runner's Far Out
1983 Dual Ch. Krissys Kaptain Kay-Cee
1984 Fld. Ch. Jaron's Brittany
1985 Dual Ch. Bandee-Britts Red Jinx

Winners ABC Amateur

1951 Int. Ch. Diane de Beauch, U.D.
1952 Domino de Klemanor
1953 Fld. Ch. Belloaks Ginger
1954 Dual Ch. Holley Haven Duchess
1955 Holley Haven Dan
1956 Fld. Ch. Ferdinand of Leeway
1957 Dual Ch. Saxon of Fredan
1958 Fld. Ch. Ferdinand of Leeway
1959 Dual Ch. Belloak's King
1960 Fld. Ch. Gladwin Smokey
1961 Fld. Ch. Jeff of Minnahaha
1962 Ferd's Cannonball of Leeway
1963 Fld. Ch. Epper of Siouxland
1964 Fld. Ch. Tiger's Jocko
1965 Fld. Ch. Rendezvous Skipper

Field and Amateur Field Ch. Sholdebrand Bandee Baronett, owned by Dr. W. Steven and Tarey Rudd.

National, Dual, AFC Cinnabar's Ami Roc de 'Edwards, owned by Chuck and Carole Alff and bred by Robert Edwards. Roc began his show career at 6 months by earning his first major, topping three champions to win Best of Breed. He finished his championship at 18 months and earned his Amateur championship at four years.

21

The American Brittany Classics

As NOTED IN THE history of the breed, Brittanys spread rapidly about North America. Very shortly after their introduction, they spread from Mexico to British Columbia, and from Southern California to New Brunswick and Nova Scotia. This meant that the Brittany was being used on all kinds of feathered game—woodcock, prairie chicken, grouse, partridge, quail and pheasant.

When national trials came into being, it soon became evident that dogs from one section of this vast area might have to work on game birds with which they were not familiar. Moreover, a dog that could perform superbly on one type of game might always be in the shadow because at particular trials it would have to work other species. The American Brittany Club solved this problem by setting up its Classic Stakes. These were to be—and are—just slightly less important than the National Championship events. They are officially given by the American Brittany Club, but regional clubs act as hosts for the events.

The classics are limited open all-age events for Brittanys only. They are the Pheasant Classic, Quail Classic, Prairie Chicken Classic, Grouse Classic, Gun Dog Classic and Chukar Classic. The American Brittany Club limits the entry to dogs that have qualified in other events. For example, a dog must have won a first place in a derby or open all-age in order to qualify. In some cases Winners has been withheld, and some classic events have not been held every year.

Here are the winners in each classic since their beginning:

Pheasant Classic

1964   Ch. White Flash's Nikki
1965   Fld. Ch. Juchoir's Chocolate Candy
1966   Fld. Ch. Juchoir's Chocolate Candy
1967   Baroness Allamuchy Babs
1968   Foltz's Freckles
1969   Dual Ch. Les-Lee's Red Ryder
1970   Dual Ch. Tigar's Jocko
1971   Dual Ch. Black Butte Ricochet Trooper
1972   Fld. Ch. Brandy's Bullet
1973   Dual Ch. Pacolet Cheyenne Sam
1974   Senator TJ
1975   Le Pradalan
1976   Dual Ch. The Little Joker
1977   Spartan Town Squire
1978   Dual Ch. and AFC Ch. Hi-Spirit Buck
1979   Sir Christopher IV
1980   Fld. Ch. Del Oro's Mint River
1981   Fld. Ch. Lit'l Scip Of Brandy
1982   Fld. Ch., AFC Ran-Bo's Royal Rereua
1983   Fld. Ch. Markar's Bet I M
1984   Duke Of Brittmont
1985   Dual Ch. Markar's Jac's A-Dan-D

Quail Classic

1962   Detective Neal Of Kaymore
1963   Kaymore's Joe Of Weymouth
1964   Scuffletown Quito
1965   Le Bonabe
1966   Le Petite Blanche
1967   Rendevous Skipper
1968   Worrelwind's Bucky Weaver
1969   Skysan
1970   Augustus Of Rivers
1971   Fld. Ch. Sodak Sandy Sioux
1972   Bluegrass Tex
1973   Tondee's Sandy Valley Duke
1974   Nat. Ch. and Fld. Ch. Augustus Of Rivers
1975   Fld. Ch. Ringo De Britt
1976   Fld. Ch. Copper Creek Bobb

Fld. Ch. Juchoir's Chocolate Candy, (left) a Pheasant Classic winner with breeder-handler Nicky Bissell. The dog at the right is Fld. Ch. Juchoir's Bronze Bigwig with owner Grant Chadbourne.

This group of field winners all were sired by Dual Ch. Pierrot de Fontaine Vallee out of Juchoir's Shady Lady. All carry the "Juchoir" prefix. They are (l. to r.) Fld. Ch. Light Lodestar with James Rookard, Fld. Ch. Chocolate Candy with owner Larry Prefountain, Fld. Ch. Bronze Bigwig with owner Grant Chadbourne, Fld. Ch. Termison Tiger with owner Dr. Heap, Bright Bangtail with owner William Summey and Dual Ch. Shady Scamp with owner William Brown.

1977 No Records
1978 Fld. Ch. Tall Oaks Bandolero
1979 Perry's Rustic Prince
1980 Fld. Ch. Tucker Of York
1981 Fld. Ch. First Place Jake
1982 Fld. Ch. Timber's Little Wish
1983 Fld. Ch. Jacks Or Better
1984 Dual Ch., AFC Perpetuator Of Connie
1985 Far Out's Bandit

Prairie Chicken Classic

1964 Waykan Pete
1965 First Place Withheld
1966 Not Held
1967 First Place Withheld
1968 Juchoir's Choctaw
1969 Suzabob's Rip Snorter
1970 Ch. Majestic Jake
1971 Fld. Ch. Augustus Of Rivers
1972 Dual Ch. The Little Joker
1973 Fld. Ch. Mac Ago-Go
1974 Fld. Ch. Ringo De Britt
1975 First Withheld
1976 First Withheld
1977 Dual Ch. Le Pradalan
1978 Fld. Ch. Havapal Skippy
1979 Dual Ch. Charley De Brett
1980 Fld. Ch. Britthaven Simpatico
1981 Fld. Ch. Havapal's Skippy
1982 Jug
1983 Fld. Ch. Markar's Be I.M.Magic
1984 Wild Honey Ace
1985 Foot

Grouse Classic

1961 First Place Withheld
1962 First Place Withheld
1963 Event Cancelled
1964 Summit Star
1965 Not Held
1966 Kipewa's Breton Belle
1967 Fld. Ch. Laumore's Dappled Desire

1968 Dual Ch. Joel's Copper Jaques
1969 Ch. Suzabob's Hum Dinger
1970 Aud's Barney Boy
1971 Not held thereafter

Chukar Classic

1975 Yellowstone Gus
1976–1977 Not Held
1978 Fld. Ch. Simon's Ruff-Shod O'Dee
1979 Fld. Ch. Goldtone's Bonanza
1980 J. D. Of Lost River
1981 Fld. Ch. First Place Jake
1982 Fld. Ch. Simon's Ruff-Shod O'Dee
1983 Dual Ch. J. D. Of Lost River
1984 Fld. Ch. Moore's Amare Ha Frost
1985 Fld. Ch. Tate's Second Edition
1986 Maxwell's Nellie Of Almaden

Gun Dog Classic

1980 Fld. Ch., AFC Sucios Mister Chips
1981 Fld. Ch., AFC Hopper's Robber
1982 Fld. Ch., AFC Jack Flash O'Dolly
1983 Fld. Ch., AFC Timber's Little Wish
1984 Fld. Ch. Ben's Sport
1985 Fld. Ch., AFC Stedl's Bombin Ban-Jo
1985 (Ret) Fld. Ch., AFC Stedl's Bombin Ban-Jo

22

How a Brittany Becomes a Champion

THE AMERICAN KENNEL CLUB sets up the rules governing the awarding of championships. In the case of field championships, it consults the parent clubs, or governing bodies, of all the breeds in a given classification. For example, it sets up rules for Brittanys, Pointers, German Shorthaired Pointers, German Wirehaired Pointers, English Setters, Irish Setters, Gordon Setters, Vizslas, Weimaraners and Wirehaired Pointing Griffons. These are all pointing breeds.

The awarding of championships at field trials is based partly on performance, and partly on the competition. A dog has to win 10 points to become a field champion. This applies to all of the pointing breeds listed above. A dog can win points only by winning first place in a regular stake.

The regular stakes are Open Puppy, Open Derby, Gun Dog (Open or Amateur), All-Age (Open or Amateur), Limited Gun Dog (Open or Amateur) and Limited All-Age (Open or Amateur). The point schedule is as follows:

```
4 to 7 starters  ............................ 1 point
8 to 12 starters  ........................... 2 points
13 to 17 starters  .......................... 3 points
18 to 24 starters  .......................... 4 points
25 or more starters  ........................ 5 points
```

Now the general rule for pointing dogs is that the dog must win its points in at least three licensed or member club trials. It must have won at least one three-points or better Open All-Age, Open Gun Dog, Open Limited All-Age or Limited Gun Dog Stake. It cannot count more than two points each which have been won in Open Puppy and Open Derby stakes. And not more than four points of the ten can be counted if won in amateur stakes.

For Brittanys, there is an additional condition that makes the winning of a championship much more difficult. It must have won a three-points or better Open Gun Dog, Open All-Age, Open Limited Gun Dog or Open Limited All-Age Stake in which only Brittanys were eligible to compete.

There are both national and national amateur titles open for competition to Brittanys. These can be won only at National Amateur and National Open championship stakes, which are held only once in each calendar year. The rules for eligibility to compete in such trials are made by the American Brittany Club. But they are subject to American Kennel Club approval.

The winner of such a stake gains the title of "National Brittany Field Champion of 19-" or "National Amateur Brittany Field Champion of 19-." The winning of these titles does not automatically carry with them a field championship title. But the conditions for entry make it certain that the dog that wins is already a field champion, or will become one by winning. The point rating given above applies in the National Open Championship Stake.

Conformation Championships

It is customary to speak of championships won in conformation as "bench championships." For at least 70 years, all dog shows were benched. Now benched shows are rare. But the term "bench" championship still remains. In France, people often speak of a "beauty" championship.

As in the field, conformation championships are won on a point system. A dog must win 15 points. At least six of these points must be won at two shows with a three-points or better rating each and under two different judges. Some of the balance of the points must be won under a judge or judges other than those referred to above.

Championship points are awarded in winners classes only. The so-called regular classes are Puppy, Novice, Bred-by-Exhibitor, American-Bred and Open. If a dog wins first, it gets a blue ribbon, and then it enters the Winners class. It competes there with the other class winners for points.

Championship points are based upon the number of actual competitors in the regular classes. The dog awarded Winners Dog or Winners Bitch then gets the championship points. The dog that gets Best of Winners may get extra points by doing so. Let us suppose that the Winners Dog won three points and the Winners Bitch five. If the dog now is awarded Best of Winners, he would be entitled to five points, that being the number won by the bitch. He cannot add on the three points he won to make eight. That is, he cannot win double points. The most points that can be won at any show is five.

If a dog wins Best of Breed over champions, it can count these dogs in

Dual Ch. Pierrot de Fontaine Vallee (left) is distinguished as one of the great performers and sires in the breed. Shown with him is Ch. Juchoir's Some Shoveller. Both dogs are owned by Mrs. Nicky Bissell.

Dual Ch. Destry, owned by Frank Vulgamore.

Dual Ch. Jacques des Rocheuses, owned by Lucas Ruiz.

figuring championship points. If the dog goes from the classes to first in the Sporting group, and then on to Best in Show, it would be entitled to the highest point rating won by any dog in the group or in the show.

Let us suppose a Brittany won only one point in breed competition. If it now wins the group over an Irish Setter who had won three points in its breed, then the Brittany would be credited with three points instead of only one. If it wins Best in Show over a Maltese who won five points in its breed, then the Brittany would be given five points.

The American Kennel Club divides the country into seven divisions. It then makes up point ratings for each division by a complicated system. This is based upon the number of dogs of a breed registered in the entire country, the number registered from a given division, and the number being shown in that division. The purposes are to make it reasonably difficult for a dog to win a championship, but not so difficult that it cannot win one.

Canadian Bench Championships

Canadian Kennel Club rules for winning a championship are roughly the same as those of the American Kennel Club. There are these differences. A dog must win 10 championship points under at least three different judges. In figuring championship points, champions are counted, provided the class dog defeats them. It must defeat dogs of its own breed at least once, or it must place in groups in which five or more breeds are competing. It is important here to point out that, in Canada, a dog must compete in all classes for which it is eligible, or any points it may have won will be canceled. Thus, if a dog wins five points in its breed and goes Best of Breed, it must compete in the group or it will lose its points.

The Canadian Kennel Club also divides its country into zones. Point ratings are figured by breed only, and are not divided by sex as in the United States. At the present time, the point ratings for Brittany Spaniels are the same in all parts of the country. One dog, if it gets Winners, receives one point. Three dogs get two points, four get three, six get four and eight get five.

Canadian Field Championships

To become a field champion in Canada, a Brittany Spaniel must win 10 points at licensed field trials under Canadian Kennel Club rules. At least three of the points must have been won in an unrestricted senior open stake, and not more than two points can be won in puppy stakes. An unrestricted stake is one in which all pointing breeds are allowed to compete. Senior stakes are all stakes other than puppy or derby stakes.

In puppy stakes with five or more starters, the winner gets one point. In

Ch. Cimmaron's Timeless Tiffany shown going group fourth under Melbourne T. L. Downing at Marquette KC with owner-handler, Christine Ward. Tiffany finished her championship at 18 months in the Bred-By-Exhibitor class.
Booth photo.

Ch. Danaris Damifino winning a Best of Breed under judge Virginia Hardin. Owned by D. and N. Harris.
Booth photo.

Dual Ch., Amateur Field Ch. Greenlane's Majestic Lady (Windagail's Dancer's Shady Duke ex Dual Ch. Suzabob's Regal Duchess). Owner-handler, Ed Lepp, Paisley, Ontario, Canada. She was shown to her show championship by Ted Palmer.

derby stakes with eight or more starters, the winner gets two points. The rating for senior stakes is as follows.

	First	Second	Third
6 to 7 dogs competing	1	0	0
8 to 11 dogs competing	2	1	0
12 to 15 dogs competing	3	1	½
16 to 19 dogs competing	4	2	2
20 or more dogs competing	5	3	2

The official stakes at Canadian trials are the Open Puppy, Open Derby, Gun Dog (Open or Amateur) and All-Age (Open or Amateur).

Please note that in Canada the Brittany is still officially the Brittany Spaniel.

Ch. Torbec Little Rover, owned by Gordon and Michele McIntyre.

23

Official Field Trial Classes

American Kennel Club

OPEN PUPPY. For dogs six months of age and under fifteen months on the first advertised day of the trial.

OPEN DERBY. For dogs six months of age and under two years on the first advertised day of the trial.

GUN DOG STAKE (Open or amateur). For dogs six months of age and over on the first advertised day of the trial.

ALL-AGE STAKE (Open or amateur). For dogs six months of age and over on the first advertised day of the trial.

LIMITED GUN DOG STAKE (Open or Amateur). For dogs six months of age and over on the first advertised day of the trial who have won first place in an Open Derby Stake or have placed first, second, third or fourth in a Gun Dog Stake. A field-trial-giving club may give an Amateur Limited Gun Dog Stake in which places that qualify a dog have been acquired in Amateur Stakes only.

LIMITED ALL-AGE STAKE (Open or Amateur). For dogs six months of age and over on the first advertised day of the trial who have won first place, second, third or fourth in any All-Age Stake. A field-trial-giving club may give an Amateur Limited All-Age Stake in which places that qualify a dog have been acquired in Amateur Stakes only.

In an Amateur Stake at a licensed or member field trial, all dogs must be owned and handled by persons who, in the judgment of the Field Trial Committee, are qualified as amateurs.

Ch. Stillmeadow's Rambler, C.D., owned by William McClure. *Nicholls photo.*

Dual Ch. Jacque of Connie, owned by C. Kent Lipsey.

Canadian Kennel Club

OPEN PUPPY STAKE. From January 1st to July 1st in each year, for dogs whelped on or after January 1st of the year preceding, and from January 1st to July 1st in each year for dogs whelped on or after January 1st of two preceding years.

OPEN DERBY. From July 1st to December 31st in each year for dogs whelped on or after January 1st of the year preceding, and from January 1st to July 1st in each year for dogs whelped on or after January 1st of two years preceding.

GUN DOG STAKE (Open or Amateur). For dogs six months of age and over on the first day of the trial.

ALL-AGE STAKE (Open or Amateur). For dogs six months of age and over on the first day of the trial.

At any field trial there shall not be more than one of each of the stakes described in this section, except that both open and amateur stakes may be held in Gun Dog and All-Age stakes. And no club shall hold more than two of these stakes in one calendar year unless justified by unusual circumstances and approved by the Canadian Kennel Club. Dogs running in an amateur stake must be owned by an amateur and handled by an amateur.

Here we should add another rule of the Canadian Kennel Club: "A dog is not eligible to be entered in any stake in a licensed field trial, if the judge of that stake, or any member of his family has owned, sold, held under lease, boarded, trained or handled the dog (except in an amateur stake) within six months prior to the date of the field trial.

Standards of Procedure

Both the American and Canadian Kennel Clubs have published carefully-worked-out procedures, both for operating trials, and for evaluating performances. The American Kennel Club booklet is called *Registration and Field Trial Rules and Standard Procedures for Pointing Breeds, Dachshunds, Retrievers, and Spaniels.* This booklet may be obtained by writing to the American Kennel Club, 51 Madison Ave., New York, N.Y., 10010. Single copies are free upon individual request. When ordered in quantity, the cost is 25 cents per copy.

The Canadian Kennel Club has a similar booklet, *Field Trial Rules and Regulations for Pointing Breeds.* It also has a booklet, *Standards of Judicial Practice and Field Trial Procedure.* Single copies of these are free upon request by writing to the Canadian Kennel Club, 1173 Bay St., Toronto, Ontario, Canada.

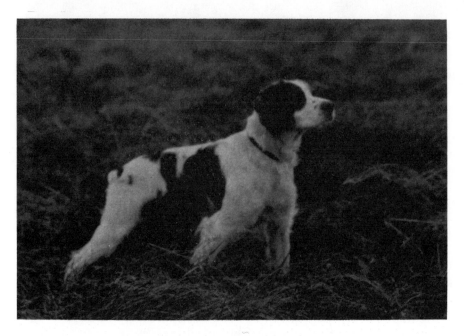

French and International Ch. Noric de Saint Tugen, owned by Mme. Marchand. Noric is also a field champion. *Dim photo.*

Gaston Pouchain, for 25 years president of the *Societe Centrale Canine* and author of the French book, *L'Epagnuel Breton,* still hunts at age 85, and, he says, "without glasses."

24

The Brittany Spaniel in France Today

by Genie Rundle, updated by Maxwell Riddle

The author is indebted to Madame Genie Rundle for the present information on the Brittany Spaniel in France. Mrs. Rundle visited with many of the great breeders of today to get this information. Although part of this has been covered in earlier chapters, there are slightly different conclusions. And therefore, the information is given just as Mrs. Rundle wrote it. This will enable readers to reach their own conclusions as to the origin and development of the breed.

ACCORDING TO THE LARGEST and most recent publication in France, *Le Grand Livre Du Chien,* published in that country in 1970, the Brittany Spaniel was only recognized as a distinct breed during the 19th century, although it had existed since the time of the Celtic flight into Brittany when the Anglo-Saxons invaded Wales, at which time the Celts took with them the Springer Spaniel. This breed, when crossed with the existing French type of working spaniel, gave rise to the type so well known today. That is to say, rustic and cobby.

In fact, the "crouching dog" of the Middle Ages is certainly the ancestor of all French types of spaniel, as well as some others with longer coats, such as the three types of setter: English, Irish and Gordon. It dates back as far as the First Crusades, at which time it was usual for the knights of France and Arabia to exchange dogs and horses they used for hunting. These, in turn, being crossed with several other types of dog then known, such as the Sloughi from the Orient, and various hunting dogs from Spain, gave rise to the original crouching dog. This dog is very often depicted in early French paintings and tapestries, and during the 16th century, became the French Spaniel. In those days the dogs were widely spread across the Brittany regions of France and were strongly built dogs with long, silky coats. It was after this that the Springer made its entry into the same territory. And thus was born the Brittany Spaniel, very similar to the one we know today.

There is a more recent account, which appears to be authentic, that was related to me by Monsieur Jacques Piraux. He is the owner of the dog with the present day's highest number of awards, though not yet a champion. He tells that 70 or 80 years ago "a gamekeeper named Lulzac entered the service of the Vicomte du Pontavice. Lulzac owned a red-and-white Welsh Springer type of Spaniel, and the Vicomte bred English Setters. These two dogs were purposely bred and their progeny gave rise to the color orange and white."

Monsieur Piraux goes on to say:

> I learned a few months ago from an industrialist who owned these dogs that only the liver-and-white Brittanies were physically able to withstand the rigorous North African climate. For that reason, sportsmen living in Morocco were the sad eyewitnesses of the general disappearance of these orange-and-whites, along with several other breeds, and setters, which could not survive the intense heat.
>
> The breed is essentially sporting, and although it can be used on big game, it is generally preferred for pointing and retrieving under all weather conditions, and in the thickest, most prickly undergrowths. The Brittany Spaniel will swim into the iciest water to retrieve its game and is tireless in all its efforts. It is one of the gentlest of breeds, willing to submit to its master's orders. It is also affectionate, sensitive and an ideal companion.

There are at the present time over 230,000 Brittanys registered with the L.O.F. of the *Societe Centrale Canine* (the official French Kennel Club), and the present annual rate of registration is about 5,000. However, since the Brittany is the most sought-after sporting dog in the world, field trials are obviously where it is most prized. The most hotly disputed competition, other than in France, is in Switzerland and in both North and South America.

In France, field trials are divided into three categories. Those that take place on partridge are held in the spring, and number about 30 held during April. During the summer—in August—five or six are held on partridge and quail. Then there are about 20 autumn trials, which include the wing shooting of partridge and pheasants, and the shooting of rabbits and hare. Retrieving is

French Dual Ch. Stop de Morwandoy. *Bonnet photo.*

An international show and field titleholder is the French
dog, Ch. Quetche De Kestellic, owned by M. Le Brosse.

Ch. Quodic De Kestellic, owned by M. Le Brosse, like his
brother Quetche, holds international titles in both field
and bench.

163

required. In addition, there are two special field trials on woodcock and snipe.

The most important trial of the year is the one organized by the *Societe Centrale Canine,* since it is here that the title Champion of France is awarded to the winner. At this trial only selected dogs can compete. Another most important trial is that held by the *Club de l'Epagneul Breton,* in which as many as 150 dogs compete in a single day.

Today the Club de l'Epagneul Breton proudly acknowledges as its head President Gaston Pouchain. President Pouchain is also at present president of the *Societe Centrale Canine,* with which the Brittany Club is affiliated. There are two vice presidents, Dr. Roguet and M. Pambrun. The secretary is M. Dages, and the assistant secretary, M. Baudot. The treasurer is M. Valeyrie, and the assistant treasurer, M. Le Chat. Other members of the committee, of which there are 12 in number are: M. Arnaud, Dr. Bazin, L. Bourdon, Combanaire, Derouet, Freville, Guyemer, Jeangirard, Labrosse, Lamour, Lelong and Moncet. The headquarters address is 25, rue du Renard, Paris, 4e. The secretariat is at 24, Place de la Chapelle, Paris, 18e.

There are now three recognized colors for the breed: liver-and-white, orange-and-white and black-and-white. This latter, although once banned in order to avoid the "blue" that was cropping up as the result of undesirable crossings, is now re-established.

Note: The L. Bourdon, to whom reference is made earlier, is Louis Bourdon, the son of Emile Bourdon, founder of the famed Cornouaille Kennels. Louis Bourdon continues the kennels of his father. Cornouaille is the Breton term for Cornwall.

The Modern French Breed Standard

General Appearance—Height: Maximum 51 centimeters (19.89 inches); minimum, 46 centimeters (17.94 inches). Ideal height for males: 48 to 50 centimeters (18.72 inches to 19.50 inches); and for bitches, 47 to 49 centimeters (18.33 to 19.11 inches). The ideal **weights** are: 15 kilograms (33.07 pounds) for males; and 13 kilograms (28.66 pounds) for bitches. A compact dog, ears short and set high, skull rounded with tight lips, coat flat, lightly fringed, fringes wavy never curly, cobby type, tail about 10 centimeters (3.9 inches) long; natural bob tail permitted.

Nose—Colored according to whether the dog is white and orange, white and liver, or white and black. Nostrils open, well shaped. **Faults:** Bare nose patches (butterfly nose), too light nostrils that interfere with scenting.

Lips—Tight with upper lip slightly overlapping the lower. **Faults:** Thick or with heavy flews.

Muzzle—Medium length, about two thirds the length of the skull. **Faults:** Too long or too short.

Skull—Medium length, rounded, median line slightly marked. Well defined but not exaggerated stop. **Faults:** Apple headed, distinct occipital

French Dual Ch. Sacha de Saint Tugen, owned and bred by Mme. Marchand, is one of 16 champions bred by this famous kennel since 1956.

Fld. Ch. Quito de Saint Tugen, owned and bred by Mme. Marchand, was winner of the 1971 national field trial championship of France. Mme. Marchand trains and handles all her own dogs.

French Ch. Querou de Cornouaille is a contemporary example of the breeding from the famous Cournouaille Kennels that contributed so strongly to American fanciers when the breed was getting started in North America.

This dog is a famous show and field winner in France. He is Pipo and is owned by M. Jacques Piraux. This liver and white is considered to be of excellent type by continental authorities.

crest, narrow or coarse. Stop heavily indented.

Eyes—Brown, in harmony with the coat, lively and expressive. **Faults:** Too light, mean, or bird of prey eyes.

Ears—Set high, rather short, lightly fringed, though the ear ought to be well covered with hair. **Faults:** Low set, pendulous, too large, or with very curly hair.

Neck—Medium length, well set on the shoulders, without dewlap. **Faults:** Too long, too slender, too short and thick-set.

Shoulders—Oblique and well muscled. **Faults:** Too straight or too angulated.

Forelegs—Muscled and bony. **Faults:** Bone too heavy or too light.

Chest—Deep, descending to the level of the elbow, sides well rounded, deep as well as wide. **Faults:** Narrow, not deep enough, slab-sided.

Back—Short, withers well defined, never sway-backed. **Faults:** Too long or sway.

Loins—Short and Strong. **Faults:** Long and weak.

Hips—Lower than the withers, set well into the loins.

Croup—Slightly falling. **Faults:** Too straight or too steep.

Flanks—Well rounded without excess. **Faults:** Fat and falling.

Tail—Level, docked if the dog does not have a natural short tail, always short, about 10 centimeters (3.9 inches), often with a little twist, and ending with a queue of hair. **Faults:** Long or bare.

Forelegs—Very straight, with pasterns slightly bent, clean and muscled. **Faults:** Pasterns too straight or falling radically, lack of feathering (elbow to pasterns).

Hindlegs—Strong thighs, stifles well bent, muscular, not cowhocked. Thighs well feathered half way to the hock. Hocks short, not too bent. **Faults:** Straight stifles, lack of feathering, too straight (hocks) or too bent.

Feet—Toes compact with a little hair between. **Faults:** Large, long, cat footed, splayed.

Coat—Flat, or slightly wavy, not excessively heavy. **Faults:** Curly or too soft.

Color—White and orange, white and liver, white and black, tri-color, or roan of any of these colors.

Summary—Thickset and strong backed. An elegant little dog, very vigorous in its movements, energetic, with an intelligent look, presenting the appearance of a full-blooded dog.

The judges should excuse, without prizes, all dogs under 46 centimeters or over 51 centimeters.

Lack of pigment is a fault on the nose. Lack of pigment on the eyelids eliminates the dog from receiving any prize. Lack of pigment is a serious fault and no dog having (a lack) of it should receive a rating of excellent. If the lack of pigment is very minor, the dog may receive a rating of very good.

Monorchids may not be shown in dog shows or compete in field trials.
The classes in a show will be in two divisions: (1) White and orange. (2) Other colors.

Comment by the Author

The French Kennel Club is somewhat more realistic than is the American Kennel Club. Thus, it recognizes that if monorchidism (only one testicle descended) is a fault, it is equally a fault in show dogs and in field dogs. It is considered in most countries to be a transmissible fault. For that reason, the French Kennel Club bars monorchids in both shows and field trials. In the United States, the fault is ignored in dogs entered in field trials.

Judging systems vary in different countries. Some in Europe and elsewhere (Brazil is an example) "rate" the exhibits. Thus, depending upon its quality, a dog might win a rating of Excellent, Very Good, Good or Sufficient. In the Scandinavian countries, which have strong Brittany entries, dogs can get first, second, third, or 0, meaning "nil" or no award. France uses the system of Excellent, Very Good, Good and Sufficient.

Only a dog winning a rating of Excellent gets a certificate toward its championship. And in case a number of dogs receive such a rating, then the judge picks the best of these for the championship rating. One dog of each sex is awarded this certificate.

A dog needs to win three of these to become a champion. But, in addition, one of these must be won at the annual Paris show. This limits the breed to two conformation champions a year. However, in the case of Brittany Spaniels, this is increased to four. The reason is that there can be two white-and-orange champions, male and female, and two in the other allowed colors.

In Europe and in South America and Mexico it is possible for a dog to win an International Championship. This is one granted under the rules of the F.C.I., or Federation Cynologique Internationale, whose headquarters are in Belgium. An international beauty championship certificate (C.A.C.I.B.) can be awarded at any licensed F.C.I. show.

In Europe, to become an International Champion, the dog must win four C.A.C.I.B. certificates in three different countries, one at least of which must be won in the owner's country, or in the country of origin of the breed. In countries outside Europe, as for instance in Mexico, and in most of the South American countries, the rule is slightly different. The dog must win four C.A.C.I.Bs under four different judges, one of whom comes from another continent. Additionally, the dog will have to demonstrate some hunting ability, including freedom from gun shyness. Puppies cannot win C.A.C.I.Bs.

International beauty and field trial champion Fifi du Costang, owned by Gaston Pouchain. She is black and white.

French Show Champions (*Champion de France de Conformite*) 1985, and their owners

Radar de L'Echo de la Foret (Gibier Tiré) à M. Provost
M'kantie du Menez Saint Mikael (Gibier Tiré) à M. le Floch
Pla'h du Menez Saint Mikael (Gibier Tiré) à M. le Floch
Sady de Loguel Lan à M. Lostec
Punch des Pigenettes à M. Dartevelle
Ska de Saint Tugen à M. Willems
Tania de L'Echo de la Foret (Gibier Tiré) à M. Mouraud
Perine de Keranlouan à M. Morin
Perine de Keranlouan (Gibier Tiré) à M. Morin
Tex de L'Echo de la Foret (Gibier Tiré) à M. Maillard
R'vampir du mas de la Combe (Gibier Tiré) à M. Covolo
Toinon du Rio des Vingt Deux à M. Herbelin
Riesling des Pigenettes (Gibier Tiré) à M. et Mme Sabatini
Sybelle de L'epi d'or (Gibier Tiré) à Mme Zazempa
Ureps du Buisson de Choisel (Gibier Tiré) à M. Terran
Sibeau du Sombretang à Mme Ganz

Courtesy R. Thenlot

25

French Field
Trial Rules

In EUROPEAN COUNTRIES, THERE are fewer specialist breeds than in the United States, Canada and Mexico. On our side of the Atlantic, a Brittany would normally be used on feathered game only. But in Europe, it might be required to prove itself on hares. It might also be required to retrieve on both land and water, and even to make "blind" retrieves.

In Europe, almost all hunting is done on foot. And so, field trials are conducted on foot. In our country, field trials for European breeds have inevitably felt the effect of our long-established Pointer and Setter trials under American Field or Amateur Field Trial Clubs of America rules. In our country, we would not dream of mixing a Springer Spaniel, a Labrador Retriever and a Brittany together in a licensed trial. But this is often done in Europe.

The rules of the French Kennel Club require two judges. Efforts are made to make all tests as nearly identical as possible. That is, in the same cover, with the same wind direction, and with similar retrieving tests. As a rule, the dogs are worked alone, that is, singly. However, if more than 18 dogs are entered, then the dogs work in braces.

The French penalize dogs that cast out so far as to disappear from sight. They expect that, in the woods, a dog will slow its pace so that it can keep in touch with its handler. Dogs are expected to cast back and forth in front of their handlers, and in crossing in front should not be farther than gun range, a maximum of about 60 yards, but with 40 being average.

Ch. Sabor Su Saristas, owned by M. Gaston Pouchain.

Tro de Keranlouan, owned by M. Guy Morin, is a French field trial champion and an international beauty champion.

Dogs are penalized for pottering. They may bump one bird, but if they bump a second, they are disqualified. When dogs are working in braces, they are required to back. Unproductive points are heavily penalized.

We require our dogs to "freeze" on point. The French follow a system used in England. The dog is expected to hold point until the arrival of its handler. Then, but only on command, it must drop into a crouching position. The reason for this rule stems from the Middle Ages method of throwing a net over the covey. The crouching dog was out of the way. The rule survives from the belief that the standing dog might interfere with the shooting.

Readers of this book will remember that in the early trials in America, game was shot over the dogs. This was the procedure in France then, and it is still the same in most trials. Official gunners do the shooting.

Steadiness to wing and shot is not required, provided the dog marks the fall and makes the retrieve promptly. But if, in breaking, the dog interferes with the shooting, then it is penalized. Such interference, for example, might occur if the dog bolted after a started hare. In a somewhat contradictory rule, the dog is supposed to retrieve upon command of the handler. In part, this refers to the dog that has remained steady, and in part to special retrieving tests.

Field trial committees can vote to eliminate water tests, provided an announcement to this effect is made before the start of the trial. When a water test is given, it is "blind." That is, the dog is sent out to retrieve game it cannot see from shore.

Land retrieves of about 20 to 25 yards are often required. In such tests, the dead bird may be placed in a ditch or heavy thicket. Some obstacle, such as a low wall or fence, is between the dog and the retrieve. The dog is expected to jump this barrier. Such retrieves are called "cold" retrieves. They are given when a dog has not had a chance to retrieve game it pointed. Heavy penalties are made against dogs that carry their game sloppily.

Though the dog is not required to be steady to wing and shot, it must remain staunch until the handler comes up. And if the bird is not shot, it is expected to remain steady, that is, it should not make a useless chase.

A dog cannot win championship consideration unless it has been on point, and preferably on birds. However, if it has been repeatedly on point on hare, it can be awarded a C.A.C. These initials stand for a certificate of ability. The dog must win four to be a champion.

French *Champions de Travail,* 1985, and their owners:

Nationaux:
Sady le Loguel-Lann à M. Lostec.
Punch des Pigenettes à Dr Dartevelle.
Ska de Saint-Tugen à M. Willems.
Tania de L'Echo de la Foret à M. Mouraud.

Perine de Keranlouan à M. G. Morin.
Toinon du Rio des 22 à M. F. Herbelin.
Sibeau de Sombretang à Mme Ganz (CH).

Nationaux de Gibier Tiré:
Radar de L'Echo de la Foret à M. Provost.
M'Kantie du Menez Sant-Mikael à M. Yvon Le Floc'h.
Pla'h du Menez Sant-Mikael à M. Yvon Le Floc'h.
Perine de Keranlouan à M. G. Morin.
Tex de L'Echo de la Foret à M. Maillard.
R'Vampir du mas de la Combe à M. Covolo.
Riesling des Pigenettes à M. et Mme Sabatini.
Sybelle de L'Epi d'or à Mme Zazempa.
Ureps du Buisson de Choisel à M. Terran.

Champions Internationaux 1985:
Rapid de la Source Enchantée à M. Molinier.
R'Vampir du mas de la Combe à M. Covolo.
Plet des Gaulis de Hetres à M. Maerten.
Poker des Pigenettes à M. Trentini.

An interesting study of two Brittanies on point, from a card of the French parent club.

26

Brittany Hall of Fame Twentieth Anniversary

T HE BRITTANY HALL OF Fame was inaugurated in 1965 with the election of 13 dogs. A committee of "old timers," composed of fanciers who had been active since before 1950, was selected to recommend the Britts to be elected. A list of early dogs was drawn up with information regarding their accomplishments and winning progeny. From this list the first 13 were selected.

The committee was in almost 100 percent agreement that the Number One place of honor in the Hall of Fame should be accorded Kaer de Cornouaille. (* indicates the original 13 Hall of Fame Brittanys.)

*Kaer de Cornouaille was imported from France in 1938. Trialed very little because of World War II, his field wins were made in very heavy competition. He was the top sire of field champions until 1962. He produced three Dual Champions, who are themselves Hall of Fame dogs.

*Dual Ch. Allamuchy Valley Uno, a son of Kaer, came at a time when the Brittany was merely standing his birds. Uno pointed his! He passed this style on to his pups. He had 10 field placements with a 2nd in the 1949 Nationals, and he produced Hall of Famer Dual Champion Uno's Jet.

*Dual Ch. Angelique de Bretagne was the 2nd Dual Champion bitch. She was a deep orange-and-white medium-sized bitch with a peanut butter smear on her muzzle. She had 18 all-age placements in Britt trials, as well as a big record in all-breed competition.

*Dual Ch. Avono Happy, a Kaer son, won the National Specialty show in 1946 and 1948. He was medium-sized with a dark orange saddle and a very cobby body. He was a big-running, gutsy dog with a mind of his own. He sired eleven bench champions, three field champions and one dual champion.

*Dual Ch. Brit of Bellows Falls was the first AKC champion and the first dual of the breed. He was a flashy orange dog with a lot of white, well proportioned and near the top of the height standard. He produced one dual and two show champions.

*Fr. Ch. Gwennec de L'Argoat held only the French title, which includes both show wins and field requirements. He was the strongest influence on the winners of the early Brittany trials, and he sired one Hall of Fame member.

*Helgramite Howie d'Acajou was a spectacular performer, owner trained and handled to his dual title. He is described as white with an orange head. He held the most all-age placements record for many years with 61 AKC placements and 3 National placements.

*Ch. Patrice de Sharvogue was the first really fine show dog. He won the National Specialty in 1943, 1944 and 1945. He was a son of Gwennec.

*Dual Ch. Patsy of Edough, a flashy orange-and-white bitch, was one of the top field winners during the first 10 years of Brittany trials.

*Dual Ch. Pierrot de Fontaine Valley was a top winning dual champion. He had 49 AKC field placements and multiple group placements. He was white-and-orange with an outstanding temperament. He was handled to wins by 13 amateurs.

*Dual Ch. Pontac's Dingo finished his field championship at 18 months and his dual championship at 27 months. Dingo won the Nationals three times. He was a light orange roan, on the large side, with a powerful ground eating drive. He produced two duals and two field champions.

*Fld. Ch. Torchy of Lionheart was a rather large orange-and-white dog who was the first field champion on the West Coast. He ran in American Field shooting dog stakes, against pointers and setters, and made a record of 17 placements.

*Dual Ch. Uno's Jet was a well-marked orange-and-white dog. He placed second in the National Derby Stake in 1950 and was third in the National Championship in 1951. In one spring season he won all but two trials on the circuit (and placed second in those!). He was an extremely nice dog and a popular sire who was near the top of the list of producers of field champions. He also sired one dual champion.

Dual Ch. Tex of Richmont was a heavily blanketed liver-and-white dog with a highly angulated rear that gave him tremendous drive. He produced 42 field winners including the dual champion Hall of Fame bitch, Pacolet Cheyenne.

Dual Ch. Towsey was a Brittany legend who won the Nationals three times (1955, 1957 and 1959). He was a rather light orange, heavily ticked and a

The famous Ch. Patrice of Sharvogue, owned by Dr. Edgar W. Averill, was best of breed at the first national Specialty. This early great narrowly missed becoming a dual champion.

marvelous mover. At age nine he won three 5-point majors on the bench.

Dual Ch. Pacolet Cheyenne was a big-running orange-and-white bitch. She produced two duals and thirteen field winners.

Dual Ch. Dingo's Little Mike won the National Specialty in 1958, placed twice in the National Open and three times in the National Amateur. He had 50 AKC placements with 10 Open All-Age firsts and was considered the nearly perfect all-around Britt.

Fld. Ch. Ferdinand of Leeway won the National Amateur Championship in 1956 and 1958. He was a large, strong running, orange-and-white male who set new boundaries on the range for a Brittany. He had 40 AKC field placements and produced 2 duals and 37 field winners.

Dual Ch. Holley Haven Duchess, white-and-orange group winner, placed first, third and fourth in the National Amateur three successive years. She won the National Dual Award in 1956.

Allamuchy Valley Warrior was never campaigned in either field or show. He produced one Hall of Fame dual champion, one field champion and nine bench champions.

Price's Sunflower Gal produced two Hall of Fame dual champions, Way Kan Jeff and Way Kan Jill, as well as 10 other field winners.

Dual Ch. Pacolet Sam was a powerful, strong dog with lots of guts. He had 39 field placements with a second and third in the Nationals. He produced four field champions, including National Champion Hall of Famer, Dual Ch. Pacolet Cheyenne Sam.

Dual Ch. Belloaks Ibby was the first bitch to win more than 50 field placements. She produced one dual.

Fld. Ch. Jeffrey of Argard was a large, well proportioned orange-and-white male who set a new kind of pace for big-running Britts. He won the Nationals in 1956, produced 21 field winners and five field champions.

Fld. Ch. Way Kan Jill won the U.S. Open twice and placed in the National Championship fresh off a litter of pups. She produced 21 field winners including National Champion Bazooka's Brandy.

Dual Ch. Way Kan Jeff was the first American/Canadian dual of the breed. A rather small male, he was a super hunting dog who was not always easy to handle. He had 56 field wins with 17 firsts and three Classic placements. He sired 20 field winners including National Champion Dual Ch. Way Kan Fritts.

Dual Ch. Lund's Trooper was the first dog of any pointing breed to earn over 100 AKC field placements. He also had two group placements in shows. He was handled entirely by his amateur owner. He is the leading sire of duals.

Dual Ch. Doctor Joe of Kaymore was an average-sized light orange roan and a lovely shooting dog. He produced four duals, three field champions and twenty bench champions.

Dual Ch., AFC Ban-Dee was National Champion in 1973 and 1974. He was the first Brittany to sire over 100 field winners. He produced a National Amateur Champion, Fld. Ch. The Real Thing, a National Champion, Dual Ch. Tomar's Ban-Dee Sam and a National Specialty Show winner, Dual Ch. Hi Ace.

Dual Ch. Pacolet Cheyenne Sam won the National Specialty Show in 1970, the National Championship in 1971 and an American Field three-hour Endurance Championship. His production record puts him near the top for the breed.

Dual Ch. Tigar's Jocko was a white-and-orange male. He had 54 AKC placements, won the National Amateur in 1964 and placed third in that stake in 1965 and 1967. He also won the National Amateur Shooting Dog Championship (American Field), a top win in longtail competition at that time. He sired 24 field winners, 11 show champions, 6 field champions and 1 dual champion.

Fld. Ch. Goldtone's Duke, a white-and-orange male, won the National Championship in 1968, and placed in 1969 and 1973. He also won several American Field Championships. He produced both show and field champions.

Ch. Sommet des Collines, C.D., has produced more titled offspring than any other bitch in the history of the breed except for Ch. Gilkey's Jessie. She ranks number one for duals and number two for field champions. She has three obedience-titled pups, one with a U.D. and a High in Trial. Her pups included Best in Show Ch. Red's Revenge and National Amateur Champion/ Hall of Famer Dual Ch. Colorado's Jumping Gypsy.

Dual Ch., AFC Char-Lee O'Dee, with 136 AKC placements, is runner-up for the number of field placements by a Brittany male. He won the National Amateur Championship in 1971 at age 10, was second in that stake and had six National placements. He is the sire of eight field champions, fifteen show champions and four duals.

Dual Ch., AFC Gringo de Britt won the National Amateur Championship in 1969 and 1970 and placed second in the National Championship in 1969. He had a total of 53 field placements, many of them after he was hit by a car and sustained a fracture that never fully healed. Gringo sired 13 field champions, 11 bench champions and 3 duals.

Ch. Copper Jill of Edwards had twenty Best of Breeds and two group placements, an exceptional show record for a bitch. She whelped twenty-three field winners, possibly the record for a bitch, with three field and two dual champions, including National Champion Dual Ch., AFC Cinnabar's Ami Roc d'Edwards.

Dual Ch. Colorado's Yankee Timber was a powerful moving roan dog with a lot of class. This 1967 National Champion has 33 AKC field placements and a good production record.

Dual Ch. Joel's Copper Jacques was a son of Hall of Famer Ferdinand of Leeway. Jake won the first National Gun Dog Stake in 1968 from 62 entries.

"Brittany," from an original painting by Roger Cruwys.

He was the holder of the All-Age first record for many years with a total of 19 Open All-Age firsts.

Fld. Ch. Kay Cee Bandit was a top-winning Derby. He was retired early after an accident, but already had won 32 field placements. He sired two dual champion Hall of Fame dogs, Ban-Dee and Gringo de Britt.

Fld. Ch. Scipio Spinks was a small liver-blanketed male. He earned 80 AKC placements with 35 firsts. He is currently runner-up for the Open All-Age firsts record with 22. He produced fifteen field champions, five bench champions and a National Champion, Dual Ch. Jumpin' Jack Flash II.

Ch., AFC Sequani's Dana Macduff ranks right near the top in the all-time show records and in the number of duals produced. At eight years of age he started his field career, and finished his Amateur Field Championship at ten years of age.

Dual Ch., AFC Colorado's Jumping Gypsy was the tenth elected bitch to the Hall of Fame. She won the National Amateur Championship in 1972 and was a granddaughter of Dual Ch. Colorado's Yankee Timber.

Fld. Ch. Holliday Britt's Bazooka, an orange-and-white male, sired thirty-five field winners, including National Champion Bazooka's Brandy, two duals and four bench champions. His 26 wins include fourth in the Futurity and third in the National Championship. He won the U.S. Open Championship once and was once runner-up. He is grandsire to Hall of Famer Fld. Ch., AFC Scipio Spinks.

Dual Ch., AFC Hello Dolly Miss Kaer was a sprightly orange-and-white bitch with 89 AKC placements. She won the National Amateur Championship in 1974 and 1975, was fourth in the National Championship in 1975, placed in two Classics, the Futurity, and was Best of Opposite Sex at the National Specialty Show once. Bred sparingly, her most notable son is Fld. Ch., AFC Jack Flash O'Dolly.

Hall of Fame

Lack of election year indicates one of the thirteen selections by the original Hall of Fame Committee in 1965.

Dual Ch. Allamuchy Valley Uno
Dual Ch. Angelique De Bretagne
Dual Ch. Avono Happy
Dual Ch. Brit of Bellows Falls
French Ch. Gwennec De L'Argoat
Dual Ch. Helgramite Howie D'Acajou
Kaer De Cornouaille
Ch. Patrice De Sharvogue
Dual Ch. Patsy of Edough
Dual Ch. Pierrot De Fontaine Valley

Dual Ch. Pontac's Dingo
Fld. Ch. Torchy of Lionheart
Dual Ch. Uno's Jet

1965
Dual Ch. Pacolet Cheyenne
Dual Ch. Tex of Richmont
Dual Ch. Towsey

1966
Dual Ch. Dingo's Little Mike
Fld. Ch. Ferdinand of Leeway
Dual Ch. Holly Haven Duchess

1967
Allamuchy Valley Warrior
Price's Sunflower Gal

1968
Dual Ch. Belloaks Ibby
Dual Ch. Pacolet Sam

1969
none

1970
Fld. Ch. Jeffrey of Argard

1971
Dual Ch. Way Kan Jill

1972
Dual Ch. Way Kan Jeff

1973
Dual Ch. Lund's Trooper

1974
none

1975
none

1976
none

1977
Dual Ch. Doctor Joe of Kaymore

1978
none

1979
none

1980
Dual Ch., AFC Ban-Dee
Dual Ch. Pacolet Cheyenne Sam
Dual Ch. Tigar's Jocko

1981
Fld. Ch. Goldtone's Duke
Ch. Sommet des Collines, C.D.

1982
none

1983
Dual Ch., AFC Char-Lee O'Dee
Ch. Copper Jill of Edwards
Dual Ch. Gringo de Britt

1984
Dual Ch., AFC Colorado Jumping Gypsy
Dual Ch. Colorado's Yankee Timber
Dual Ch. Joel's Copper Jacques
Fld. Ch. Kaycee Bandit
Fld. Ch., AFC Scipio Spinks
Ch., AFC Sequani's Dana Macduff

1985
Dual Ch. AFC Hello Dolly Miss Kaer
Fld. Ch. Holiday Britt's Bazooka

Thirteen of the original elected dogs were dual champions, and twenty of the present list were dual champions. Dual Ch. Jig of Kaymore sired five dual champions and three show champions. Lund's Trooper sired six duals and a total of twenty-two champions, show and field: seven were field champions, and two were nonchampions, but distinguished themselves as producers. I have not given biographies of the later dogs because that should be done by those individuals who knew each dog.

An interesting, albeit unidentified, painting showing a Brittany Spaniel pointing a woodcock and an English Setter backing.

Ch. Elcia's Lil'Hoss of Greenfield, owned and handled by Theda F. Stell, finished his championship at the same show where his sire, Ch. Beelflower Dirty Dan was best in show. *Ludwig photo.*

Ch. Ches-Val's Sparky, owned by Charles Dodson, is shown winning the first of three consecutive bests of breed at the Maryland Brittany Club Specialty. The judge is Glenn Sommers and the handler is George D. Edge, Jr. *Shafer photo.*

27

The Great Show Dogs

List compiled by Rita Keating, updated in 1986 by the author

BRITTANYS HAVE COMPETED IN all branches of the sport for which they have been eligible. In other chapters, we have listed the dual champions and the great obedience winners. But Brittanys have an ever-increasing recognition in the show ring. The first Brittany to win a Sporting group was Ch. Queen of Paradise, on September 14, 1946. That same year, Dual Ch. Amos of Edough won the Sporting group at Lima, Ohio. Lee Holman handled the dog, and the author was judge. He was also the judge when Cherie D'Oiseau became the third group winner at the Del Monte, California show on May 30, 1954.

One of the great show dogs of the 1960's was Ch. Miss Sue's Gad-A-Bout, C.D. He was owned by Richard and Anne Smith of Roswell, Georgia. In some 15 months he won 40 Best of Breed and 12 group placings, of which three were group firsts. Yet still the longed-for Best in Show eluded the great dogs of the times, including at least a dozen who had won groups.

The first to win Best in Show was Ch. Havre de Bois Henri, owned by Paul Vollmar, at the Livonia, Michigan, show of 1957. It is ironic that his victory came under Selwyn Harris, the judge who had once told the author he would not put up the garbage breeds but only the standard ones.

It would be 12 years before another would get Best in Show. The dog was Ch. Beelflower Dirty Dan. His victory came in 1971 at Bakersfield, California, in an entry of 2,000 dogs. He was owned by Paul and Linda Mooney and was shown by Linda.

Dan's sire and grandsire were both dual champions, and his dam produced a number of field winners. Dan himself had several placements in puppy stakes. But he was kicked in the head by a horse, and this spoiled his field career. However, he has proven himself as a sire. His daughter, Elcia's Lil' Hoss of Greenfield, owned by Theda F. Stell, finished her championship at the same show at which Dan won Best in Show. He produced two ABC National Specialty winners, Ch. Greenfield's Mister Mark and Ch. Greenfield's Le Duc de Cannelle, and through the latter, produced the Best in Show winner Mizlu's Louisiana Purchase.

Ch. Ffynant's Trouble, owned by John Mattinson, was a group winner who was denied a Best in Show ribbon. Yet, in a sense, he earned a higher honor. He sired Ch. Ffynant's Revelation and Ch. Ffynant's Happy Time. Revelation, owned jointly by Mattinson and Joan Colucchio, won five Bests in Show, two in 1973, two more in 1974 and once again in 1975. Happy Time was purchased by John Gilkey, then of Lovington, New Mexico, but later of Merrill, Wisconsin. Tony Gwinner showed the dog.

Happy Time's record is extraordinary. He won three Best in Shows in 1974, four in 1975, and three in 1976. He also won two bests in Canada—at Lion's Gate and Vernon and District. His total record was Best of Breed in five specialties, 223 Best of Breed at all-breed shows and 154 group placements. Yet the story does not end there. When bred with Ch. Gilkey's Jessie, 40 pups were born in some six litters. Twenty-five of them became American champions, and two were sold to Canadians and won championships in Canada.

One of Jessie's puppies by Happy Time was Ch. Gilkey's Jolly Time. Jolly Time won four U.S. Bests in Show, and one in Canada. He was also Best of Breed at seven specialties, Best of Breed at all-breed shows 263 times, and had 145 group placements.

Ch. Red's Revenge, known to his friends as Mugs, was a hunting companion for Vic Schoonover for four years. A sharp-eyed professional handler saw him and convinced the Schoonovers to show him. He won his championship in eight shows, and had two group four placements. He was sold to Wenzel Dvornik. Joel Evans then took charge of him, and under his handling won a Best in Show at the Milwaukee, Wisconsin K.C. show on January 27, 1974. He was then seven years old, but he continued breed victories when he was ten. In the meantime, he sired Ch. Evansport's Devilish Diver when mated to Ch. Evansport Tempestuous Tamar. John Marsman bought him. Marsman lived at Niles, Michigan and showed in Michigan and Ohio shows. He got his Best in Show at the Sugarbush K.C. at Chardon, Ohio on July 25, 1982.

Kuno Spies bought a puppy by Ch. AFC Sequani's Dana MacDuff, out of Ch. Scarlet O'Hara of Little Egypt. He was born October 28, 1976, and was named Blazer Sequani Maximilian. He became a champion, and won Best in

Ch. Ffynant's Revelation, owned by Joan Colucchio and John Mattinson, was a multiple BIS winner during the 1970s.

Alverson photo.

Ch. Ffynant's Happy Time, owned by John N. Gilkey and shown by Tony Gwinner, has eight Best in Show awards in the United States and two more in Canada.

Ch. Gilkey's Jolly Time, owned by John Gilkey, had three Bests in Show in 1979. He is a son of Ch. Ffynant's Happy Time.

Twomey photo.

Show at Kittanning on June 21, 1981.

Tobi McNeal bought a Brittany puppy sight unseen. She was an expert junior showman, and she got a group first at a puppy match with the dog she called Stuart. Its formal name was Prince Valiant's Happy Time. He was born November 27, 1978. The next year, when not yet a year old, he completed his championship by winning from the open class at the ABC National show. His Best in Show came at Lima, Ohio on June 28, 1981.

Ch. Do-Well's Jason, C.D., was acquired by Debbie Melgreen when he was three years old. He was sired by Ch. Suzabob's Do-Well, C.D.X. out of Princess Ginger Spice, and was born September 18, 1975. He won Best in Show at the Hawkeye K.C. show in June of 1980, and at the Ozark K.C. show in June of 1981. Along the way, he won a C.D. obedience degree, and won High in Trial. He is the only Britt to get both honors. He was the leading sire of show winners in 1982 and was tied for first the next year.

One of Jason's sons is Ch. Do-Well's Henri of Chesabrit. His dam is Ch. Duff's Queen of Sheba, U.D. Beverly Duff bred and owns him. His Best in Show came at the Coulee K.C. show on December 8, 1984. The Duffs live in Cottage Grove, Minnesota.

Ch. Mizlu's Louisiana Purchase was sired by Ch. Greenfield Le Duc De Cannelle, out of Faison's French Frog. Joseph Rodrigues bought him from L. D. and W. R. Clark, and included his daughter, Amy, as half owner. Amy usually showed him. His first Best in Show came January 29, 1984 at the Orange Empire show. In 1985, he won back-to-back Bests in Show. The first came at Tucson, Arizona on March 24, 1985, and the second at Kern County in California the next week. The dog survived a facial bite by a brown recluse spider.

Ch. Russett Hill M'Lord G. Chaucer was owned by David and Catherine Rigoulot, both of whom have divorced and remarried. He is a son of Ch. Ffynant's Revelation and Ch. Danas Lady Charlotte. His Best in Show came in 1977.

The 1984 National Specialty winner, Ch. Twin Oaks Vantage Point, topped his record of eight group firsts by winning Best in Show at Livonia, Michigan on April 6, 1986, and then taking the top honors at Mid Kentucky on May 3, 1986. He is owned by Clark and Mary Benjamin of Williamston, Michigan. He was bred by Linda and William Duncan, and was whelped August 4, 1983 by Ch. Twin Oaks Jackpot out of Ch. Prince Valiant's J and J. Cheri Schmitz handled him.

Ch. Carosel Tropic-Ana Of Jen-Mar was sired by Ch. Gilkey's Jolly Time, and he by Ffynant's Happy Time, for three generations of Best in Show winners. His dam is Ch. Jen-Mar's Jollyanna Of Carosel. His victory came at the Carroll K.C. under the judging of Arnold Woolf. Carosel is the kennel name of Carol and Ross Petruzzo, noted breeders and eastern professional dog show handlers. The owners are Jennifer and Maryann Breininger of Jen-Mar Kennels. His career is mostly ahead of him because he is barely 18

Ch. Prince Valiant's Happy Time, a Best in Show Winner, shown with Tobi McNeal, age 13. *Booth photo.*

Ch. Do-Well's Henri of Chesabrit (left), owned by Beverly Duff and handled by Darrell Droel, Ch. Chesabrit's Code of the West (right), owned by Darrell Droel and handled by Romoelle Droell. Henri was Best of Breed and Cody was Best of Winners under judge Clinton M. Harris. Both dogs are out of Ch. Duff's Queen of Sheba, U.D.

Olson photo.

months old at the time of this writing.

Ch. Chesabrit's Code Of The West topped a 1,600-dog show at Lake Minnetonka on June 7, 1986. He was bred by the Chesabrit Kennels of Mike and Beverly Duff. He is owned and handled by Darrell Droel. His sire is Best in Show winner, Ch. Prince Valiant's Happy Time, and his dam is Ch. Duff's Queen Of Sheba, U.D. Sheba has produced nine champions, two of which are dual champions, and Ch. Foxylady of Chesabrit, who has produced four champions.

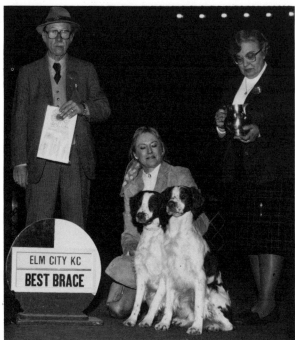

Best Brace in Show under judge Theodore Wurmser (left to right): Ch. Dowell Bretagne of Chesabrit (son of Ch. J. B. Jason, C.D.) and Ch. Ringeyes T. Sir Gala-had, C.D. (son of Ch. Marques Little Rascal, great-grandson of Ch. Dana MacDuff). Trained, shown, and owned by Mari Kennedy, Bretagne's Brittany Kennels.
Ashbey photo.

Ch. Bathsheba of Spring Hill (Ch. Hunter-lane's Copper King of L. G. ex Jessie of Spring Hill), bred and owned by Susan W. Lehosky.   *Alverson photo.*

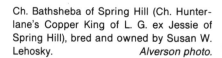

28

American Field Champions

THE AMERICAN FIELD AND its Field Dog Stud Book were the first to recognize the Brittany when it came to America. Later, the American Field was the first to recognize the American Brittany Club as the official American sponsoring club for the breed.

It has been said that the greatest single activity of the American Kennel Club is in field trials. Yet, if taken without explanation, this statement is misleading. Activity under American Kennel Club jurisdiction includes field trials for pointing breeds, flushing spaniels, retrievers, Beagles (the largest field trial group), Dachshunds and Bassets.

The American Field conducts field trials for pointing breeds. Its trials are conducted under rules formulated by the Amateur Field Trial Clubs of America. These trials exceed 750 annually, with over 2,600 stakes. The stakes are Open Puppy, Amateur Puppy, Open Derby, Amateur Derby, Open All-Age, Open Shooting Dog, Amateur Shooting Dog, and Open Championship and Amateur Championship. These may have a total of 3,000 or more Brittanys, a figure that may include the same dogs running in many events.

Dogs competing at trials under American Kennel Club rules can win points toward championships in various stakes. This is not the case in trials held under American Field jurisdiction. Under its rules, a dog can win a championship only by winning an officially designated championship stake.

In the first edition of this book, we listed 20 dogs that had won American Field championships. We repeat them here, and add those who have won since.

Dual Ch. Freck-O-Dee, owned by Stan Judd.

Dual Ch. Cindy's Chico Diable, owned by Charles Ayres and Joe Dahlheim.

Bazooka's Brandy, owned by Dan Huddleston
Bemji of LaRue, owned by C. P. Plyler
Britt's Bazooka, owned by A. H. Pillow
Carey's Freckles, owned by J. J. Carey, Jr.
Goldtone's Duke, owned by Dr. George Pester.
Gringo De Britt, owned by Dr. and Mrs. Tim Poling
Gundy, owned by Dr. C. T. Young
Holiday Britt, owned by J. T. Cahill
Jac Pierre's Pride, owned by J. E. Cohen
L'Etoile De Dingo, owned by J. W. Freeman
Miller's Desert Dust, owned by L. E. Miller
Pacolet Cheyenne Sam, owned by Ken and Erin Jacobson
S'No Fun Mack, owned by Dr. W. R. Heap
Sundown Sundown Sioux Land, owned by E. L. Darby
Tess of Chippewa, owned by Hilmer Peterson
Tigar's Jocko, owned by John Munson
Towsey, owned by J. T. Cahill
Way-Kan Jill, owned by R. B. Leverich
Way-Kan Mandy, owned by Harold Miller
Yankee Boy's Tommy, owned by J. A. Costelow

There are two major events for Brittanys only that are held under American Field jurisdiction. These are the United States Open Championship and the International Brittany Field Trial Association Championship. Though a dog may be designated the winner, the title might be withheld. Here are the winners in each of the two events since 1963. Note that the International was not held from 1978 until 1986. The U.S. Open is two-hour heats or series. Here are the winners and their owners in each of the two events.

United States Brittany Open Championship

1963   Way-Kan Jill, James Leverich
1964   Bill's Buddy Boy, Dan Huddleston, title withheld
1965   Holliday Britt's Bazooka, A. H. Pillow
1966   Way-Kan Jill, James Leverich
1967   Way-Kan Mandy, Harold Miller
1968   Bazooka's Brandy, Dan Huddleston
1969   Gringo De Britt, Dr. and Mrs. Tim Poling
1970   Pacolet Cheyenne Sam, Ken and Erin Jacobson
1971   Gundy, Dr. C. T. Young
1972   S'No Fun Mak, W. R. Heap
1973   Ban Dee, W. E. Oliver
1974   Jacolet's Wandering Star, P. D. Hinch
1975   Ringo De Britt, Paul Hinch

1976 Perry's Rustic Prince, L. L. May
1977 Red River Lady, D. E. Bradford
1978 Jacolet's Wandering Star, P. D. Hinch
1979 Jacolet's Wandering Star, P. D. Hinch
1980 Bayou's Lonesome Sue, J. C. McConnell
1981 Tall Oaks Bandolero, John McConnell
1982 Tall Oaks Bandolero, John McConnell
1983 First Place Jake, Ron Curtis
1984 La Jean's Johnnie of Connie, James and Janet Chase
1985 Homes Acres Risk, Robert and Barbara Youngs
1986 Minnehaha's Tammy, Richard Culbert
Runner-up: Markar's Jac's A Dan D, Robert Weisz

International Brittany Field Trial Championship

1969 S'No Fun Mack, Dr. W. R. Heap
1970 Jac Pierre's Pride, J. E. Cohen
1971 Carey's Freckles, J. J. Carey, Jr.
1972 Tondee's Sandy Valley Duke, S. H. Tardy
1973 Perry's Rustic Prince, L. L. May
1974 Perry's Rustic Prince, L. L. May
1975 Goldtone's Doc, L. L. May
1976 Jacolet's Wandering Star, P. D. Hinch
1977 Perry's Rustic Prince, L. L. May
1986 Vikings Yankee Dandy, Argan Johnson
Runner-Up: Far Out Bandit, Kent Brueggemann

Illinois Brittany Amateur All Age Championship

Title Withheld
1st.—Duke of Brittmont, E. R. Hart, Owner
2nd.—Blue Chip Stock, H. R. Gentsch, owner

Illinois Brittany Open All Age Championship

Lavender N Lace, Richard Culbert, owner
Runner-Up—Markar's Jac's A Dan D, Robert Weisz, owner

Mo-Kan Brittany Open All Age Championship

Markar's Bet I-M-Magic, William Greendyke, Owner
Runner-Up—Tu Tu II, Craig Cheatum, owner

Texas Open Brittany Championship

Royal Britt Starbuck Of Auten, Al and Sharon Van Wieren, owners
Runner-Up—Rimarda's Rhapsody, Bruce Frederick, owner

194

Dual Ch. Markar's Jac's A Dan D owned by Robert G. Weiss.

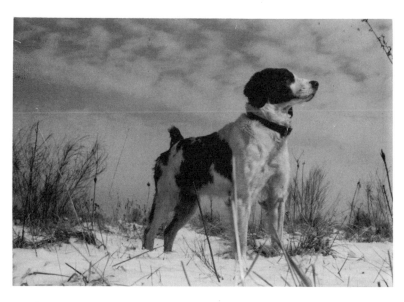

Dual Ch., Amateur Field Ch. Chipp Britt Jill, owned by Lloyd Conable, Jr., National Field Champion 1975. First female to win a National championship.

Nebraska All Age Brittany Championship

Tu Tu II, Craig Cheatum, owner
Runner-Up—Charlie's Angel IV, William Charlesworth, owner

Oklahoma Open Brittany Championship

Lobo's Cotton Candy, Bob and Lou Lanham, owners
Runner-Up—Jacolet's Kona Wind, John Henderson, owner

Michigan Brittany Open All Age Championship

Franklin County Bandit, Mary Jo Wirth, owner
Runner-Up—La'Jean's Johnny Of Connie, Jim and Janet Chase

If one consults the list of dual champions, it will be noted that a number of American Field champions are also dual champions. These include Markar's Jac's A Dan D, Markar's Bet-I-M-Magic and Jacolet's Kona Wind. Two dogs deserve special mention. Jack Flash O'Dolly is a four-time American Field champion, with a number of field wins in American Brittany events. Tall Oaks Bandalero is a two-time American Field champion and won the National Open championship in 1982.

The Derby Winners 1986

Illinois Invitational Derby Classic

Winner—Bay Arbor Abe, Barbara Wade, owner
Runner-Up—Air Alex Wilbanks, L. T. Manck, owner

Mo-Kan Open Derby Classic

Winner—Cherokee Maiden of Azlin, Brad Woodruff, owner
Runner-Up—Tu Tu II, Craig Cheatum, owner

Victorie Brittany Derby Classic

Winner—Moore's Fantastic Kate, Bobby Fox, owner
Runner-Up—Shoal Creek Spanky, Tom Dunn, owner

Michigan Brittany Open Derby

Winner—Jehovah Jirah Jumping Jinny, Joe Colgeazier, owner
Runner-Up—Wildwind J. J.'s Katie, Toney Vescoso, owner

29

The Dual Champions

THE MEN AND WOMEN WHO founded the American Brittany Club were determined to keep the Brittany a dual-purpose dog. They could see what had happened in other breeds. For example, the English Springer Spaniel had been split into two varieties—show and field. The last English Springer dual champions won the honor in 1942. The show dogs grew larger. Field trial dogs were supposed to work at a pace consistent with a hard day of hunting. But instead, they became race horses that seldom worked more than 15 minutes in a heat. English Setters had long been split into two varieties. Only recently has an English Setter of show type won a dual championship.

Viszlas, German Shorthairs, German Wirehairs and Gordon Setters have kept the dream of producing dual champions. But the sum total of all of these breeds has not equaled the record of a single breed—our Brittany. There have been—and are—240 dual champion Brittanys. And so far as the author has been able to determine, this total is greater than that of all other dual champions of any breed.

We have a very great debt of gratitude to pay to those who founded the American Brittany Club. Their foresight has made possible the proud record Brittany owners of today have kept as their goal.

The complete list of dual champions follows. But to it we list two who have crossed into Canada and won dual championships there as well. They are Dual Ch. Bernie's Butch and Dual Ch. Way-Kan Jeff.

Britt of Bellows Falls
Aotrou Mac Eochaidh
Avono Happy
Allamuchy Valley Uno
Dingo's Little Mike
Penny's Happy Pepi
Avono Hapte
Tex of Richmont
Helgramite Howie D'Acajou
Helgramite Chip
Helgramite Tarquinious
Helgramite Shamandre
Helgramite Howie
Pierrot de Fontaine Vallee
Remarkable De Fontaine Vallee
Pacolet's Sam
Pacolet's Whist
Pacolet's Cheyenne
Pacolet Cheyenne Sam
Kaymore's Megs
Jig De Kaymore
Detective Neal of Kaymore
Belloaks Ibby
Belloaks King
Belloaks Highflyer
Uno's Jet

Angelique De Bretagne
Holley Haven Casey
Holley Haven Duchess
Towsey
Way-Kan Jeff
Joel's Drole
Fredan's Buddy
Lund's Trooper
Trooper's Little Frenchman
Tigar's Jocko
Molko's Mike of Jacques
Sue City Sue
Appanoose Rust
Doctor Joe of Kaymore
Birch Hill Tawny
Juchoir's Shady Scamp
Lewis's Ringo
Tietjen's Red Raider
Ouragan Jerry's Bob
Ultra-Mend Maisie
Faulkner's Reddy
Bernie's Butch
Begg's Royal Duke
Majestic Jake
Genii's Colorado Ladd
Foltz's Freckles

Uno's Chief
Pontac's Dingo
Albedo Valley Dingo
Skippy Allamuchy Luke
Penelope De Evanston
Gallinacious Doc
Lamonte's Rebel
Shenango Valley Dingo
Amos of Edough
Patsy of Edough
Mandy of Edough
Wippy de la Vallee Bourault
Bonaire Doc
Britt of Blaisey Blas
Saxon of Fredan

Spicks of Mugho Hill
Dusty's Shining Chevalier
Sir Robert of Beelflower
Skipper of Siouxland
Way-Kan Fritts
Eva's Trooper Jorinda
Suzabob's Humdinger
Mar-Ko Valkerie
Beau'Pere
Knox's Starbelle Broons
Chaplin's Golden Arrow
Kaymore Dapper Dan
Black Butte Ricochet Trooper
Early Times
Juchoir's Trooper Jill

Dual Ch. Patway's Ramblin Rocky on point. Rocky is the only *7th generation dual champion* and is owned by Robert A. Bowell.

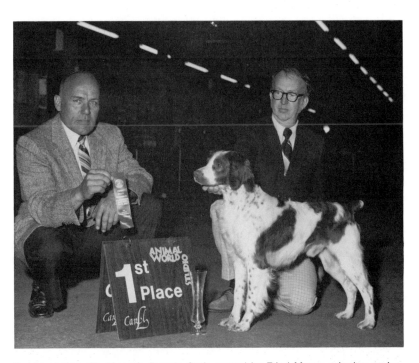

Dual and Can. Ch. Moore's Brandy Cork, owned by Ethel Moore, winning under judge Wayne B. Fessenden. *Animal World Studio photo.*

Tigre de Klemanor
Evergray's Tic Toc Bobby
Paul's White Flash
Freckles VII
Penny's Happy Peppi
Sue's Jim Dandy Jigger
Rusty of Beelflower
Joel's Copper Jacques
Brooks De Becque
Rusty of Highbrow
Mel's Red Rover

Jacques Des Rocheuses
Suzabob's Hedgerow Happy
Freck O'Dee
Marmalade Sarah
Colorado's Yankee Timber
Pike's Peak Rambler
Tondee's Sandy Valley Duke
Char-Lee O'Dee
Sequani's Dana O'Teed
Sequani's Des Colline, C.D.
Sequani's Spade of Kennisau
Sequani's Roi Des Collines, C.D.
Sequani's No Ka Oi of Moonbabe
Sequani's Pride of Rufus
Sequani's Marjo Boisvert
Sequani's Cin-Ban De Mar-Ed
Bobby Day's Friar Tuck
Buster Boy IV
Le Pradalan
Kidogo Sam Stacy
Timm Valley Jenny
Li'l Brother Easy
Winterton's Jocko
Perry's Rustic Prince
Jacolet Pride
Way-Kan Bing

Rock Brook's Andy O'Dee
Blaze'N Pinto
Lady Margo Parker

Cindy's Chico Diablo
Dixie Du Blanche Happy
Destry
Tipco's French Rebel
Holley Haven Heide II
Grouse Feathers
The Circuit Contender
Faircrest Polyjet
Suzabob's Gigolo
Jacque of Connie
Chipp Britt Jill

Mike Bazooka of Tejas
Shot Gun Liz
Gringo De Britt
The Little Joker
Coveymoore's Bomarc
Jock Scott of Big Meadow
Sodak Sandy Sioux
Rufus Rastus Johnson Brown
Yancher's Ra Pa Lu
Ban Dee
Merchant of Breton's Lightning
Killey
Hi-Spirit Bazooka's Pistol
Reynold's Sir Lancelot, C.D.X.
Paul's Goldtone Whiskers
Windy Hill Charlie Brown
Majestic Jake
Blue Grass Tex
Nehl's Little Bit's, T.D.
Colorado's Jumping Gypsy
Freck's Boy Pete
Don Juan De Britt
Sassy De Britt
Hello Dolly, Miss Kaer
Majic Muff Heckle
Lady Amber VI

Jeff's Tic Toc Brandy
Harmony Lane Cinamon Ho-Boy
Timber's Marquis De Colorado

Golden Gypsy Timber
Charley Debrett
Edwards Sam of Grouse Hollow
Lost River's Copper Diggins, C.D.X.
Bi-Mar Cheyenne Kit
La-Pitt Dave-O Duke
Hedgerow's Cheyenne Buck
Willow Run Ike
R J's Brandy Sniffer
DeCampo's Miss Tuffy Brown
Ffynant's Jokers Wild
Triple Crown Sandy DeColline, U.D.
Moonbabe's Kawananakoa
Tomar's Ban-Dee Sam
Sheeba Viking Queen
J D of Lost River
My Little Teddy Bear
Ramblin's Chocolate Dandy
Willo's Highland Ruff'N Ready, C.D.X.
Hi Ace
La-Pitt Buck
Bi-Mar's Special Edition

Cinnabar's Ami Roc De Edwards
My Sunny Boy
Goldtone's Doc
Dinar O'Dee
Smokestone Dynamo
Brought Mars Jiver De Campo
Peppers Prince
Hope's Maximilian Robespierre
Hi-Spirit Buck
Sweet Seasons Call Me Oats, C.D.
R & D's Rocky Mountain Timber
Timberex
Ban-Dee's Elkanak of Shiloh
Jumpin' Jack Flash II
Suzabob's Brigadoon Rhett
Kidogo's Dixie 'D
DeCampos Sed Ruff Brown
Char-Lee's Beau Rascal
Auten's Morning Star
Bullet's Buckshot
Perry's Rustic Zip
Britt's Red Jinx

Bi-Mar J J Tyrone
Greenfield Wind Song
Dolly-Mae-Madison
F and S Count Geoffery
Marjo's Honey
Marjo's Cisco Kidd
Rustic Prince's Rebel
Scipio's Little Chick
Hope's Perseverance
Hope's Trace of Rust
Hope's Princely Pauper
Jen-Mar's Chelo Del Prado, C.D.
Jacolets Kona Wind
Lobo's Cotton Candy
Rob's Hi Ra
Sunnyvale Skipper

Perpetuator of Connie
Country Cousin Sweet Sue
Willow Run Cheyenne Down Pat
Hybrittin's Hocus Pocus
Hi-Scor Dixie De Britt
Moore's Brandy Cork
Commanders-O Neo-Valley Tuffy
Oak Grove Andrew
Timberline Tracy De Marquis
Markar's Jac's A Dan D
Markar's Bet I M Magic
Patway's Ramblin Rocky
Hot Asphalt
Tiffany Rose of Lakewood
Kipp's Trooper Rochambeau
My Little F. Blossom
Kinwashkly Red Patches
Sequani's Kwail Kall Jud

30

Alan Stuyvesant

O F ALL THE PIONEER importers who gave America the solid basis in Brittany bloodlines that made possible the startling growth of the breed, three names stand out: Louis Thebaud, René Joubert and Alan Stuyvesant. Of the three, Alan Stuyvesant stands above the others because of his continued heavy imports and his judicious spreading of them across the country. But who was he?

He sometimes said, humorously, that his family had built New York City. The first Stuyvesant of record was Peter. In 1645, he was named governor of New Netherlands, of which New Amsterdam was the capital. He arrived in 1647, battle-scarred with a wooden leg and ornamented with silver rings. He was not especially well liked, and he was forced to surrender New Netherlands to the British, who made New York the new capital. In his later years, Peter Stuyvesant lived on his estate, *Bouwerie,* from which came New York's famous Bowery.

In the following centuries, the Stuyvesant name became prominent in the building of New York. Alan's mother was Elizabeth, Princess Alesandre de Caraman-Chimay of France. Alan and his brother, Lewis, spent much time on her estate. Both spoke fluent French and both graduated from Princeton where Alan was welterweight boxing champion. Both were well known as big-game hunters, for they had accompanied Theodore Roosevelt, Jr. on his Asian hunting trip. When World War II broke out, the brothers donated an ambulance and served with it, first in France, and then in North Africa. Lewis was wounded. For a time they were prisoners of war, but Alan was repatriated and returned to America. Alan became a captain and was parachuted into

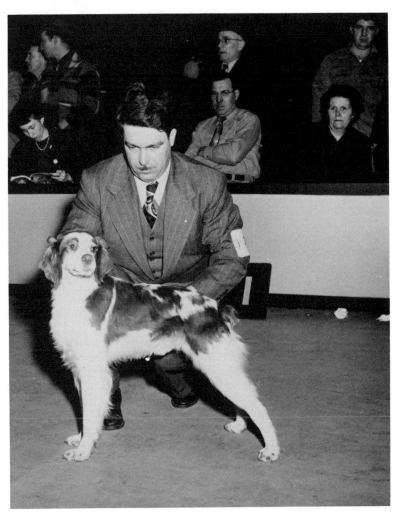

Ch. Tudor du Roc' Hellou, owned by Alan Stuyvesant, finished his bench championship at the International Kennel Club of Chicago.

occupied France where he served as liaison with the Free French underground, and those on the outside.

Alan managed the family estate, Tranquility, which was next to the Rutherfurds, who were related to him. The Rutherfurds raised Fox Terriers, and one Rutherfurd dog, Ch. Warren Remedy, was Best in Show at Westminster in 1907, 1908 and 1909. But Alan became interested in Brittany Spaniels. He had imported some from France before the war, and he bred others. He believed that the French stock had been depleted. He proposed to have American breeders send dogs to France. Dogs bred by Stuyvesant, Walter Oberlin, Jack Whitworth and Lucian Ufford were sent over.

Now pick up the story as told by Gaston Pouchain, whose great French book *L'Epagneul Breton* was published by Robert Thenlot, editor-in-chief of the collection *Revue Du Chien*. M. Pouchain is now 85 but "hunts without glasses."

After the war, the stock of Brittanys was reduced, although larger than one might have expected. Above all it was still a valid stock. A good omen for the competitions which, however, were not to begin again before 1946.

One morning, at the office of the Parisian section, I received a telegram from the United States. It informed me of the arrival of an American accompanied by three bitches which he wished to offer to the club in order to re-establish the race of Brittanys, which he thought to be almost extinct as a result of the war. I sent my friend Bonnet to Le Havre first in order to invite this kind American to come to Paris, then to take delivery of the three females.

Having arrived in Paris, this American proved to be very pleasant, and he told me his story immediately. He was called Alan Stuyvesant and he told me his ancestors had built New York. "I am very fond of the Brittany," he told me, "and I am a member of the Brittany Spaniel Club. I live in New Jersey where I am an architect. At the time of the invasion of Normandy, I was a lieutenant and I parachuted into Sainte-Mere-L'Eglise."

He and I became friends immediately. After a pleasant week in Paris, Alan Stuyvesant returned to the United States. He took with him a son of Poilu that I had offered him in order to thank him for his gesture. That dog had a brilliant career across the Atlantic. Above all he brought new blood which was very necessary there, as is still the case today.

Stuyvesant had left, but he had promised to return—to come back each year to Paris in the spring to renew the blood of the Brittanys of his country, and also to attend our trials, and likewise to spend some time in Brittany. But I shall speak of that later.

Just as he had promised, our friend Alan Stuyvesant came regularly each year in spring to France, and more particularly to Brittany, in order to "fill up on Brittanys." During one of these stays, I drove him to Brittany with one of his American friends who had come with him from the United States. On the way, we stopped at Le Mans for lunch, and that American noticed on another table a plate of snails. He asked me if that was good, and upon receiving my affirmative reply, he ordered a dozen of them which he feasted on . . . unfortunately while drinking Coca Cola and not a good wine. At the end of the meal, he asked me what a snail was. Since he knew no French and I knew no English, I drew him one on the menu. I thought then my last hour had arrived. Stuyvesant was laughing heartily, but his American friend screamed furiously: "You made me eat slugs." I hastened to reassure him, and we arrived with smiles at the Breton Special at Rennes.

The following year, Alan Stuyvesant came once again to Paris. At three o'clock in the morning, someone rang my doorbell non-stop. I got up and asked: "Who is there?" "It's Alan," he replied simply. Still in my pyjamas, I opened the door and found Stuyvesant. I wanted to know right away whether a serious accident had happened to him. "No," he replied, "in America, one goes to a friend's house at any hour." "In that case, all is well . . . come on in."

Shortly after, however, he explained to me that in coming he had left his car on a bridge of the Seine, that he had forgotten which one, and that he could not find it again. I understood right away and I advised him to go to bed, telling him that I would take care of the matter in good time. In fact, in the morning, the car could not be found on any bridge, neither on the St. Michel bridge, nor on the others. Then I went to see the police commissioner (a friend of mine), in order to find out if by chance there had not been brought to his attention a small car abandoned on a bridge and belonging to an American. He saw red immediately. "Send him to me, your American," he announced furiously, "and I'll teach him to block with his car all the traffic on the Arcole Bridge." I pleaded the cause of my friend, explaining his glorious conduct at the time of the Normandy invasion, mentioning his Legion Of Honor. Finally the commissioner calmed down and, a decent chap, he authorized me to return the car to Alan, who was very happy that the whole affair ended so well and so simply.

We went together to see Allaire, whose daughter was married to an American. Since my friend was supposed to cross the Atlantic to visit his daughter, Stuyvesant arranged things so that he might be a judge on that occasion for the class of Brittanys in New York.

That year, Stuyvesant, after attending the field trial of the Club, returned to his New Jersey with Allamuchy Valley, a descendant of Tudor de Roc Hellou, who won his championship, as well as with Allamuchy Valley Addie, a descendant of Iane de Cornouaille.

Another year, Stuyvesant was coming to France to get me, for I was to be judge of the Brittanys at Madison Square Garden of New York. As the *Queen Mary* was turning to enter the harbor, Alain [Alan] slipped and unfortunately fell down a metal staircase leading to the hold, smashing his skull in the fall. The stewards coming to clean, discovered him only the next morning. He was at death's door. Transported by plane to the American hospital at Neuilly, he was to die shortly after, medical care having been given to him too late. A police commissioner, having found my address in his papers, informed [me] of his death, and I had to go identify him at the morgue. I then immediately gave notice of his death to his nearest relative in Paris, the Count of Caraman Chimay. This gentleman immediately made the necessary arrangements. A Mass was celebrated in the American cathedral on the Avenue Georges V, and the body was transported by plane to New York.

Rumba de L'Argoat, the last dog imported by Alan Stuyvesant. *Jones photo.*

Officers of the American Brittany Club posed for this photo in November of 1950. They are (l. to r.) Alan Stuyvesant, Coy Conwell, Walter B. Kleeman, William Averill and Howard Clements. *Shafer photo.*

With Alan Stuyvesant, I lost, we all lost a great and sincere friend. Thanks to him the relations between the French and American Brittany Clubs could have developed well, for the betterment of the breed in the United States.

Note: M. Pouchain is in error on two points. Alan was a captain, not a lieutenant, and the ship was not the *Queen Mary,* but the *United States.* It left to return to America before the French could investigate the tragedy.

This picture, taken in 1945, shows Jilo (background) and Kaer de Cornouaille on point. Both dogs were imported and owned by Alan Stuyvesant. *Jones photo.*

Ch. Gilkey's Jessie shown with her Handler, Tony Gwynner under the late Herman Cox, Judge. Owned by John N. Gilkey.

Bill Francis photo.

31

Gilkey's Jessie—A Probable World Record Holder

OVER THE MORE THAN 50 years that the author has been writing about dogs, investigating claims, sometimes validating them, sometimes not, there have been claims of six or seven champions in one litter. Oddly, the dam usually has failed to produce champions in later litters. Some of the great production litters came at a time when a new breed was making its debut. In earlier times, in these rare breeds, one could combine the sexes to make points. The animals would then be shown against each other—that is, all of the litter mates. It sometimes happened that each one in the litter would beat its litter mates, and thus all became champions. However, the American Kennel Club finally eliminated the system.

At the time that Ch. Ffynant's Just Jay Jay was mated with Gilkey's Jezebel, no one could have guessed that an extraordinary female puppy would be in the litter. She was whelped August 30, 1971. She was named Gilkey's Jessie, and in time she became a champion. John Gilkey lived at that time in Lovington, New Mexico. He also owned Ch. Ffynant's Happy Time, and he decided to mate the two.

The litter was so promising that he made repeated matings between the pair. Jessie was never mated to any other dog. In all, she had 40 puppies, and 25 won American championships. One of the 25, Gilkey's Jamboree, went over into Canada, and there won a championship. Still another, Gilkey's Apricot Brandy, was sold to a Canadian owner before being shown. Under its Canadian owner's name it also won a Canadian championship.

So, depending on how you wish to figure it, Jessie produced 27 champion puppies, or 26 plus one international (that is, Canadian and American), champion. Here then is a list of Jessie's champions.

Gilkey's Judith
Gilkey's Jamboree
Gilkey's Joshua
Gilkey's Jolly Time (a major Best in Show winner and sire)
Gilkey's Happy Time Repete (In 1976 number eight in producer's list)
Gilkey's Janet
Gilkey's Time Again
Gilkie's Jeannie
Gilkey's Jeremiah
Gilkey's Double Time
Russell's Happy Days
Gilkey's What A Time
Gilkey's Spring Time
Gilkey's High Time
Gilkey's Right Time (Bred by Gilkey and Jacqueline Diskin)
Gilkey's One More Time
Gilkey's Time For Everything
Gilkey's Third Time Around
Gilkey's Valentine Candy
Gilkey's Romance Time
Gilkey's Valentine Day (Tom W. Green, owner)
Gilkey's Valentine Forever (Mary C. and Quentin S. Dagenhart, owners)
Gilkey's Valentine For Baron (George G. Russell, owner)
Gilkey's Valentine Cupid (Cleon F. Richards, owner)

The accuracy of this champion's list has been certified by Harold and Irene Schlintz of H.I.S. Publications, researchers extraordinary, who compiled it for the author. The Canadian championships of Gilkey's Jamboree and Gilkey's Apricot Brandy have been certified by the Canadian Kennel Club.

Ch. Gilkey's One More Time shown going BB under judge Arnold L. Woolf. Owned by William and Elaine Bierie. "Morey" had been retired for several years but took BB from the Veteran's Class at the Michigan Brittany Club specialty, August, 1985 and went on to win the Sporting Group.

Ch. Gilkey's Jolly Time, owned by John N. Gilkey of Merrill, Wisconsin, shown with the author and handler, Tony Gwynner.

Morry Twomey photo.

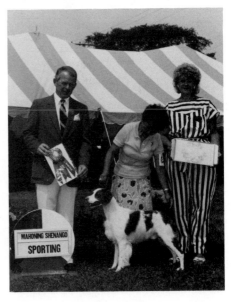

Ch. Shannon Creek Happy Pierre (Prince Valiant's Happy Time ex Gilkey's Happy Daze) shown winning the Sporting Group under Dr. Bernard E. McGivern, Jr., handled by Yoko O'Shell, Agent for owners Robert and Fukue O'Shell.

Fld. Ch. Suzabob's Frisco Frannie, owned by Gerald Supplee.

Ch. Suzabob's
Freckled Miss,
owned and
handled by Edwin
Jeffreys, Jr.
Ashbey photo.

32

Suzabob—A Study of a Kennel Record

SUCCESSFUL ANIMAL BREEDING IS a great and complicated art. It requires dedication, the ability to conquer the tragedy of failures and the determination to go on. But the best-bred dogs in the world cannot win without skilled training and, yes, some occasional luck. Neither can dogs win show championships if they are not given some training. Nor can they win titles in obedience unless they are given competent training. All must face heavy competition.

In this chapter, I am taking some dozen years from the records of the kennel of Robert and Suzanne Young of Selinsgrove, Pennsylvania. The record is outstanding for a number of reasons. First, there is the record of multiple winners that have carried the Suzabob kennel name. Second, the sires and dams indicate how matings were made. Third, the winners have scored in three branches of the sport: conformation, field trials and obedience. Fourth, the number of sportsmen who have bought Suzabob puppies, and then have carried on the kennel name, is itself proof of the reputation Suzabob dogs have earned. And finally, anyone studying the record must take great pride in the incomparable ability of the Brittanys themselves. No greater proof of their all-around ability could be obtained.

The Youngs bred their first litter of Brittany puppies in 1954. The period this chapter describes is from 1969 through 1982. There has been a period of relative inactivity, but the Youngs are still engaged in the sport, although to a lesser extent. They bred a litter of puppies in December of 1985.

The Eastern New England Trial of 1970 was a memorable one for the Suzabob Brittanies. All four placings were won by dogs from this breeding. First through fourth (l. to r.) are Dual Ch. Suzabob's Hum Dinger, owned by Robert Young; Fld. Ch. Suzabob's Frisco Frannie, owned by Gerald Supplee; Dual Ch. Suzabob's Gigolo, owned by Nancy Dilliplane and Fld. Ch. Suzabob's Errol of Flynn, owned by James Dilliplane.

Dual Ch. Suzabob's Hedgerow Happy (Dual Ch. Shenango Valley Dingo ex Ch. Suzabob's Seminole Sadie).

NATIONAL AWARDS

Dual Ch. Suzabob's Hedgerow Happy—NATIONAL SPECIALTY SHOW WINNER—1969 and 1974

Dual Ch. Suzabob's Hum Dinger—NATIONAL GROUSE CLASSIC WINNER—1969

Ch., AFC Suzabob's Rip Snorter—NATIONAL PRAIRIE CHICKEN WINNER—1969

Ch. Suzabob's Dolly Dimples and Debbie Young (age 12)—NATIONAL JUNIOR FIELD TRIAL HANDLER—1967

DUAL CHAMPIONS	Date Finished	Owner
Dual Ch. Suzabob's Hedgerow Happy Sire—Dual Ch. Shenango Valley Dingo Dam—Ch., AFC Suzabob's Seminole Sadie	September, 1969	D. Buster San Francisco, CA
Dual Ch. Suzabob's Hum Dinger Sire—Dual Ch. Uno's Chief Dam—Queen of Sylvan	December, 1970	Robert Young Selinsgrove, PA
Dual Ch. Suzabob's Gigolo Sire—Ch. Suzabob's Bobo, C.D. Dam—Ch. Suzabob's Lucky Leho	September, 1971	J. Dilliplane Etters, PA
Dual Ch. Willow Run Ike Sire—Ch. Suzabob's Land Rover Dam—Suzanne L'Ange	March, 1979	J. Urbanski Linder, VA
Dual Ch. Suzabob's Brigadoon Rhett Sire—Dual Ch. Suzabob's Hedgerow Happy Dam—Suzabob's Willowbritt Polly	April, 1979	P. Snyder Sellersville, PA

FIELD CHAMPIONS		
Fld. Ch., AFC Suzabob's Rip Snorter Sire—Fld. Ch. Pin Oak Guy Dam—Dual Ch. Suzabob's Hum Dinger	September, 1969	H. Robb Tinley Park, IL
Fld. Ch. Suzabob's Errol Of Flynn Sire—Ch. Suzabob's Bobo, C.D. Dam—Duned In Amber	October, 1969	J. Dilliplane
Fld. Ch., AFC Suzabob's Frisco Frannie Sire—Dual Ch. Tigar's Jocko Dam—Leeway's Ferdline Penny	September, 1971	G. Supplee Doylestown, PA
Fld. Ch., AFC Suzabob's Cassanova De Lorre Sire—Fld. Ch. Suzabob's Errol of Flynn Dam—Ch. Suzabob's Bo-Jean	October, 1975	J. Dilliplane
Fld. Ch., AFC Suzabob's Don Juan De Lorre Sire—Fld. Ch. Suzabob's Errol of Flynn Dam—Lady of Hanover	March, 1977	J. Dilliplane
Fld. Ch. Suzabob's Jet Sire—Dual Ch. Suzabob's Gigolo Dam—Ch., AFC Suzabob's Seminole Sadie	April, 1978	E. Kerr Berlin, NJ

AMATEUR FIELD CHAMPIONS	Date Finished	Owner
Ch., AFC Suzabob's Seminole Sadie	July, 1973	R. Young
Fld. Ch., AFC Suzabob's Rip Snorter		H. Busby
Fld. Ch., AFC Suzabob's Frisco Frannie	1975	G. Supplee
Fld. Ch., AFC Suzabob's Don Juan De Lorre	March, 1977	J. Dilliplane
Fld. Ch., AFC Suzabob's Cassanova De Lorre	October, 1977	J. Dilliplane

BENCH CHAMPIONS

Ch. Suzabob's Dolly Dimples   September, 1961   R. Young
Sire—Luke of Edough
Dam—Queen de Coeurs

Ch. Suzabob's Bobo, C.D.   August, 1962   R. Young
Sire—Fld. Ch. Passamonte's Jet Commander
Dam—Ch. Suzabob's Dolly Dimples

Ch. Suzabob's Diamond Chip   May, 1966   M. Gottschall
Sire—Fld. Ch. Chip's Get   Harrisburg, PA
Dam—Suzabob's Diamond Lil

Ch. Suzabob's Pride of Gayterry   May, 1966   B. Kline
Sire—Ch. Suzabob's Bobo, C.D.   New Cumberland, PA
Dam—Pa'tridge of Gayterry

Ch. Suzabob's Bo-Jean   July, 1966   B. Kline
Sire—Ch. Holley Haven Beau
Dam—Ch. Holley Haven Dixie

Ch. Suzabob's Lucky Leho   March, 1968   R. Young
Sire—Tigre of Fairhaven
Dam—Pawnee Princess

Ch. Suzabob's El Capitan   November, 1968   M. Stone
Sire—Ch. Suzabob's Bobo, C.D.   Dillsburg, PA
Dam—Suzabob's Trixie

Ch. Suzabob's Desert Rose   November, 1968   R. Cox
Sire—Dual Ch. Uno's Chief   Tucson, AZ
Dam—Ch., AFC Suzabob's Seminole Sadie

Ch. Suzabob's Honey Boy   January, 1969   J. McSweeny, Jr.
Sire—Ch. Suzabob's Bobo, C.D.   Pittsburgh, PA
Dam—Harvester's Honey

Ch. Suzabob's L'Andre De Mergol   May, 1969   M. Gottschall
Sire—Ch. Suzabob's Bobo, C.D.
Dam—Suzabob's Trixie

Ch. Suzabob's Tomahawk   May, 1969   G. Daub
Sire—Dual Ch. Uno's Chief   Hudson, MI
Dam—Mistex Duchess of Richmont

Ch. Suzabob's Lady Golden Rod   July, 1970   R. Walters
Sire—Dual Ch. Uno's Chief   Harrisburg, PA
Dam—Ch., AFC Suzabob's Seminole Sadie

Ch. Suzabob's Bebo Britt Sire—Ch. Suzabob's Bobo, C.D. Dam—Juchoir's Bee	August, 1970	C. Rodamer Harrisonburg, VA
Ch. Suzabob's Freckled Miss Sire—Ch. Suzabob's Bobo, C.D. Dam—Pin Oak Cindy	May, 1971	E. Jeffreys Warminster, PA
Ch. Suzabob's Guaranteed Sire—Ch. Suzabob's Bobo, C.D. Dam—Dual Ch. Faircrest Polyjet	August, 1973	S. Stapinski Glen Lyon, PA
Ch. Suzabob's Do-Well, C.D., C.D.X. Sire—Dual Ch. Suzabob's Gigolo Dam—Ch., AFC Suzabob's Seminole Sadie	October, 1973	E. Salmons Liberty, IL
Ch. Suzabob's Land Rover Sire—Fld. Ch. Suzabob's Errol of Flynn Dam—Suzabob's Clementine Rose	May, 1974	R. Young
Ch. Suzabob's Gun Moll Sire—Ch. Suzabob's Bobo, C.D. Dam—Dee Cee Sifflett	July, 1974	J. Tighe Blairstown, NJ
Ch. Suzabob's Miss Teed, C.D. Sire—Ch. Suzabob's Bobo, C.D. Dam—Dual Ch. Faircrest Polyjet	August, 1974	D. Groff Bridgton, NJ
Ch. Suzabob's Hickory Buddy Sire—Ch. Suzabob's Bobo, C.D. Dam—Suzabob's Hickory Honey	November, 1974	M. Stone
Ch. Suzabob's Holly Hill Friskie Sire—Ch. Suzabob's Land Rover Dam—Ch. Suzabob's Holly Hill Miss	August, 1975	B and H Donnell Southampton, PA
Ch. Suzabob's Five O'Clock Shadow Sire—Ch. Suzabob's Bobo, C.D. Dam—Triple 'S' Skeets of Hedgerow	October, 1975	R. Young
Ch. Suzabob's Holly Hill Miss Sire—Dual Ch. Suzabob's Gigolo Dam—Ch., AFC Suzabob's Seminole Sadie	April, 1976	H and B Donnell
Ch. Suzabob's Antique Shotgun Sire—Ch. Suzabob's Land Rover Dam—Suzabob's Cinnamon Ginger	August, 1977	R. Ploude Manchester, CT
Ch. Terlo's Aces & Eights Sire—Ch. Suzabob's Land Rover Dam—Ch. Terlo's Miss Fizz of Beauchamp	1977	W. Carlevaro Maitland, FL
Ch. Suzabob's Hedgerow Hunter Doc Sire—Dual Ch. Suzabob's Hedgerow Happy Dam—Suzabob's Willobritt Polly	September, 1977	W and N Newcomb Wilmington, DE
Ch. Suzabob's Brandwine Poppie, C.D., C.D.X. Sire—Dual Ch. Suzabob's Hedgerow Happy Dam—Suzabob's Willobritt Polly	April, 1978	C. Price Wilmington, DE

Winners at the 1963 Quail Classic included (l. to r.) first—Kaymore's Joe of Weymouth, owned by James B. Bell, Jr. and handled by Phil Morehouse; second—Wood's Pontiac Dingo, owned by John St. Paul, III and handled by Jane Thompson; third—Rusty of Highbrow, owned and handled by Ernest Facer; fourth—Dual Ch. Belloaks King, owned by James B. Bell, Jr. and handled by Phil Morehouse. He is posed here with Martin Best. *Hemmer photo.*

Ch. Suzabob's Canadian Sunrise going BB under Morley Thornton, shown by Sue Young (Mrs. Robert Young), Suzabob Brittanys.
Steven Klein photo.

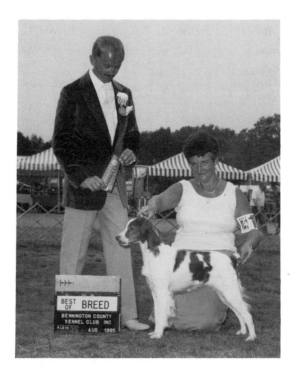

218

Ch. Suzabob's Hun Harrasser Sire—Ch. Suzabob's Land Rover Dam—Suzabob's Cinnamon Ginger	1979	Lynda Fisher Clinton, MT
Ch. Suzabob's Brandwine Britches, C.D. Sire—Ch. Suzabob's Land Rover Dam—Ch. Suzabob's Brandwine Poppy, C.D., C.D.X.	October, 1979	C. Price
Ch. Suzabob's Canadian Sunrise Sire—Ch. Suzabob's Do-Well, C.D., C.D.X. Dam—Slaney's Sarrah Davey	August 12, 1985	R. Young

OBEDIENCE DEGREES

Ch. Suzabob's Bobo, C.D.	May, 1966	D. Young
Ch. Suzabob's Miss Teed, C.D.	1975	D. Groff
Suzabob's Valleyview Chipper, C.D. Sire—Ch. Suzabob's Bobo, C.D. Dam—Suzabob's Razzle Dazzle	1975	E. Jeffreys
Ch. Suzabob's Do-Well, C.D., C.D.X.	1976	E. Salmons
Ch. Suzabob's Brandwine Poppie, C.D., C.D.X.	1977–1979	C. Price
Suzabob's Ralfee Elle, C.D. Sire—Ch. Suzabob's Land Rover Dam—Karden's Penny	December, 1978	D. Young Petty
Deb-A'Rays Jake of Hunterlane, C.D. Sire—Ch. Suzabob's Land Rover Dam—Hunterlane's Blackberry Brandy	1979	P. Borst
Ch. Suzabob's Brandwine Britches, C.D.	November, 1980	
Suzabob's Benjji, C.D. Sire—Ch. Suzabob's Land Rover Dam—Suzabob's Shade de Lade	October, 1982	S. Young

CANADIAN AMATEUR, OPEN AND FIELD DOG CHAMPION

Suzabob's Regal Duchess Sire—Suzabob's Lone Eagle Dam—Suzabob's Frisco Friskie	Peter Dolynski Beamsville, Ont. Canada

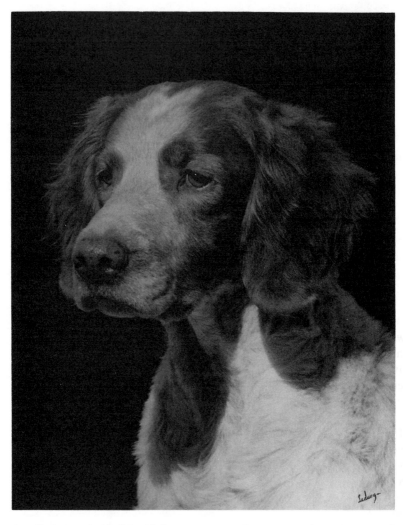

Ch. Frenchman's Yankee Nickel, owned by Dorothy MacDonald, has built a fine show record and is a Specialty winner. This appealing head study by Joan Ludwig was made for the cover of *Pure-Bred Dogs—American Kennel Gazette. Ludwig photo.*

33

How to Prepare Your Dog for the Shows

WHEN THE AMERICAN STANDARD was written, those who took part in constructing it had in mind a dog that could leave the field and be shown on the bench. They visioned a dual-purpose dog, as the Brittany Spaniel then was. And they intended to keep it one. That their judgment was correct is proven by the astonishing number of Britts that have won both in the field and at the shows.

Most sporting dogs cannot compete successfully in both branches of the sport. For example, the standard for the American Cocker Spaniel says: "The ears, chest, abdomen, and posterior sides of the legs should be well feathered, but not so excessively as to hide the Cocker Spaniel's true lines and movement or affect his appearance and function as a sporting dog." One who sees the modern Cocker Spaniel in the ring will recognize that the appearance and function of the animal as a sporting dog have been destroyed. The American Cocker Spaniel has, therefore, disappeared from the sporting scene. The English Springer Spaniel is popular both as a show dog and as a pheasant dog. Yet one who studies the show dogs and those who compete in field trials must believe that he is looking at two different breeds.

It was to avoid this divergence of type and the formation of two radically different breeds that the Brittany standard was drawn. But standards are useful only so long as breeders and competitors adhere to them. It is often said that the judge is the custodian of the standard. If, in judging Cocker Spaniels, the judge applied the standard, he would withhold all awards. Yet judges

Ch. Auten's Admiral Bird (Dual Ch. Sequani's Spade of Kennisau ex Ch. Auten's Misty Morning), bred by Ron and Carol Auten and owned by Tom Davenport and Ron Auten. *Alverson photo.*

Pix-O-Dee Sioux and Ch. Evansport's Star of David, owned by Joel K. Evans and Douglas Birchfield, were best brace in the Sporting group at the Chain O' Lakes Kennel Club under the late Nelson Groh. Mr. Evans handled the pair to the win. *Ritter photo.*

know that Cocker Spaniel show-dog people want their dogs the way they are being prepared and shown. So, in the long run, it is the breeders and exhibitors who must protect their dogs by breeding to the standard.

Before showing a dog in the ring, each Brittany owner should check it against the standard. This is difficult to do. Hundreds of people read standards, look at their dogs, and then say: "He fits the standard perfectly." Yet the dog may be a pathetic specimen. Still, there are three points that the owner can check. The first is height. Is your dog too tall or too small? The second concerns color. Does it have black in its coat, or a nose so dark as to appear black? Is it the tri-color—liver, white and tan? And does it have an excessively long and heavily feathered coat? To ask it differently, does it have so much coat that it will require excessive trimming to make it presentable?

Measuring the height of a dog is quite difficult. Not one owner in a thousand has the standard measuring equipment required by the American Kennel Club for making official measurements. Moreover, two persons skilled at measuring dogs, can come up with two different heights. And finally, owners are always inclined to give their dogs the benefit of a half inch or so. But an exact measurement is not usually required. That is, it is important to know only that the dog is neither over 20½ inches at the withers, nor under 17.

A very simple device can be made to determine this. Most hardware stores and building supply houses have soft iron dowel rods. One should get a 48-inch or longer piece with a diameter of three-sixteenths of an inch. This can be put into a vice and can be lightly pounded and bent to form a three-sided wicket, such as is used in croquet. The wicket should be 20½ inches tall. If a 48-inch dowel rod is used, then its width will be 7 inches. If a longer rod is used, the width can be seven or eight inches, not wider. The ends are then cut off to make the height exactly 20½ inches.

Place your dog in a show position. It should be standing with its forelegs perpendicular to the ground, and parallel to each other when viewed from the front. The head should be held up in its normally alert position. The wicket is then set under the hair at the highest point of the shoulders, where they join the neck. If the wicket does not touch the ground, then the dog is over 20½ inches tall, and so has a disqualifying height. A similar wicket can be made for determining whether or not a small dog is too small to qualify. But in this case, if there is space between the cross bar of the wicket and the shoulders, then the dog is too small.

The "guillotine" type measuring device used by the AKC was ridiculously inaccurate, especially when done by measuring committees who often had no experience. The author made his own wickets. These were accurate, but could be used only to tell whether a dog should be measured by a committee. However, the wicket made the committee measurements look very inaccurate. The AKC ordered the author to stop using the wickets. The AKC then developed adjustable wickets, and a new procedure was set up.

Now the judge had to measure the dog. The handler had to pose the dog himself. The judge lifted the hair at the withers, brought the wicket up from behind and set it on the highest point of the shoulders. If the dog was over, then the wicket did not touch the ground. If the dog was believed undersize, then the wicket did not touch the shoulders. Only one measurement could be taken.

The judge is the custodian of the standard. So it is his duty to measure questionable dogs. But exhibitors also are custodians of the standard. So any exhibitor in the ring has the right—and duty—to demand a measurement of any dog thought to be over or under the standard. If an exhibitor waits to demand a measurement until it is obvious that the questionable dog is going to win, then he, or she, is guilty of bad sportsmanship and can be penalized by the AKC.

The question of proper color is more easily handled. Any person who is not sure of the color of the dog's nose, for example, can take it outside into the bright sunlight and get an exact answer. But here again, owners are apt to give their dogs the benefit of a doubt, which the judge will not do. And here again, the owner who tries to claim that this black is really only a very dark brown is merely being dishonest with himself.

There is a final physical test that each person who intends to show a dog should make. This is to discover whether the dog has both testicles. The American Kennel Club rule is that a dog must have two normal testicles normally placed in the scrotum. If he does not, then the judge must disqualify him. The owner can save a lot of future embarrassment if this check is made before the dog is taken into the ring.

Many an embarrassed and startled owner will tell the judge: "Well, he had two when we checked him yesterday." What has happened is this. The dog is inexperienced. He is a house dog. This is the first time he has been around a thousand dogs. He has never known the strange noises, the strange surroundings, and all the strange people. In fright, he tends to draw the testicles up the scrotum and close to the body. He may even draw them into the body, assuming that the inguinal canals are large enough to permit this. So something more than a check is necessary. Before taking a dog to a dog show, the owner should accustom him to strange noises, strange places and dozens of people who will want to reach down and pet him.

There is a tendency to "over prepare" a Brittany for the show ring. Owners should always remember that excessive trimming destroys breed character. The Brittany is not a "pretty dog." He is one of the greatest of all working dogs, and he should look the part. Owners should remember that the standard was drawn by sportsmen who wanted to insure that a great field dog could leave the trial course and enter the show ring the same day.

Overtrimming is probably practiced by the professional handlers more than by those who handle their own dogs at shows. The professional handlers recognize that, for most breeds, a dog show is simply a beauty contest. So they

Ch. Spot of Edwards, a liver and white, bred, owned and handled by R. B. Edwards.

Ch. Mist'Dee's Star of Hope (Ch. Hope's Sea Captain ex Misty Meg), bred by Henry E. Kowala and owned by Delia and Mervin L. Fritz. *Alverson photo.*

Ch. Kay Cee's Copper Arrow (Birch Hill's Arrow ex Brookmont's Ban-Dee Victory), bred by M. Vagos and owned by Robert J. and Carolyn L. Unger.

Alverson photo.

226

try to make their dogs beautiful. Judges admire beauty, too. But there are some who recognize that beauty in a Brittany consists of soundness, conformation to type and of the marvelously muscled body the Brittany has, or should have.

The tendency is to use clippers on the neck and shoulders, and even on the back and on the rib cage. The reason for doing this is to accentuate the length of neck and the layback of the shoulders. Clipping the top of the back may accentuate the topline. But it also robs the Brittany of its tight, beautifully weather-resistant coat. For 25 years it has been said that if Brittanys were to win groups and Best in Show awards, then they would have to be trimmed in this way. Yet Brittany owners should be more interested in breed competition, in making champions and in displaying their dogs as they should be shown than in winning groups. And, it follows that they should be teaching judges to know that the over-trimmed Brittany should be penalized, not rewarded.

This is not to say that all trimming should be avoided. The hair on the neck and shoulders may become unkempt. A heavy neck-and-shoulders ruff does make it appear that the neck is too short and the shoulders too straight or upright. Some thinning and smoothing can be done, but clipping, never. The groomer must always keep in mind Brittany breed character.

Brittanys differ from other spaniels in not being excessively hairy about the feet. An occasional dog, however, will show this characteristic. In such cases, hair should be shoved upward between the toes and then cut off. Hair on the top of the foot tends to make the foot appear flat. The nails should be trimmed. Long nails tend to flatten out the foot. They are a hindrance in the field, since they catch on brush and slow forward motion. And they prevent normal action of the toe and foot muscles. They should be clipped back to, but not into, the quick. This is easily visible in the Brittany foot, being a pinkish area fed by a blood vessel.

If toenails have been allowed to grow too long for too long a time, it might not be possible for the owner to cut them back far enough without causing both pain and bleeding. In such cases, consult a veterinarian. He may anesthetize the dog, cut the nails deeply back, and then stop the bleeding. The nails and quick will then adjust back to normal. After that, the owner can cut the nails. There are several types of nail clippers. One has very heavy blades that meet. The other has a sort of guillotine blade that is enclosed in a track. This is probably easier to use for most people.

Unless the dog has just come off a field trial course, as would be the case when field trials and bench shows are held together, it should be clean. A bath is best given two days before the show. If the dog is bathed just before the event, the hair is apt to be soft, fluffy and ruffed up. Professional handlers prevent this by pinning a bath towel about the dog after it has been partially dried out. The hair will then lie flat or will be slightly wavy, as a Brittany coat should be.

Most professionals "chalk" the white on their dogs. This imparts a brighter white, and makes the dog look cleaner. It can be done with the Brittany in those areas where the white is pure. That is, in nonticked or nonroaned areas. But the owner should remember that there are rules about the preparation of a dog for the show ring. Chalk, or any other cleaning substance, must be brushed out before the dog enters the ring. If the judge pats the dog and a cloud of dust rises, he must immediately dismiss the dog. Coloring matter is not permitted. You cannot use color materials to make the orange brighter or the liver darker. If the judge finds coloring on his hands as he examines the dog, it will be dismissed immediately. And if he suspects dye, more serious consequences may result.

The teeth should be checked for tartar. Of course, this should be done occasionally whether or not the dog is to be shown. But no dog should be taken into the ring with heavy tartar deposits on its teeth. A veterinarian can remove the tartar. Many are willing to show the owner how to split it away, so that later trips to the veterinary hospital are not necessary.

Unkempt hair that destroys the appearance of the ears, where they join the skull, can be trimmed off. The eyes should be checked for matter. The dog is given a final brushing. And he is ready to enter the ring.

34

How to Show
Your Brittany

SHOWING DOGS IS AN art. That is why professional handlers are so successful. But the pros work at it. If owners worked just as hard to prepare their dogs—and themselves—they could be as successful as the handlers are. In fact, many owner-handlers can beat the professionals. They can and they do.

Early training to pose and to walk properly on leash are sometimes unpleasant for the dog. So it is wise to do this training when the dog is hungry—for instance, just before mealtime. The dog quickly understands that following training it will get a meal. So it pays attention to you and works enthusiastically. This is all the more true if the dog is fed once a day.

The first step is to teach your Brittany to pose. Common expressions for this are: "Stack your dog," and "Set up your dog." To learn how a dog should pose, study magazine pictures of Brittanys being posed, and also those of other sporting dogs. Also, study the pictures in this book. You might take as an example the picture of Fenntus du Cosquerou, one of the first of the breed to come to this country. Do not study the pictures of Cocker Spaniels. They are posed far differently than are other sporting dogs. What may be right for them is incorrect for Brittanys.

After you have gotten a fairly good concept from studying pictures, try setting up your dog. At this point, many handlers lift the front end of their dogs, either by a hand under the rib cage just behind the legs, or by the neck. They then let down the front so that the forelegs are perpendicular to the

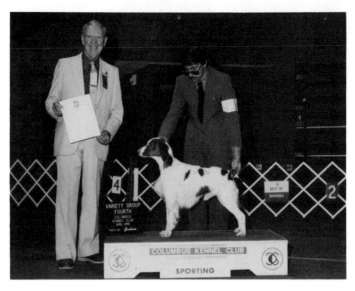

Ch. Why Not Campari on Ice shown winning a Group 4th under judge Thomas M. Gately at the Columbus KC. Breeder/owners: John Wood (handling) and Dianne Kroll. *Graham photo.*

Ch. Woodstock's Lady Valentine (Ch. J. W. Woodstock ex Double Duffy Treat Maggie), bred by Donna M. Cheek and Dwight R. Conley. Owned by Jane and Bill Theobald, "Lady" was Best of Opposite Sex at the American Brittany Club August, 1985, Specialty. The handler was Nancy Morabito. *Alverson photo.*

Spring Hill's Suzan Lee (Ch. Shannon Creek Jacques ex Ch. Cleopatri of Spring Hill), bred and owned by Suzan W. Lehosky. *Alverson photo.*

ground. If, then, the front legs are not quite true, they will take each leg by the elbow and set it properly. Do not lift the leg at the foot or pastern since you can never quite get the leg into true position in that way. A true position is one in which the legs are perpendicular to the floor or ground when viewed from the side, and parallel to each other when seen from the front.

The handlers then turn their own bodies slightly and attend to the rear end. While the left hand holds the dog in position by the collar or leash, the right hand is placed at the stifle joint. The leg is lifted and placed into proper position. The same procedure is used to set the other leg. Often, when the second hind leg is set, the dog will try to move the other forward. Say "no" sharply, and then reset the legs.

When the hind end is true, the back pasterns, often called the hocks though the hock is really the joint, are perpendicular to the ground when viewed from the side, and parallel to each other when seen from behind. Now a Brittany should have some angulation at the stifle and hock joints. In particular, it is the angulation at the stifle joint, formed by the upper and lower leg bones, that provides the drive needed by a great field dog. So try to set the hind legs to indicate as much drive as possible.

If you have set the feet too far back, the foot pads will not touch the floor. The dog may begin to slip, since it cannot get safe footing. Also, if set too far back, the hock joints will be pulled inward, and the feet will tend to toe out. You will then have set the dog into a cow hocked, and very faulty, position. If the legs are set too far under, the dog will appear to be too straight in stifles (insufficient angulation) and there will be a tendency to roach back.

When one first starts to pose a dog, the dog will try to put its head down. Lift the head, give a sharp command, and if necessary, slap the dog lightly and upward under the chin. The dog's second reaction will be to roach its back and pull its hind legs under it. But once again you scold the dog and reset the hind legs. Once the dog is in position, compliment it, and stroke it along the back until it relaxes. Sometimes it helps to stroke gently under the chin. After your dog has held the position for a minute or two, compliment it, walk it around on the leash for a minute or so, and then repeat the entire exercise.

If you watch Doberman Pinscher handlers, you will notice that they scratch or tickle their dogs on the undersides of their tails. Doberman Pinschers have about as much tail as does a Brittany. The purpose is to get the Doberman to raise the stump, or tail stub. This creates an illusion. It makes the back appear short, since the back line is broken at the tail.

Now a Springer Spaniel is supposed to be square when measured from the ground to the highest point of the withers, and from there to the root of the tail. But a Brittany should be square when measured from the ground to the highest point of the withers, and from the breast bone to the back side of the thighs just under the tail. This means that the Brittany is a tall, leggy spaniel. So getting it to raise its tail stub will help to show the judge that this is exactly

Ch. Tuway's Jolli Judi (Ch. Tuway's Kaymore Flash, C.D. ex Ch. Suzette De Brentwood, C.D.), owned and bred by Wayne Fessenden, was the winner of the 1969 Dual Futurity. She is shown here being owner handled to a win under judge Phil Marsh. *Petrulis photo.*

International (FCI) and Mexican Ch. Tuway's Holliday Marc (Fld. & Amateur Fld. Ch. Holliday Britt's Ed ex Ch. Tuway's Jolli Judi), owned by Wayne Fessenden, is the first American-bred international champion of the breed. Here he is making a win under the author at Mexico City.

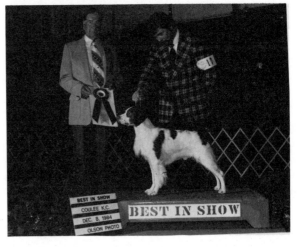

Ch. Do-Well's Henri of Chesabrit is shown going Best in Show at the Coulee KC under Robert Waters. He is shown by Darrel Droel for owner Beverly Duff.
Olson photo.

what it is. But you must study your dog. If the dog's chest is slightly shallow, or if it appears to be because all the hair on the underside of the chest has been pulled off during field work, your dog may apper to be too leggy. In that case, you won't want to get the tail stub elevated.

You should practice all this in front of a knowledgeable show-dog person. Or you can practice in front of a full-length mirror. In the latter case, you may not be able to get the entire dog's reflection from the mirror at one time. Then first set up the dog so that you can see the front half with a side view. When you are satisfied that you have set the legs properly, lift the dog around so that the reflection is of the front. Check to be sure that the legs are parallel to each other. Then look down to be certain that they are also perpendicular to the floor. Repeat this with the hind half of the dog. Again view it from the side and from the rear, and check particularly to see that you have not made the dog cow hocked.

So far, we have said nothing about the head except that you should keep it elevated. Now you want to show the neck in a lovely, convex arch. So do not elevate the head until the nose points toward the ceiling. To do so may force the neck into a concave, or ewe-necked, position. Try to keep the head in a more natural position, its top line parallel to the floor, or only slightly tipped above parallel. Sometimes you can shove the head backward just slightly to give the neck a convex arch. But if you shove it back too far, you will make the neck look too short, and the shoulders too upright, or straight.

Having set their dogs into proper show position, most handlers try to keep them alert by "baiting" them. Some use a squeaker, or a toy, such as a toy mouse. These are fine for terriers and toy dogs. Others use a bit of dog biscuit. But the most successful baiting material is a chunk of liver boiled hard. Some handlers will even allow their dogs an occasional nibble. But successful baiting, too, requires practice. For you must teach the dog to maintain its position while being alert to the boiled liver.

Once you have taught your dog to pose, to allow you to set it up in show position and to hold that position, you take the next step. The dog must learn to hold its position in the presence of other dogs. And it must learn to allow strangers to handle it, as judges will. These people should handle the muzzle, look at the ears, touch the shoulders, lift a front foot, put slight pressure on the back, check the hip sockets, perhaps lift a hind leg and, if the dog is a male, check its testicles.

You must teach your dog to permit examination by both men and women. A judge hears something like this a hundred times a year: "My dog doesn't like men." Or "He isn't used to men." Or "He's afraid of women. I think their skirts frighten him." The judge, however, cannot accept such excuses. He can only tab the dog as being shy, or as having some other personality problem. He will penalize the dog accordingly.

Similarly, it is necessary for the dog to learn that it must pose quietly in

Ch. Richard's King Henry (Ch. Ti War Chip de Triumph ex Jo-No's Mike's Springtime Sandy), owned and handled by R. B. Edwards, was the #2 Brittany in America on the Phillips ratings in 1970. He is shown making a best of breed win under judge Theodore Gunderson. *Booth photo.*

Ch. Ju-Di's Peggy Sioux, owned and handled by Richard Pocock, was best of breed at the Western Pennsylvania Kennel Association under the late Virgil Johnson. *E. H. Frank photo.*

the presence of other dogs. This is not difficult if you have other dogs. If you haven't, then ask neighbors to come over to your yard, with their dogs on leash, while you pose yours. This will require only a few lessons, but they will be invaluable. Also, pose the dog along the street, so that it gets used to standing quietly while cars, trucks, children on bicycles and tricycles and running children are passing by.

The next step is to teach the dog to walk, or to trot, on leash. For this, it is best to use a show lead—one that is both a collar and a leash. Fasten the leash so that it is directly under the chin. You do this in order to teach your dog to move with its head up. Only in this way can the judge check the dog's movement when it is coming toward him.

At first, the dog will fight the lead and will try to force its head down as it moves. Usually, a few gentle jerks upward are sufficient to correct this. When the leash is too tight, or when the dog fights it, gagging or light vomiting may occur. This is a natural reaction. But when it happens in the ring, the judge can only register the thought that, either the dog has been badly trained or it has a personality defect. Either way, it can be a mark against your dog.

When the dog's legs propel it along in a straight line, the animal is said to be true in movement. If the body is slightly turned so that the dog is moving forward at an angle, the dog is said to be crabbing or sidewinding; that is, the hind end is slightly to the right or left of the front end. You will get the idea if you first move a ruler lengthwise in a straight line, then turn it slightly but move it along the same line.

Often, crabbing is due to lack of training, or simply to sloppy gaiting. This may sometimes be corrected by gaiting with a tighter leash. But ideally, you want the dog to move truly while on a loose leash. So a better method is to gait the dog along a sidewalk. If the dog crabs to the left, then walk with the dog between you and the outside edge of the sidewalk. He must then move truly, or his hind legs will keep falling off the walk. You can do the same thing by putting the dog between you and the curb.

Sometimes an owner will gait his dog so slowly and with the leash holding the head so high that proper movement is impossible. When viewed from the side, the dog's action may appear to be a hackney type, with the front legs being lifted too high. In such cases much forward motion is lost. Or the dog may be held back so that all four legs move forward with very short, mincing steps. Practice until your dog will move forward at its fastest stride, without breaking into a gallop, and without getting out of a true forward line. Your dog cannot move truly unless you adjust your own movement to its best gait. So learn to rate yourself with your dog. Have people watch and criticize as you move together.

Gaiting, too, should be done along busy streets so that your dog will become used to the rumble of trucks, the shouting and passing of children and the presence of other dogs. Take it to shopping centers. Let people bend down to pet it. Make it gait and pose in parks, in auto repair shops or wherever there will be unusual noises. The judge simply cannot accept such excuses as: "He does this beautifully at home." Or "He doesn't like to show in buildings." Or "These strange noises scare him."

Before you take your dog into the show ring, study the breeds and classes that are judged before your class. Be present at least an hour before the hour scheduled for judging your breed. This will help to get the dog used to the show. It will also give you an opportunity to study the way the judge conducts his ring. For example, if the judge has the dogs set up and then examines them before gaiting them, then be prepared to set your dog up after the first ring go-round. If he gaits them straight out and back on a narrow mat, be prepared to do that, and that only. Don't stupidly ask him if you should gait straight out and back when that is the way he has gaited a dozen dogs before you. If he wants you to move your dog in a triangle fashion, or out and then back and forth across the ring in a "T" pattern, he will tell you to do so.

There is another reason for being at least an hour ahead in reaching the show. Let us suppose that the judge's ten o'clock assignment shows six Chesapeake Bay Retrievers, then seven Pointers, and then ten Brittanys. If the judge judges at a normal rate of speed of 25 to 30 dogs an hour, you could expect that Brittanys will be judged at or after 10:30. But some of these dogs may be absent. In that case, you will be judged earlier—at 10:15 A.M. if half the others are absent. Finally, you should report to the ring steward and get your arm band at least 20 minutes before actual judging of your breed starts. In this way, the judge will not be held up.

Most judges do not care whether dogs are lined up in catalog order or not. If one does, he will ask his steward to bring them in in that order. This usually facilitates checking the entries in a big class. But what the judge does want to see is your arm band number. Be sure that you turn your arm band so that the judge can see it easily. He is not interested in the dog food advertising on it. But in hundreds of cases that is about all he can see. The judge who must ask to see a number 100 times, or who must take 500 extra steps, and lean around 100 arms, is likely to get irritated before the day is over.

When the judge lines up the dogs and ask exhibitors to pose them, allow plenty of room between the dog in front of you and the dog behind. Only in that way can you set up your dog without cramping it, or yourself and the judge. Do not allow yourself to get stuck at the end of the line and in a corner where you will be partially hidden from the judge. If the entry is large enough to require two sides of the ring and you are at the end of the long side of the L, turn your dog to round off the corner. In this way, the judge will get a perfect look at your dog.

It is customary to set the dog in show position, and then to remove the leash. This is to prevent the leash from breaking the flowing lines of the dog. If your dog has been well trained you can do this safely. But practice this a dozen times before you attend the show.

American and Mexican Ch. Tuppence Halfpenny, owned, bred and handled by Dorothy Macdonald, is the first Brittany to hold championships in both Mexico and the United States. *Ludwig photo.*

Ch. J.J.'s Judd of Ja-Dor, owned by John Chokran, is the sixth champion out of Dual Ch. Sue City Sue. He is shown making a win under Judge Heywood R. Hartley. *Gilbert photo.*

If you are fortunate enough to get Winners Dog or Winners Bitch, then you must compete for Best of Breed. (In Canada, Winners Dog and Winners Bitch compete, and then the Best of Winners only enters to compete with the champions for Best of Breed. But in the United States both Winners Dog and Winners Bitch compete with the champions for Best of Breed.)

The best handlers make a careful study of judges. They watch them constantly. In this way, they learn that judges have certain guidelines. They are tough on dogs with bad feet, they like great angulation of the hind legs, they are "head hunters." You, too, should study judges. By watching the judge as he passes on the breeds ahead of yours, and in your own, you may get some valuable tips on how to present your dog.

There are some "don'ts" you should make a part of your dog-showing bible. Don't enter the ring and say: "Hello judge, it is nice to see you out our way again." Or "Glad to see you back again." Or "It's good to have a competent man on our breed for once." Dozens of exhibitors make this mistake. The judge is bound to think that you are simply buttering him up, currying favor. And all the other exhibitors will be sure of it.

If you know the judge, don't rush up to talk to him before the judging. And don't take him out to dinner the night before or invite him for the night after. Other exhibitors will be sure that both you and the judge are dishonest. Wait until the judging is over, then talk to him or invite him out to dinner, even if you have lost. A famous judge once said: "A judge is the most popular man in the world before a show, and the loneliest afterward."

Don't ask the judge what he didn't like about your dog. He might have liked it very well. Any faults in it may have been very minor. He may simply have liked another dog better, and upon a matter of viewing that is impossible to explain—overall balance. You can ask an opinion on young puppies. Many people take puppies to the show just to get outside opinions on the prospects—opinions from other exhibitors and from the judges.

If you lose, don't get mad at the judge or at your dog. If it is a good dog, there will be other shows and other judges. Two very competent judges may differ in the way they total the merits and faults of two dogs. In a very important sense, both of them may have sound judgment. So you thank the judge for doing a good job, and decide that tomorrow will be another day, and a winning one.

Ch. Bret Gainier Anderson, C.D.X., owner-trained and handled by Carolyn Elizabeth Anderson, going BB under Clint Harris at Chattanooga. *Graham photo.*

Ch. Carosel Tropic-Ana of Jen-Mar, owned by Jennifer and Mary Ann Breininger, pictured going Best in Show under judge Arnold Woolf. He was a group winner at 10½ months and had a Best in Show at 18 months. *Ashbey photo.*

35

Early Field Training
for a Brittany Puppy

UNTIL RECENTLY, IT WAS a rule in field-dog training that no dog should be given formal training until it was eight months to a year old. The key word in the rule is "formal," or precise and severe training. It was felt that precise, steady training would ruin a puppy's spirit, shorten its range and perhaps make it bird shy. The rule still holds, as far as severe training goes. But careful and detailed study of puppies now indicates that a six- to twelve-weeks-old puppy can be given some basic training that may make it possible for the puppy to develop into a great field dog.

Studies at the Jackson Memorial Laboratory at Bar Harbor, Maine and elsewhere have shown that the period from six to twelve weeks is the most critical in a puppy's life. During it, the puppy's mind is most receptive. The puppy is trying very hard to adapt itself to its environment. Lessons learned during this period are normally learned for life. Bad habits learned at this time will be difficult to break; good habits become the springboard upon which good adult behavior is launched.

Every person has seen a seven-weeks-old puppy happily waddling along on a string held by a child. The puppy has already learned to walk on a leash. This is an important first step. The puppy has taken it without the shock that it would get if leash broken at six months. It is important for a field dog because it means that the puppy can be taught to stop and point, and to hold that point during a flush. If taught during this period, the puppy may never break a point.

An eight-week-old litter of Brittany puppies—future masters of the bird field.

Once the puppy has been taught to walk on leash, a game-bird wing can be put in the grass ahead of it. As the puppy moves along, every cell in its nose is gathering in odors. As the new and strange odor reaches its nose, the puppy stops to savor it. Now instinct awakens in all the other cells of the puppy's body. "This," they will whisper to the brain, "is the odor a thousand generations of bird dogs ahead of me were taught to find. This is the reason that I was bred."

The puppy is on leash. It stops momentarily to get the meaning of the odor. The owner can now apply light leash pressure, and can steady the puppy by voice while also assuring it that the odor is a proper one for puppy to savor. After a few lessons the puppy will stop automatically.

The next step is to fasten the wing to a fishing line at the end of a fishing pole or fly rod. The owner can restrain the puppy in a point while "flushing" the wing. It sounds simple, and it is. The puppy is pointing, and is being held steady by light leash pressure, while something exciting is being "flushed" in front of its nose. A conditioned reflex is being set up to point, and to remain steady to flush.

During this period, one must use great caution. No lesson should last longer than two minutes. Any long lesson will tire the puppy and make it hate all training. But a series of one- or two-minute lessons, repeated half a dozen times a day, can be permanently learned while remaining fun. The owner must constantly restrain himself from making the lesson too long. Too short a lesson is still better learned than one too long. Every lesson must be accompanied by plenty of compliments and voice assurances, and plenty of petting. And there must be adequate rest and play periods in between.

Every puppy loves to rush out to retrieve things. But they don't always want to bring them back. Instead, they would prefer to romp off with them. Formal retrieving lessons can come later. But "fun retrieving" can be taught at this time. The puppy is kept on a light cord line. The object to be retrieved is thrown out a few feet ahead of the puppy. It rushes out and grabs the object. The owner simply draws the puppy to him while complimenting it. This lesson can be repeated three times. It is play, but even play can be tiring if repeated too often. The lessons can be repeated at intervals every day. The object at this time is simply to condition a reflex action in the puppy to rush out to retrieve, and to return to its owner's hand.

Probably every owner of a prospective field dog worries about the possibility that his dog will be gun shy. The causes of gun shyness, noise shyness or storm shyness are not known. Sometimes all three occur in the same dog. But this is not always true. A Brittany owned by the author would be sent into epileptic convulsions during an electrical storm, but he was not gun shy. And a gun-shy Springer Spaniel was not afraid of other noises.

It must be your aim to make gunfire a part of your dog's life. In a six- to twelve-weeks-old puppy this is easily done, though only if the dog does not have some pathological fault in respect to noise. The owners of puppies sometimes fire cap pistols just before feeding. They wait until the attention of the puppies is diverted at the far end of the run. They then fire the pistol, and call the puppies to their meals. The puppies come to associate the firing with the pleasures of eating. The puppies also learn to rush to the sound of gun fire. A shot fired into the air has helped many an inexperienced and lost dog to find its owner.

Sometimes an owner holds a puppy in his arms while another dog points. He then flushes the bird, and puts the puppy into the warm scent left by it. Later, he can hold the puppy either in his arms or in the scent while someone at a distance fires. It is not necessary to kill the bird. For example, it can be a pigeon tied to the end of a fishing line and "planted" in light cover. As the pigeon reaches the end of the line, it is brought down and the gun is fired. The trained dog is then sent out to make the retrieve while the puppy watches. Here the puppy is learning the excitement of hunting. It picks up this excitement from the scent, the flush and shot and the excitement shown by the other dog as it rushes out to make the retrieve.

Every dog must gain field wisdom. It can gain a part of this during the six- to twelve-weeks period. It must learn to climb banks, to search for holes under fences, or to jump through holes in the fences or over the tops. It must learn to cross streams, either by searching for a shallow place or by swimming. As it gains field wisdom, it will also gain the confidence to cast out and away in searches of birdy cover.

You must remember not to tire your dog by too-long walks or running while still so young. If you tire it too much, it may lose interest. And too much running may injure bones before they have had a chance to change from cartilage into hard, strong bone. So make your field walks short, but with a purpose. One trainer used to take six-weeks-old puppies in his hunting coat while training other dogs. He would set the puppy down into a warm scent, then let it work out the area, then pocket it again.

The owner can take a puppy to a creek bank. He can set the puppy down along the water's edge, or he can let the puppy find its own way down the bank. Puppy wants to be with master, so if the owner simply walks over the bank, the puppy will find its own way down. If then, the owner walks across the creek at a shallow spot, the puppy will follow. There can then be lessons where the puppy must swim or get left behind. The same procedure can be followed in going up a bank. The owner selects one that will not be too hard. If the puppy cannot climb it, the owner simply walks along the bank to a spot where the puppy can climb up.

The same procedure is followed at fences. At first, the puppy will not know how to search for a hole under the fence. So the owner climbs the fence, then walks along until there is an opening. He may have to show the opening to the puppy the first time. After that, the puppy will conduct its own searches.

Jumping through holes is more difficult to teach. The owner may have to pull a leash through the hole, then tug upward gently until the puppy gets the idea. A simple method is to teach the puppy to jump over low objects. The owner puts puppy on a leash, walks to the barrier and, though it is not so high that he must jump, he pretends to jump over. The puppy will get the idea quickly. Jumping through holes then is simple to teach. Of course, you deliberately make your walks include things that puppy can and will have to jump.

In all these lessons, it is important not to help the puppy unless it is absolutely necessary. Do not help it up or down a bank. It may come to depend upon you always to help it. Once you've shown it how to jump, never help it again.

People sometimes speak of a dog's homing instinct; that is, the ability of a dog to find its way home. This may indeed be an instinct. But much of it is training and acquired knowledge. We know a man who deliberately tries to lose his puppies. He takes them to an area of woods and flat lands and ravines. While the puppies are busily exploring, he slips away, and returns to the point from which the walk began. The puppies, suddenly finding themselves without a guiding master, become panicked. But only for a minute. They quickly get to work to backtrack. The owner helps very young puppies by trying to leave extra-deep footprints in spongy turf. In his first lessons, he is not more than 25 yards away. He then gradually lengthens the distance. At first, he may help with a couple of voice calls, but not afterward. Puppies taught in this way can never be lost in the field, and they quickly acquire great boldness and field sense.

Most Brittanys, even though working to a man on foot, hunt at some distance away. They learn the position of their master by his occasional voice calls. These are no more than unintelligible cries, but the dogs recognize their masters' voices and position themselves accordingly as they hunt.

Yet there are times when the dog must respond, must quit hunting and come to heel. This can be taught to very young puppies. You can use your own vocal whistle, or a wind whistle. You may have taught the puppy to come to the feed dish when a cap pistol is fired. You can fire your gun in the field to make the puppy respond. Or you can teach it to come to its meals when you whistle. Of course, you have to use imagination.

For instance, you might have someone take the dog a short distance away just at feeding time. Then you blow your whistle, and set down the food dish. Or you wait until the puppy is around the corner of the house, then blow the whistle. What you are doing is imprinting in the dog a reflex action to come instantly upon that whistle call.

Another method is to put the dog upon a light long cord. Then when the puppy is going away from you, you whistle, snub the dog short, and then begin to draw it in to you. Puppy may put on the brakes. But you continue to draw it in, and you praise it as you do so. When it reaches you, you pet and compliment it. This lesson must be repeated again and again until the puppy automatically turns and comes to you when you blow that particular whistle.

In this chapter, we have been writing solely of early field training. Yet field dogs should be bold and confident under all circumstances. So they have to gain experience under many and varying conditions. During this period, you should be taking your puppy into the home. It needs to know about hardwood floors and waxed composition floors, about rugs and home noises. And it must meet a lot of strangers. Among these strangers should be cats and chickens. A cat or a kitten will quickly teach a small puppy to respect it. One scratch on the nose and puppy learns its lesson permanently. A grown dog, however, might become a cat killer once one has scratched it. Nothing can be more embarrassing than to have your fine hunting dog rush into a farmer's yard and chase and kill his cat, or his chickens. If you have a cat in your home, the lesson will be learned at six weeks of age. If you haven't, then take your puppy to visit a cat or, preferably, a kitten.

And take it to a farmer's chicken yard. Here use a training rope; for instance, a builder's chalk line. Tie one end to puppy's collar. Let it drag the rope. If it starts to chase a chicken, say "no" sharply, and at the same time upset the puppy. Remember that a sharp upset is much better than a few weak jerks. Be stern enough so that only one or two lessons are sufficient. But after such lessons, work with your pheasant wing, so that puppy quickly learns that one is forbidden, and the other is its way of life.

If at the twelfth or fourteenth week, these lessons are mostly stopped, the puppy will still not forget them. The puppy can then be taken out of training, so to speak, and just allowed to grow. But field romps in all sorts of cover should be continued, so that the puppy continues to grow in field wisdom. Then when formal training begins, puppy will be bold and confident. He'll quickly return to the responses you taught him as a baby, and he will become an easily trained and experienced field dog.

Ch. Flint's Kinwashkly Queen, C.D., 12 years old, foundation bitch for Kinwashkly Brittanys owned by Rick and Leslie Andreas. "Queen" has produced 1 dual champion, 1 field champion, 8 bench champions and 11 other field winners.

Jacolet's Kona Wind is the sixth generation of dual champions and the sire of Dual Ch. Sunnyvale Skipper. Both dogs are owned by John and Adele Henderson. Kona Wind has been a multiple winner at all-breed pointing dog trials.

36

Yard Breaking
the Brittany

Y ARD BREAKING IS THAT part of field training that can
be done in your backyard. But it is more than that. It is obedience training. It
can, and should, be given to all puppies whether or not they are ever going to
compete in field trials or in dog shows or obedience trials. It is the basic
obedience that makes a better companion of every dog.

You should teach your dog to heel both while on a leash and when free of
it, to sit when you stop, to sit and to lie down upon command, to come when
called and to carry and retrieve. All these things can be taught in your
backyard, on the sidewalks in front of your house, in special trips to shopping
centers, or to places where there are people and animals that will tend to divert
your dog's attention.

Heel and sit can be taught in one lesson. The dog should heel on your left
side. The reason is that most people are right handed. So they carry things in
the right hand. They also carry their gun on the right side. But, if you are left
handed, you could teach the dog to heel on the right side. Here we assume you
will have the dog walk at heel on your left side.

Start walking. Say the dog's name and a stern "heel." Jerk on the leash to
pull the dog up to your heel. If it tries to go ahead, jerk lightly to bring it back,
and again command "heel."

After you have walked 20 to 30 steps, stop and command "sit." Instantly
grasp the dog's collar with your right hand, and the skin of the rump with your
left. Pull backward with both hands, and downward with the left. The dog is

Ch. Millette's Happy Go Lucky, owned by Rosita and Robert Richway. *Alverson photo.*

Ch. Suzabob's Land Rover, owned by Robert E. Young.

thus forced to sit. Make it hold this position for a minute or so. If it tries to get up, restrain it, and repeat the command "sit." Now start forward and command "heel." Walk 20 to 30 steps, and then stop and repeat the "sit" exercise.

As in most training exercises, do not make the mistake of making lessons too long. Work with the dog for five minutes. Then allow a rest period of half an hour. Follow with another 10-minute lesson. Give four or five such lessons a day.

Sometimes the dog will pull ahead so hard that the pressure on the neck made by the collar makes the dog choke. If fairly severe jerks and the "heel" command do not bring the dog back to heel, there is a simple method for correcting the error. Use an umbrella, a cane or just a long stick. If the dog pulls ahead, tap it lightly on the nose. This will cause it to back up. After a few times, the stick can simply be used as a guide. It can be held ahead of the dog, and it will not pull ahead. Sometimes a cane or umbrella can be swung back and forth as a pendulum.

If the dog is being trained for the field, or for simple home obedience, it is not necessary to have it walk close to your side. If it is to compete in obedience trials, then close heeling is required. A simple method of teaching close heeling is to do the exercises along the edge of a sidewalk, or along a street curb. If along a sidewalk, then walk close enough to the left edge so that the dog must stay close to your side or get off the sidewalk. If on the street, walk along the left side, with the dog between you and the curb. This method is particularly good for dogs that tend to walk with the forelegs near you but with the hind end pointing away. That is, the dog is crabbing.

Different dogs require different lengths of training for any given exercise. But an important factor in training is attention. The dog who will not give you its attention is difficult, or even impossible, to train. Most Brittanys give you their attention and they learn quickly. So for most of them, the heel and sit lessons should be well learned within three days. But if you are training your first dog, remember that you are also training yourself. So, since you are not an expert, a somewhat longer period may be required.

The next step is to teach the dog to heel and sit "free." That is, to work free of the leash. Always start each lesson by repeating first those previously learned. So give your dog two minutes of work on leash. Now, with the dog sitting at your left heel, take off the lead, while cautioning it with your voice to remain sitting. Now command "heel" and start walking forward. But be prepared to grab the collar and give a slight jerk if the dog does not instantly respond. Be prepared also to grab the collar and jerk the dog back if it tries to go ahead. Here again, the cane, umbrella or long stick can help to guide the dog.

If your dog has learned its first lessons well, it should learn to heel and sit free within a maximum of three days. But again, remember to start each day with heeling and sitting while on the leash. You will be really amazed at how quickly your dog learns to obey while off the leash. Yet the lesson will not be fully learned until you have worked the dog under all sorts of conditions, such as while other dogs are in the yard, while children are running and playing nearby, and where there are many people, as at a shopping center.

Sit and stay is the next lesson. If your puppy lives in the house, this can be simply—and quickly—taught at feeding time. Mix up the dog's food. Then have your dog sit in a corner. Command it repeatedly to sit and stay while someone else puts down the food dish in a far corner of the room. Be prepared to grab the dog if it starts to rush for its food. Make it sit again. And then place the palm of your hand in front of its nose as a warning. If it ignores the command and hand, grab it again, and again force it to sit. After a moment, remove your hand and say "okay" or some other signal that will tell the puppy it can go to its food.

If you are feeding twice a day, the lesson can be repeated twice a day. But you can also practice using dog biscuits. Your next step is to make the dog sit in the corner while you put down the food dish. Put the dog in the corner as usual, then caution it to sit, and keep the palm of your hand out toward the dog. Then get the food dish, back away from the dog and carefully set down the dish. If the dog "breaks" and rushes toward the food dish, catch it on the way. Carry or drag it back to its corner, and then make it sit for a moment before letting it go.

Carrying it back can be both a correction and a mild form of punishment. The best way to carry it is to grab the puppy by the scruff of the neck and by the skin on the rump. No dog likes to be carried in this way. But in dogs as lightly made as the Brittany, the method is harmless but very effective.

The next step is to practice outside. Take the dog into the yard. Practice your heeling on and off a leash. Now command the dog to sit. Step carefully in front of it. Keep repeating the command "sit," and use the palm of your right hand as a restraining signal. Now back slowly away. If the dog breaks, catch it and carry it back to the spot from which it broke. Repeat again and again, always backing away.

When the dog will remain sitting until you say "okay" or give it a hand signal by dropping your hand, or both, you are ready for the next step. Back away as before. Now turn around. The dog may break. If it does, start over again. Once it will stay when your back is turned, try something new. With the puppy sitting, stand in front of it, command it to sit and stay. Turn your back and begin to walk away. If the puppy breaks, carry it back to the spot from which it broke, and start over again. At first, walk slowly away. Later, move away rapidly.

Now you are ready for the next lesson. This is to teach the puppy to sit and stay while you are out of sight. You can sit the puppy at one end of the yard, then walk into the garage, or around the corner of the house or barn. If

250

1980 National Specialty winner, Ch. Greenfield Le Duc De Cannell, owned by Joseph and Amy Rodrigues and shown with Amy, age 8.   *Ludwig photo.*

puppy breaks, try to catch it before it reaches you, scold it, and return it to its spot. You can figure that the puppy has not learned the lesson thoroughly until you can stay out of sight for several minutes.

At first, you will want the puppy to sit in its position until you have returned to it and have placed yourself so that the puppy is at your left heel. Later, you can let it come to you when you call. But, if you start to let it do this too soon, you may be teaching it to break and not to wait until the command to "come."

This lesson must be practiced under all sorts of conditions. If your puppy is a house dog, then you should practice making it sit in one room while you are in another. Later, you must practice where there are other people and other dogs to distract it. One of the lamest of excuses is "Well, he does this perfectly at home . . ."

You must also teach your dog to lie down, and to stay there until told it can get up. An occasional dog cannot be taught this. It is the author's experience that such dogs have some degree of inherited shyness. When lying down, they feel defenseless and become frightened. If you cannot teach your Brittany to lie down and to stay there while you are out of sight, then it might be wise not to use the dog for breeding. A further such test is to make the dog lie down in the dark and stay there while you move some distance away.

There are various ways to teach a dog to lie down. One is to make it sit. Then grab its front legs and upset it, while commanding "lie down." Restrain it in the lying-down position while complimenting and soothing it. Another method is used with a leash. Have the puppy sit. Place the leash under the arch of one shoe. Now pull up on it while commanding "lie down." As you pull up, the puppy's head and neck are forced down. When puppy is squatting on both hind and front legs, shove it over onto its side.

However you do it, compliment the puppy but restrain it from getting up. Finally, you can tell it to sit and allow it to take that position. It is important to teach it the difference between sitting and lying down. Remember also to practice this lesson under all sorts of conditions. To do so is to give the puppy confidence in both you and in the world about it. And this is important whether you are to train the dog for field or obedience work.

Jumping, if properly taught, is one of the fun lessons for dogs. A simple way is to put the dog on leash, then to approach and to walk over a low barrier. If the puppy balks, step back to its side. Walk back a few steps, turn and again approach the barrier. As you step over, command "jump" and lift upward on the leash. Forced in this way, the puppy will try to jump the rest of the way. Compliment it with petting and by voice. Repeat again and again, and as the dog learns to make the jump, begin raising the barrier.

Also, take the dog off leash and walk over. As you raise the barrier, begin running to it, and jump over yourself. Then as you continue to raise it, run alongside while the dog jumps over.

252

The dog is not well trained until it will jump over at your command. First, sit the dog a few steps away, then stand a few steps away on the far side. Face the dog, call it and command "jump." Be prepared to rush forward and to stop it if it tries to run around. Set it directly in front of a very low barrier, step over, and then command "jump." Eventually, the dog will get the idea and will jump over at command, even when you are some distance away and order it to go forward and to jump.

Also, the dog is not well trained until it will jump over a variety of barriers or objects. The author once knew an obedience-trained Standard Poodle that could get perfect scores in Utility work. It was a perfect jumper over the standard jumps used in obedience work. But this dog would balk at a low field fence, and would refuse to jump over an overturned chair or other object. So practice with your dog. You might even practice having it jump over a kneeling youngster.

In similar fashion, teach it to broad jump. Standard broad jump hurdles, as used in obedience trials, are easily made. These are boards four-feet six-inches to five feet long. They are supported by end pieces that are six inches high at the forward edge, and four inches at the near edge. This gives them an upward and forward slope. You can make two or three of these, with four being ideal. One can be five feet long, the second, four-feet ten-inches, the third, four-feet eight-inches and the fourth, four-feet six-inches. In this way, they can be nestled together so as to take up the space of only one when not in use. They should be painted flat white. Practice with these until the dog will race to them and leap over three or four when well spaced.

In obedience trials, a Brittany would be required to jump over a barrier one-and-a-half times its height. Thus a Brittany 20 inches tall would have to jump a 30-inches-tall barrier, and clear it without touching it. In the broad jump it would be required to jump 60 inches clear. So you should practice until the dog will leap such a distance. But also practice having it jump over brooks or ditches. Remember that you are teaching the dog to do the unusual as well as the usual. If you practice making it do unusual things, you will be giving it the confidence to do things at your bidding that it has not done before.

Retrieving should also be taught during yard breaking. As written earlier, retrieving comes naturally to very young puppies. But it is play, not work. The difference is that you must teach your dog *must*. When you order it to retrieve it *must* do so. Also, during play retrieving, the puppy will tend to chew on the object; it will want to take it in the opposite direction, and it will not want to give it up.

It is the author's belief that a dog should be taught to carry before it is taught to retrieve. If it is taught to carry first, then it will always retrieve with style later on. There will also be less danger of hard mouth—the condition in which the dog either chews the game or crushes it in its mouth. Teaching the dog to carry is done in two steps. The first is simply teaching the dog to hold something in its mouth until told it can give the object to you; that is, can put it into your hand. This lesson can be taught in the home or in the backyard. The object can be anything. A newspaper rolled up and tied is excellent. A block of wood can be used. You may even use a block of wood to which a pheasant or pigeon wing has been nailed.

Have the dog sit. Kneel beside it. Command "hold" or "carry," though the former is to be preferred. Place your left hand over the dog's muzzle and squeeze between the teeth. The dog is then forced to open its mouth. Place the object to be held—dummy is a good word for it—in the dog's mouth. Command "hold it." The dog will try to spit out the dummy. But prevent this with your right hand. At the command "okay" take the dummy. Repeat this four or five times. You may have to slap upward under the chin to get the dog to hold the dummy. If so, do it lightly, while using a commanding tone of voice.

As soon as the dog understands and will hold the dummy until told to release it into your hand, you are ready for the next step. Put a leash on the dog, but fold it into your hand until only a foot is left between your hand and the dog's neck. As the dog holds the dummy, command "fetch," and begin to draw the dog forward. If it tries to spit out the dummy, warn it to "hold it" or repeat the command "fetch." You probably will have to hold the dummy in the dog's mouth a few times. But a Brittany will ordinarily get the idea very quickly.

Now lead it about, warning it to "fetch" and praising it. Once it will carry the dummy, begin to praise it continuously. Then have the dog sit and deliver the dummy to hand. Now praise and pet it with all the enthusiasm you can muster. In this way, the dog will become immensely proud to carry something for you, and it will do so with great style.

If the dog shows any tendency to chew on the dummy, drive some blunted nails through it in such a way that any attempt to clamp down on the dummy will bring pain, but will not puncture the mucous membranes of the mouth. The dog will quickly learn to carry gently, or as field people say, "with a tender mouth." Practice until the dog will carry for at least 100 yards.

The dog is now ready for actual retrieving lessons. Place the dog in a sitting position. Kneel beside it. Throw out the dummy and command "fetch." If the dog does not move, draw it to the dummy by the leash, pull its head down by force on the collar, and force the dummy into the mouth. Then, still commanding "fetch," return the dog to the spot from which you started. In most cases, the dog will carry the dummy, since it has already learned to carry. But, if it drops the dummy, scold it with a stern "no." Then again draw its head down and force the dummy into the dog's mouth. Once you have returned the dog to the spot from which the dummy was thrown, make the dog deliver to hand, as in the carry exercise. Then praise it and give it much petting.

We have said that carrying and retrieving can be taught in the home or in the backyard. It is important that whatever spot you choose be one free of distraction. You want the absolute attention of the dog. No other dogs or other people should be about. But once the lesson has been learned, practice before other people and in the presence of other dogs. Dogs enjoy showing off both for people and other dogs. But also, they learn to work under all conditions.

The last step in retrieving is to teach the dog to carry and retrieve all sorts of things. These should include your gloves, a small basket with a handle, a pigeon, pheasant, woodcock or other upland game, and ducks. Of course, you can teach the retrieving of game by using the wings of various game birds. These can be tied to rolled-up newspaper, or nailed to a block of wood. But finally, the dog must retrieve live game unharmed. If you have followed this system carefully, the latter will be no problem.

Probably dogs like to retrieve pigeons least of all. So use a live pigeon for this. There are two methods to do this. One is to tape the wings to the body and to tape the feet together. The latter is necessary to keep the pigeon from scratching tender mouth tissues. Taping the wings to the body also helps to protect the pigeon from injury. The second is to lock the pigeon's wings. This is done by folding the wings above the body. Then the left wing is crossed over the right, and the right is hooked over the left. The pigeon's wings are sufficiently loose to permit this without breaking them. But use care. Also, tape the legs together. The pigeon's body is now exposed and a small, young dog will have an easier carry.

A final step in yard breaking is to teach the dog to beware of automobiles and trucks. Take the dog on leash along any highway. Walk along the shoulder, but do not have the dog at heel. That is, use a long leash or rope and let the dog wander onto the highway itself. Then, as a car or truck comes along, give the dog a tremendous jerk over to the shoulder. After a few such lessons, the noise of any approaching auto or truck will cause the dog to rush to the side of the road. This lesson could save your dog's life.

Ch. Torbec Tag, owned by T. G. and Michelle McIntyre.

37

Final Field Training of the Brittany

IT IS BEYOND THE scope of this book to try to tell the reader how to give the final lessons in field work. But there is one major lesson that every person who wants a field dog or a field-trial dog must learn. Perhaps the following story will illustrate the point.

The author once interviewed the owner of a Coonhound that had just won the national championships in competition against some 500 dogs. This is his story.

I had a pretty good bitch. She was a real cooner, and every hunter in Kentucky and West Virginia knew her, and knew how good she was. Well, sir, I bred her to the greatest dog any of us knew about.

She had eight pups. And by golly I just made a vow to keep every darn one of those pups. I wanted to train them all until I made mighty certain which was the best one.

But the boys from everywhere heard about those pups. So they would come around with a jug of hard cider, or maybe a bit of moonshine. And we'd sit under the old apple tree in the yard and talk about hounds and coons.

And every one of those guys told me what a wonderful friend he had been to me. And every one of them told me about all the favors he had done for me. And how I really owed him one of those pups.

And you know how it was. They got every one of those pups away from me except an ugly marked kind of runty pup which nobody wanted. Well, sir, that's old Buckeye Joe. Yes sir, the same Buckeye Joe that just won the money.

Dual Ch. Joel's Copper Jacques, owned by John G. and Ellyn Lee, holds an all-time record for the breed as winner of 16 open all age stakes. He is shown here with his handler, Lee Holman. *Brown photo.*

You ask me the secret of why he's the national champion. Heck, I don't know. Except this. He's been worked on coon 365 nights a year ever since he was old enough to run a trail.

The all-important ingredient in the making of a champion is experience. So you've got to get your dog out into the field, and into game fields, as often as possible. You can't take it out just two weeks before the hunting season and expect it to be a top-grade performer.

Among other things, the dog must get toughened up for the work. It must get rid of excess fat, must strengthen muscles, must harden its foot pads, must tighten its toes. There is evidence, too, that the dog must sharpen its nose. After a long layoff, or an illness, a dog may have to learn over again how to interpret the various windborne odors that come to him. Perhaps one can say that it must gain "re-experience."

Many dogs are trained on planted game. But there is vast difference between the planted pheasant and a wild one. The planted pheasant is less strong physically. Its odor may be different. It will lack experience in running, dodging and hiding—those faculties the wild pheasant has sharpened by a summer of escaping from predators. When working such game, the dog may make unproductive points and may be accused of being dishonest or of having a faulty nose. Yet the fault may be lack of experience. After being shot at for a couple of days, pheasants tend not to fly but to run, dodge and hide. It then takes a highly experienced dog finally to pin the bird.

Many dogs will have to learn to run on a drag line. Some will have to be broken of chasing rabbits. There was a brilliant young derby dog who could never be broken of chasing deer. Every dog must be taught to back, that is, to honor the point made by another dog.

There are many books that cover all these subjects thoroughly. You can find them listed in libraries under the names of such authors as Henry P. Davis, William F. Brown, Er M. Shelley and Richard A. Wolters. If you will be doing some woodcock shooting, then you ought to learn all you can about the famous timberdoodle. Check your library for John Alden Knight's *Woodcock,* and Bennett's *Training Grouse and Woodcock Dogs.*

Dog books, by the way, are usually kept in the technology division of the larger libraries. But also, you should visit old- and rare-book stores. Many of the best books on bird-dog training are now out of print. Do not confine yourself to one book. The best trainers are better in some phases than in others. Your problems will be partially unique. So study all the books you can, and choose the methods that seem to give the best solutions for your problems.

You ought also to seek help from thoroughly experienced Brittany field people. There are some great amateurs and some supremely competent professionals. Perhaps you can arrange to work out with a top amateur. Chances are he will know the best places in which to train.

This last is an extremely important point. You must not discourage a young dog by forcing it to work for hours in unproductive cover. You yourself should be on a constant search for birdy areas in which to train. And your training should include some use of planted, or at least released, pheasants. You can space out the time between birds as the dog gains experience. As he gains experience in coming onto point over many birds, he will be less likely to become discouraged when working barren territory. And you need to give him some barren territory. If you give him too many birds in too short a time, he may then become a quitter if he has to hunt for half an hour without finding a bird.

Now there is a difference between a field dog and field-trial dog. The difference is in competition. In a trial, you will need as much experience as will your dog. So you should plan to attend as many trials as you can. Follow every brace, and study the work of dogs and handlers, both on the back course and in the bird field. Finally, enter your dog. Only in competition can you gain the experience both you and your dog will need. Don't worry about losing. The best handlers and the best dogs lose at times.

Ask experienced handlers, including the professionals, to watch you and your dog. Then ask them to tell you what you did wrong. Most of them will tell you. The next time, you won't make that mistake. A mistake you should not make is to think your dog should be the winner. You are wrapped up in the performance of your dog. You'll give it every advantage in your own mind. So will other owners in assaying the performance of their dogs. But the judges see all the dogs. They take notes. They try to figure out the winners impartially. Sometimes they make mistakes too, since often they have to make instant judgments on controversial points. Forget all that. Just try to correct your dog's mistakes, and hope for better luck at the next trial.

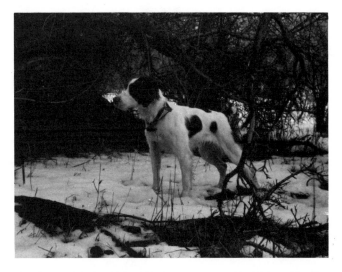

Ch. Kinwashkly Bambi Sue, field winner, owned by Rick and Leslie Andreas, Kinwashkly Brittanys.

FIVE GENERATIONS of Kinwashkly Brittanies (from left):
1. Ch. Flint's Kinwashkly Queen, C.D., 12 years old, foundation bitch owned and shown by Leslie Andreas.
2. Dual Ch. Kinwashkly Red Patches, Queen's son, 10 years old, shown by Meryle Lehr.
3. Dual Ch. Kinwashkly Brown Sugar, 7 years old, Red's niece, shown by Debbie Zimmerman.
4. Ch. Kinwashkly Sugarpatch Tina, 3 years old, Sugar and Red's daughter shown with Amy Andreas.
5. Kinwashkly BanDee Patches, 6 months old, Tina's son shown by Al Hawley.
Queen, Tina and BanDee Patches are field trial winners.

38

A Great Amateur Writes About Field Training

by Ejner Lund

(Author's Note: Because of his great record in training and handling his own dogs at field trials, we have asked Ejner Lund to give you his personal advice on field training. Mr. Lund is the owner of Dual Ch. Lund's Trooper, Dual Ch. Faulkner's Reddy and Dual Ch. Black Butte Ricochet Trooper.)

I HAVE BEEN ASKED TO put down a few notes on our experience in starting puppies. We have really started only a few, so perhaps I am not the greatest expert on this.

Our experience has been to get the pups out at the earliest opportunity. Eight to ten weeks is not too early to begin letting the pup explore the wonders of nature, and to let it get used to the environment, strange noises and excitement. Let it explore on its own. In other words, let it develop its natural instincts naturally. Don't be overprotective. The "college of hard knocks" can be a wonderful teacher.

Don't overdo the workout. If you are working an older dog along with the pup, be sure to pick up the pup as soon as it shows signs of tiring. Then carry it along. Something exciting often develops, such as birds or rabbits flushing. This will help to stimulate the pup's interest. Soon it will show enthusiasm and start ranging out on its own.

262

Dual Ch. Lund's Trooper, owned by Ejner (handling) and Gilda Lund, has established a record as one of the leading sires of all breeds. He has fathered a total of 22 champions including six duals. This is truly a most outstanding accomplishment.

If the pup is not starting to run as well as you might like, don't ever try to chase it out. This would only frighten the pup and cause it to quit running altogether. Be encouraging and run forward. Act excited and shout "atta boy," or "atta girl," as the case may be. The pup will see your excitement and try to beat you. If you get a few good casts, pick the pup up and show it that you are very pleased. Then call it a day.

If you are trying for a field-trial dog, don't make your lessons too long. You don't want the pup to think it has all day to explore at its leisure. Ten or fifteen minutes is ample to start with. Later, as the dog develops, you can lengthen your outings to a time similar to what is required in the appropriate stakes.

When the young dog really starts to run, the tendency of most novice handlers is to overhandle. They are afraid that the dog is not going to turn when it should. If a pup has been taken out regularly—several times a week, if possible—it will turn when it comes to a point where it has trouble keeping track of you. If you think it may be confused or be getting lost, let out a few good war whoops so it knows where you are. But don't call the dog. You will soon see it swinging in from somewhere. It will enjoy working for you when it finds you are not a killjoy. You will find it will not be a runaway dog, but a bold and enthusiastic explorer.

As it gains experience, you can guide it into running the type of ground heat you want by keeping close watch on the way it patterns. If it side-casts too much, give it a war whoop or whistle to get its attention. Then start running to the front. It will swing forward on seeing you do it.

As soon as it is going in the right direction, slow down to your regular pace again. Watch it closely to see that it continues. If it is running well to the front, but onesided, right or left, again a whistle or loud war whoop should be given to get its attention. Then start running forward. Remember, this should be always forward, but to the opposite side, so that the dog will swing with you. When it responds, again slow down to your regular pace. Be ready to repeat as necessary. In most cases your dog will soon be running and quartering as you want him to do.

In getting the dog's attention, never call it. You do not want it to come in. This is not desirable, and it will cause your dog to be penalized in trials. Should it happen that it does come in, run toward your dog. Yell "no" when it gets close. It will soon realize that you don't appreciate its coming in to visit.

Also, it must be remembered that, if you run your dog where no game is to be found, it will not run with enthusiasm for very long. No good will come from this. Wild birds are far better than planted birds. Many bad habits are formed from too many planted birds. The puppies quickly learn that they can catch them. Some will quit pointing, or they may develop a habit of crowding their birds. This is because the dizzied birds won't flush naturally. A pup can seldom catch a wild bird since, if crowded, it will flush.

264

Don't worry if your dog isn't holding point. That will generally come naturally with experience. That is, unless the dog has been allowed to catch the birds. In that case, some training may be necessary. Do not be in too much of a hurry for finished training. A lot of good dogs have been ruined by an over-anxious owner. Such training as "coming when called" and such other obedience as knowing that you mean "no" is good for the dog. Every pup is an individual, and should be trained as such. Give kindness and praise. Remember that being firm will accomplish a lot more than will roughness and harsh treatment.

When the dog approaches two years old, and you see that he is pointing staunchly, it is advisable to consult a good trainer. Breaking a dog is not difficult if it has been brought along properly and the person is experienced. But the age of two is a critical time. And since it is easy to ruin a dog by too much pressure, you should consult an expert.

Bringing along a young dog can be a wonderful and rewarding experience for anyone. You need only a reasonable amount of time and patience. And of course, the time to develop the "know how."

Fld. Ch. Rufus Rastus Johnson Brown, a liver and white dog, bred by Mrs. Nicky Bissell, is shown on point at the 1971 National Open Championship, in which he placed fourth. Handler Lyle Johnson moves forward to flush the bird. The mounted observers are (l. to r.) Ronald Stevenson, owner; Ken Jacobsen, reporter; and Leslie Tichenor, judge.

Ch. Toffe Idoc de Basgard, owned by Dr. J. E. Talbott.

Ch. Sir Jacob of Rey River Ranch, U.D. taking a group placement under the author, handled by Sandra A. Weddell for owner, John G. Helleis. *Kohler photo.*

39

The Obedience Winners

OBEDIENCE IS THE THIRD branch of sport in which Brittanys compete. Somewhat understandably, Brittany competition in obedience trials has lagged behind bench and field. The greatest interest of Brittany owners has been in field trials and in show competition. But show competition has lagged somewhat behind field work, and obedience trials are mostly a part of dog shows.

When the first edition of this book was written, four obedience titles could be won. These were Companion Dog (C.D.), Companion Dog Excellent (C.D.X.), Utility Dog (U.D.) and Tracking Test (T.D.). Dogs can now win awards for advanced work beyond the above titles classes, and can win an Obedience Trial Championship (O.T.Ch.). A Brittany could, of course, score a grand slam by winning field, show and obedience championships.

Fifteen show champions have won U.D. titles. In the following list it will be noted that at least one field and amateur field champion has won a tracking title. American Britts who have won U.D. titles total 55. Of these, 14 were listed in the first edition of this book. Two of the fourteen were show champions. Since that time, 13 more champions have won U.D. degrees.

We repeat here the earlier winners of U.D. titles.

Ch. Diane de Beauch (also Canadian Ch. and U.D. title holder.)
Ch. Pete's Gimlet
Trixie Of Edough
Fluvanna's Buck
My Boy Pepper

Fancy Stepper
Prince Of Spots
Dot Of Belleau
Star Omnion
Yellow Hammer
George's Plain Jess
Penelope Of Robin Drive
Ma-Petite Dor'ee
Gabrielle Du Blanc De Pris

Those winning Utility Degree titles since the original list follow, along with their owners.

Arways Banner McGray, Wayne E. Smith
J J's Special Magic, John and Linda Chokran
Daniel Chico Djohn, Ernest Daniels
Ch. Andrew De Bretagne, Patricia A. John
Pekovich's Ginger Brandy, Anthony W. and Joy Keckovich
Ch. Turner's Crossroad Samantha, Betty J. Bobzien
Ginger Sage of Lafayette, Bobby L. and Sue B. Armstrong
Curtis's I am Sonny, Curt A. Curtis
Autumn's Sweet Gypsey Rose, Linda and William Vesterfelt
Bonny Dune, Jean E. Haworth
Ch. Sir Jacob Of Rey River Ranch, John H. Helleis
Ch. Chocolate Sundae's Jill, George and Dorothy Nordland
Ch. Trailin Travis Of Aquarius, Barbara and Clifford Pantke
Annemarie's Little Taffy, Victor and Annemarie Curtis
Moonbabe's Hilaka, Winifred L. Chrones
Ch. Sequani's Toro Des Collines, Carmen J. Giovacchini
Ch. Molly's A Lady, Bruce M. Wright
Ch. Cinderella Of Lafayette, Bobby and Sue B. Armstrong
Jumping Jenny, Dolores and Carl Goller
Sunshine Brandy, Lawrence Giffin
Breinger's Toby, Mary Ann Breininger
Young's Tache Speckled Sun, Donald E. Young
Austin's Sabrena, Mrs. L. L. Austin
Aspen's Frosty Mora, Nancy Giffin
Come Saturday Morning, Sharon Buchler
Ch. Del Chico Del Prado, Leslie and Donna Casselberry
Ch. Duff's Queen Of Sheba, Mr. and Mrs. Michael Duff
Bazooka Ginger Delight, Cathryn J. and Jeffrey J. Nixon
Taffy, Carey M. Appleby
Ch. Bradach's Dooble Good, Helen and Catherine Hoveison

Ch. Windy Hill's Sweet Bippy (Dual Ch. Lund's Trooper ex Ch. Edgewater's American Beauty), owned by Rich and Mary Sabit. She is shown with her handler Robert Eldridge. *Ritter photo.*

Ch. Windy Hill's Troopers Tuffy (Dual Ch. Lund's Trooper ex Ch. Edgewater's American Beauty), owned by Robert Edwards and bred by Al Langan. *Olson photo.*

Dual Ch. Baron de Brentwood, C.D. (Fld. and Amateur Fld. Ch. Holliday Britt's Ed ex Ch. Nedbalek's Ginger), owned by Wayne Fessenden. *Petrulis photo.*

Rusty's Little Judge, Dennis R. Laird
Beau Jasper Of Langer, Thomas and Mildred Frame
Aimee De Bretagne, Ann M. Sarich and Joy E. Peckovitch
Russel's Peggie, Steve P. Russel
Fld. Ch., AFC Dark Sky, Robert and Carolyn Unger
Ch. Curtis's Midnight Bandit, Curt and Carla Curtis
Aspenwood's Shady Lady, Larry Giffin
Ch. Evansport Brandy Wine, Christine W. Weber
Rita White Shadow, Andrew and Irene Peterson
The Mark XI, Donald E. Zack
Tina Marie XI, Donald E. Zack

At least one dog has won an Obedience Trial Championship. He is Lafayette King Trooper, owned by Bobby and Sue Armstrong. And Fld. Ch., AFC Ja's Susie Towsey has also won a tracking degree to add to her list of titles. Her owners are John and Linda Chokran.

Here are the names and owners of Brittanys who have won Tracking titles.

J J's Special Magic, U.D.T., John and Linda Chokran
Pekovich's Ginger Brandy, U.D.T., Anthony and Joy Peckovich
Curtis's I am Sonny, U.D.T., Curt A. Curtis
Moonbabe's Hilaka, U.D.T., Winnifred L. Chrones.
Autumn Sun, Linda W. Kipp
Ch. J J's Pride N' Joy, U.D.T., John and Linda Chokran
Prince Valiant Spring A'Rival, Floyd, June and Nancy Frame
Curtis's Oregon Trooper, Curtis and Carly Y. Curtis
Lady Bridget XXV, Bill and Hazel Tragese

Ch. Suzette De Brentwood, C.D. (Fld. & Amateur Fld. Ch. Holliday Britt's Ed ex Ch. Nedbalek's Ginger), owned and handled by Wayne Fessenden who is handling her to a win under the late Lee Murray. *Alexander photo.*

40

Obedience Trials
and Training

A BRITTANY SHOULD BE owned first of all for companionship. But people and dogs have always happily expanded that companionship in sport. For an owner and a Brittany there are three branches of sport in the dog game. These are dog shows, field trials and obedience trials.

In the early years of obedience, many people condemned show dogs as being stupid. Many people claimed that mongrels were smarter than purebreds, and that purebred runts were smarter than their show-dog litter mates. But it was quickly realized that obedience-trained dogs could compete against each other at dog shows. And so a fascinating new sport was developed. It became an instant crowd pleaser at the shows. But it did more than that. It became one of the greatest advertisements for purebred dogs. And perhaps more than any other single thing, it taught the public the value and pleasure of a well-trained dog.

The Brittany's destiny has always been the hunting fields and secondly the field trials. But there are owners who, for one reason or another, cannot take their dogs to the field. They may have the time to compete in the shows, but not every dog will be good enough to win a championship, or even championship points. For them, there is still the obedience trial.

A goal for all Brittany owners should be a dual dog—bench and field, bench and obedience or all three. Then the dog and owner will get the most out of their companionship. And they will always be presenting to the public a breed of dog worth owning. They will be advertising the breed by performance, and in ways that words cannot do as effectively.

Victoria At-A-Girl, owned and trained by Jewel Walton. This Brittany has the distinction of being the only living dog to hold three *Dog World* Awards of Canine Distinction. She made this record by winning her C.D., C.D.X. and U.D. degrees in consecutive shows with a composite score of 197. She was twice highest scoring dog in show.

Ch. Miss Sue's Gad-A-Bout, C.D. was a winner on the bench and in obedience competition. The dog is shown winning the Sporting group under the author at the Oak Ridge Kennel Club.

For the most part, obedience trials are held in conjunction with dog shows. Thus, it is possible for a dog to compete in conformation classes and obedience trials at the same time. In England, both dog shows and obedience trials have grown so large that it is seldom possible to hold the two on the same grounds. This may happen in America, and it is already the case at many indoor shows in Canada. But where possible, Brittany owners should take advantage of the joint events.

One constantly hears show people say that obedience training ruins show dogs. This is absurd. The more training one gives to a dog, the better the dog becomes. Experience in the obedience ring gives the dog greater confidence in the conformation ring. Among reasons given for the "ruination" theory are that the obedience dog gaits too close to the handler, and therefore neither freely nor truly, and that when stopped, the dog automatically sits instead of standing. But dogs quickly learn that the show ring is not the obedience test. They will have gained the courage in the obedience ring to gait gaily and correctly in the show ring. And obedience dogs are taught to stand for examination. Finally, the number of dogs that win championships and obedience titles is an obvious proof that obedience training does not hurt the show dog.

Here let us point out again that the well-trained dog is a joy to own. And it will be the pride of every person in the neighborhood in which it lives. Neighbors are often a little hostile toward the dogs on the street, and with good reason. But they love to brag about the well-trained dog down the street, and about the responsible owner who has trained that dog. So obedience training and obedience trials can be a continuous source of joy.

In an earlier chapter, we have pointed out that yard breaking for the field dog is almost identical to obedience training for the show dog. In fact, obedience training developed in the 1930s out of the centuries-old yard-breaking procedures. If you have given your puppy any of the early training outlined in this book, obedience training for competition should be easy.

If, when you read this, your dog is an adult, do not make the excuse that it is too old to train. The old proverb, "You can't teach an old dog new tricks," doesn't apply to dogs. It was invented by men to excuse their own laziness. In the very early beginning of obedience trials, a 10-year-old Dalmatian won all three obedience titles, C.D., C.D.X., and U.D. (Companion Dog, Companion Dog Excellent, and Utility Dog), in one year. Since a Brittany is one of the most easily trained of all dogs, it follows that you can start it at any age. But the younger you start it, the longer you will enjoy its good manners.

You should also try to find a group training class in your neighborhood. Such classes are given all over the United States. Sometimes, the trainers should not be allowed to conduct classes. But the majority will give at least the minimum amount of training in preparation for the novice obedience classes. The value of such classes, aside from the ability and wisdom of the instructors, lies in the fact that your dog must learn to be obedient in the presence of a dozen other dogs, and under other distractions.

If such classes are not available, you can train your dog alone. But you must practice in the presence of neighborhood dogs, at shopping centers where many people are passing by and even when people are tempting the dog in some way—for instance, tempting the dog to get up when you have ordered it to lie down and stay put.

If you train at home, you will need something more than just a book on obedience training. You will need the latest copy of the American Kennel Club's booklet *Obedience Regulations.* Single copies of this can be obtained without charge by writing to the American Kennel Club, 51 Madison Ave., New York, NY, 10010. Since, in a given week, the AKC gets as many as 50,000 letters, address yours to the "Publications Department," or to "Obedience Regulations." This booklet gives the general regulations. And then it very carefully outlines each step of each exercise. It also explains scoring procedures and maximum scores allowed for each exercise or part of it. It also gives, by word and by drawing, specifications for building your own bar, high jump and broad jump standards. The dumbbells used are not easily made at home. But you can purchase these at all dog shows and at some pet shops.

There is some danger in obedience training. This is that you will train so severely as to bore your dog. Or, too much competition may bore the dog, who must repeat the same exercises over and over. Competition in the show ring helps to avoid this. But you must always be careful not to overtrain your dog. This is less of a problem in field work because conditions are always different—different wind conditions, different cover, and so on. But in obedience competition, the tests are always the same, and every effort is made to keep them identical, not only for each dog, but at trial after trial.

There are some slight differences in procedures in Canada, Mexico and Bermuda. So sometimes it helps if you take your dog to one of these countries. Many people do this by arranging to attend the foreign shows while on vacation. In Canada, a club can give two shows in the same building on a weekend. In some cases, three shows are given, so your dog has a chance to complete a title in a single three-day weekend. And, of course, it can win a bench championship at the same show. Bermuda offers four shows in one week during early November and in March. Mexico City has four shows on the same grounds over two successive weekends the last of November and early December.

These shows offer sufficient differences to keep your dog excited and interested. They offer you a chance to win foreign titles. And you have unusual opportunities for vacation fun and sightseeing at the same time.

In closing this chapter, we are quoting the purpose of obedience trials, as given in the AKC booklet *Obedience Regulations.*

Obedience trials are a sport and all participants should be guided by the principles of good sportsmanship both in and outside of the ring. The purpose of obedience trials is to demonstrate the usefulness of the purebred dog as a companion of man, not merely the dog's ability to follow specified routines in the obedience ring. While all contestants in a class are required to perform the same exercises in substantially the same way so that relative quality of the various performances may be compared and scored, the basic objective of obedience trials is to produce dogs that have been trained and conditioned always to behave in the home, in public places, and in the presence of other dogs, in a manner that will reflect credit on the sport of obedience. The performances of dog and handler in the ring must be accurate and correct and must conform to the requirements of these regulations. However, it is also essential that the dog demonstrate willingness and enjoyment of its work, and smoothness and naturalness on the part of the handler are to be preferred to a performance based on military precision and peremptory commands.

To this, we can only add that when you get into the obedience ring for the first time, the chances are the dog will make fewer mistakes than will you. So don't expect to make winning performances until you have gained plenty of experience yourself.

41

The American Brittany Club

THE AMERICAN BRITTANY CLUB is a member club of The American Kennel Club. It is also recognized by the American Field as the official breed sponsor. The American Brittany Club is composed of many regional or local clubs, located from coast to coast and from north to south.

Brittany owners will find a breed club reasonably close. Those clubs hold regular meetings to discuss breed problems. They conduct training sessions, fun trials and informal match shows. Each club also holds a licensed field trial in the spring and in the fall of each year. Many also hold licensed unbenched shows, either in conjunction with one of their field trials, or at other times of the year.

Membership in one of the regional clubs carries with it an automatic membership in the American Brittany Club. Cost is $15.00 a year. Memberships run from January 1st to December 31st. A half-year membership is available after July 1st for $11.00. You can join a regional club in your area. Or, if no club is close, you can join the American Brittany Club as a member at large. Thus, Brittany owners in Canada, Mexico, Alaska or the Caribbean Islands can join. Hawaii has its own regional club.

If you elect to join a regional club, you make application to join directly to it. If you wish to join the parent club as a member at large, then make your application directly to it. The address is: The American Brittany Club, 2036 N. 48th Ave., Omaha, NE 68104.

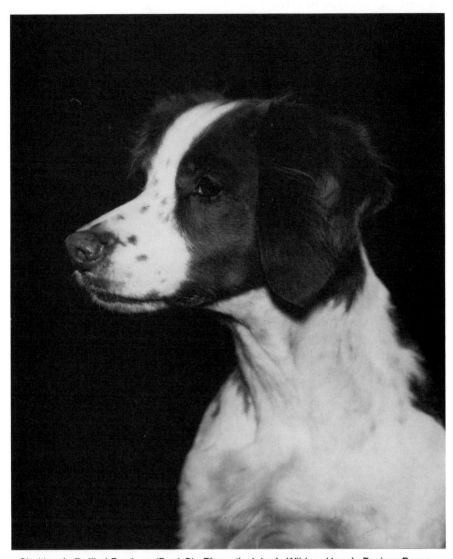

Ch. Hope's Ruffled Feathers (Dual Ch. Ffynant's Joker's Wild ex Hope's Desiree Berna-dotte), owned and shown by Tom and Judy Tighe, Hope's Brittanies. "Feather" made the front cover of the *Pure-Bred Dogs—American Kennel Gazette* showing her front movement to promote the slide shows on breed standards. Her rear movement and head study for expression are also part of the slide show. *Ashbey photo.*

The parent club publishes a monthly magazine called *The American Brittany*. Either type of membership entitles you to receive the magazine without cost. This magazine is sent to members only, although single copies can be bought for $1.50 each. The magazine is one of the most distinguished breed publications in America. It has repeatedly won national honors in the annual competitions sponsored by the Dog Writers Association of America.

In 1958 more than 50 breed magazines were submitted in the awards competitions of this organization. At that time, Dr. S. Allen Truex was editor. The judges gave the magazine first place. This is extraordinary, if one considers that Dr. Truex had to put the magazine together during whatever time a dog fancier and a doctor has to spare. Twice since, under Dr. Fred Z. White as editor, the magazine won either first or honorable mention. Again, publishing and editing the magazine had to be done in Dr. White's spare time. Dr. White also won honors for special articles contributed to the magazine. Mrs. Nicky Bissell continued the high quality of the magazine. She is one of the greatest statisticians in the history of any breed. The magazine continued its distinguished editorship with Rheta Cartmell, and now Mrs. Ella Conable. It should be said that no club magazine, for any breed, has had so great a group of editors.

Both the magazine and the American Brittany Club have grown so large that it has been impossible for one person to be executive secretary and magazine editor. Mrs. Velma Tiedeman of the Nebraska Club has taken over the job of executive secretary. And Mrs. Ella Conable, the latest to be named to the life membership list, has become editor of the magazine.

Given below are two lists of life members. The first is a list of those elected to this honorable position who have passed over to the happy hunting grounds where all Brittany lovers can have their dogs forever. The second is a list of living life members, showing the year they were elected and the region from which they come.

Deceased Life Members

	Year elected
Dr. Chester Keough	1942
René Joubert	1942
Lawrence Richardson	1942
Alan Stuyvesant	1952
Paul Dawson	1951
Jack Mayer	1951
Jerome Halle	1955
Walter Kleeman	1956
Coy Conwell	1956
Lucien Ufford	1957
Howard Clements	1960

William E. Averill	1960
James B. Bell	1964
Dr. Fred Z. White	1964
W. E. Stevenson	1965
Bob Buick	1965
Howard Crippen	1968
Thurmond McWarter, Sr.	1968
Henry Holleyoak	1968
Jack Whitworth	1970
Clarence Goering	1972
B. Len Rix	1977
LaReine Pittman	1978

Life Members—1986

1974	Nicky Bissell, Sherwood, Oregon	Oregon
1969	Dr. R. C. Busteed, Canyon, Texas	Member at Large
1985	Ella Conable, Orchard Park, New York	Pennsylvania
1984	Richard Culbert, Sioux Falls, South Dakota	Ringneck
1980	Amos Greer, Gladwin, Michigan	Michigan-Saginaw
1974	Lee Holman, Whittington, Illinois	Illinois
1976	John G. Lee, North Port, Florida	Central Florida
1976	Ellen Lee, North Port, Florida	Central Florida
1969	John W. Lee, Zionsville, Indiana	Greater Indianapolis
1973	Ruth Lee, Zionsville, Indiana	Greater Indianapolis
1981	Ejner Lund, Napa, California	Northern California
1980	Everett Metzger, Tacoma, Washington	Oregon
1971	Gerald Price, Concordia, Kansas	Midwest
1944	Maxwell Riddle, Ravenna, Ohio	Ohio
1975	George Wilson, Flint, Michigan	Michigan-Saginaw

There are 88 functioning regional clubs in the United States, including Hawaii. They are members of the American Brittany Club. As in any organization, officers change. Those wishing to join can apply directly to the American Brittany Club, or to the nearest regional club.

To obtain the names and addresses of the current officers of the American Brittany Club, write to the American Kennel Club, 51 Madison Ave., New York, NY 10010. From the American Brittany Club you may obtain information regarding the regional clubs.

This gathering of early Brittany pioneers includes (from left) Ed Borger with Edandot Gilly, judge Jerome Halle, Paul Bone and Nicky Bissell with Juchoir Tuffy, owned by James and Helen Rookard. Gilly was Best of Opposite Sex at the 1961 ABC Specialty and Tuffy was Best of Breed.

42

Some Thoughts on Color

IN CHAPTER 4, WE wrote about the tailless Brittany. At one time, a controversy raged in France on this subject. The argument even spread to the United States and Canada. Many people thought that a dog born with a tail should not be registered as a Brittany. A tailless dog was to be forever a mark of the purity of the breed, as well as a distinctive feature.

Had such a provision been kept in the standard, all other features, including hunting desire, nose, pointing instinct, stamina and coat would have been sacrificed for a feature that has nothing to do with hunting ability. Eventually, good sense won out and the argument was dropped. As an aside, in the early days in the United States some converts from pointer and setter ranks wanted a long-tailed Brittany. This idea, too, was finally dropped, though not until after long and sometimes bitter arguments.

Now a somewhat similar situation exists as to color. Recently, a Brittany oldtimer said to the author "Juan Pugibet had those awful liver-and-white dogs." Well, there was nothing wrong with them. And in any case, Pugibet had both colors.

The early Brittanys in the American Kennel Club records were listed as being of various colors. Among them one finds orange-and-white, white-and-orange, liver-and-white, white-and-liver, red-and-white, white-and-red, lemon-and-white and mahogany-and-white. There were dogs spotted with these colors, ticked with them and there were roans. All of these dogs had one ability in common. They could hunt. The original prejudice against any but orange-and-white—or white-and-orange—seems to have come from Alan Stuyvesant. And because he was the greatest of all importers, orange-and-

Fld. Ch. Fisty
Miss Kaer, owned
by Nathan
Butchard.

An early liver and white, Gar Roux, bred by Donald L. Benjamin.

Ch. Britt A Cocoa (Field Ch. Radar's Buc Shot De Ran ex Ch. Auten's Morning Star), bred by Ronald E. and L. Carol Auten and owned by Darlene and Anthony Carlesimo. Shown by Ron Auten, Agent.
Alverson photo.

Ch. IdaBritt's Freddie. He is pictured completing his championship at the Northern California specialty under judge Rutledge Gilliland, handler Frank Houska. He is owned by Bob and Joann Reimers. *Bennett Associates photo.*

white came to dominate the American sporting scene. These dogs simply were numerically superior.

The great performances of Gwennec de l'Argoat, under the handling of Hall of Famer René Joubert, quite naturally focused the attention of Midwest sportsmen on orange-and-white dogs. Howard Clements and Allamuchy Valley Luke had a similar influence in the Chicago area. Fenntus, Gwennec's Pascey II and others of that day also tilted sportsmen in favor of the orange-and-whites.

Still, the other colors were fairly well represented. John C. Weiler was a pioneer breeder who seems to be nearly forgotten today. On December 8, 1935, his Franche's Smarty (a daughter of Franche du Cosquerou), whelped a litter that included Margot de Basgard, a mahogany-and-white bitch. The sire was Keryvon de Basgard. Weiler had both colors, and Franche's Smarty produced both. When bred to Gwennec de l'Argoat, she produced Dr. Chester Keough's noted Mirabile Dictu, an orange-and-white. Weiler sold the mahogany-and-white, Spring Hill Sandy, to Julien Clark of Natchez, Mississippi.

Louis de la Fleche, one of the early importers and pioneers, bought dogs from l'Abbe Feurgard. And from them he got both orange-and-white and liver-and-white. Basgard got both colors because l'Abbe Feurgard bred for performance, and without regard to color. Keryvon de Basgard was orange-and-white, Keryvette liver-and-white.

Juan Pugibet and Dr. Keough had the same philosophy. Thus, Dr. Keough imported the liver-and-white Leltic de Pradalan from Jean Quemener. Leltic (often misspelled Lettic) was by Fanch de Pradalan out of Follette II de Pradalan.

Weiler's Pouponne du Stormally was also mahogany-and-white. Pouponne was whelped January 19, 1936, by Franche du Cosquerou out of Hase de la Casa Blanca. Thus, Pouponne represents a crossing of the best blood of the dogs imported by Thebaud and Pugibet.

Howard P. Cline's Ch. Benedictine MacEochaidh was the first liver-and-white to win a bench championship. Whelped September 9, 1941, the sire was Idoc de Cornouaille, the dam Leltic de Pradalan. Benedictine was the tenth dog to win a show championship.

Here, perhaps, there should be a word of explanation. Dual Champion Britt of Bellows Falls, bred by Edgar Lutz of Montrose, Pennsylvania, and owned by Lucien Ufford of Bellows Falls, Vermont, was the first dog to win an American Kennel Club field championship and the first to win a dual title. He was whelped July 15, 1941. There is an old saying that "records live, opinions die." But in the case of Britt of Bellows Falls, all the records seem to be wrong. The American Kennel Club stud book, which is the official breeding record, lists Britt as having been white with liver markings. Neither the author nor anyone else who personally remembers Britt considers this to be correct.

Moreover, Britt was by Kaer de Cornouaille out of Oged of Casa Blanca. Both were orange-and-white. It would be impossible to get liver-and-white from such a breeding.

Earlier records have listed Kaymore's Megs as having been the first liver-and-white dual champion. If Britt of Bellows Falls was truly white-and-liver, then he would rank as both the first liver-and-white field champion and the first liver-and-white dual champion.

However, the earlier records are wrong in another respect. Dr. R. C. Busteed's Broad Archer of Richmont is listed as a dual champion. This is an error. He was a field champion only. He was also liver-and-white, and he was certainly one of the great field dogs of his day.

To return from this rather lengthy aside, there have been—and are—some very great liver-and-white dogs. And we have shown that some of the very good producers yielded both colors. The rule must always be to breed for type and performance, and both come in both colors. Those, therefore, who hold a prejudice against one color may be limiting their breeding success, and may be harming the breed as well.

Earlier, we have mentioned Dr. R. C. Busteed. He is a professor of genetics at the West Texas State University at Canyon. He is surely one of the world's greatest geneticists, and he has been "practicing what he preaches" for 30 years. His success is legendary. Dr. Busteed has bred brother and sister together for at least 15 generations. This is the closest possible inbreeding. Others who have tried this have generally failed. Often, they have lost size and breeding potency, and sometimes disposition or basic health. Dr. Busteed's dogs have lost none of these.

In this section, we are interested only in color. Since the early days, enough liver-and-white Brittanys have performed brilliantly to prove that color is not truly a factor in field performance. In the chapter on the Brittany Spaniel in France, a French breeder reported that orange-and-whites had died out in North Africa because they could not stand the intense heat. On the other hand, the liver-and-white dogs prospered. It is difficult to believe this, except as it proves that the liver-and-whites have stamina and nose not affected by intense heat. Aside from this, behavior and performance are too complex to ascribe them to one factor, in this case color. Orange-and-white dogs taken to North Africa may have come from a strain that carried factors for weak performance in heat that other orange-and-whites would not have inherited.

In the United States and Canada, black is a disqualifying color in Brittanys. But this offers no problem. American and Canadian dogs are totally free, hereditarily, of any gene for black. Unless someone should import a French Brittany that carries a black gene, there can never be a black Brittany in either country. As Dr. Busteed has pointed out, any Brittany in America that shows up with black is a mongrel. Should this happen, the situation

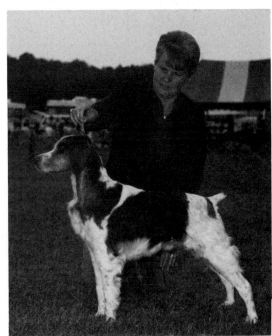

Ch. Starline's Pretty Boy Pete (Ch. Mitzy's Blue Ridge River Cholly ex Ch. J Bi's Precious Little Starlet, C.D.X.), bred by Carol Ann D. and Joseph W. McCabe and owned by Carol Ann D. McCabe and Irvin Harris.
Alverson photo.

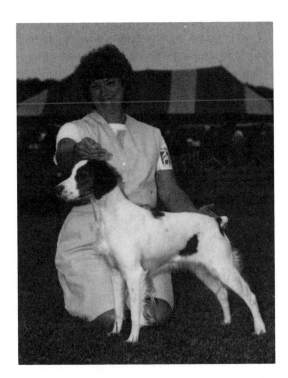

Ch. Kell-Kawn's Kade-Did (Ch. Do Well's J B Jason, C.D. ex Cast-a-Britt Jill De Bandit), bred by Dianne D. and Allison L. Park and owned by Sheryl M. Ball.
Alverson photo.

should be reported to the American Kennel Club, and an investigation made so that the dog's registration papers can be destroyed.

The current policy of the American Kennel Club is to register any dogs whose papers seem to be in order regardless of disqualifying factors. Thus, the AKC will register a white Boxer even though such a dog would be disqualified in the show ring. This permits unscrupulous breeders to cut the throats of legitimate breeders by advertising—and selling—"rare white Boxers" at prices that cannot be obtained for properly colored dogs. But, since black cannot occur in pure bred Brittanys in North America, the presence of black would indicate a mismating. If, then, the matter were to be brought to the attention of the American Kennel Club, it is possible that the registration of that litter, and its puppies, would be cancelled.

Liver is the result of a gene that is dominant over one for orange, so that a dog with both genes will invariably be liver. If two liver dogs, both of which contain hidden genes for orange, are mated, some orange pups may result. Such pups are pure for orange, and can only produce orange. Factors for roan and ticking appear to be different, that is, to differ from each other.

This chapter is not meant to be a treatise on genetics. Its purpose is only to try to place the question of color in its proper perspective. There are far more important matters for breeders of Brittanys to consider. These are stamina, nose, pointing instinct, intelligence and shyness, to name but a few.

43

American Brittany Registrations

AS TOLD EARLIER, J. R. Joubert, brother of René, told about buying Brittanys for Louis Thebaud. He brought two of them to this country, and accompanied Mr. Thebaud to the American Kennel Club, which promptly recognized the breed and registered the dogs. Edir Du Mesnil was the first to be registered, and was given the number 949896. The second dog was Clap de Callac, named after a Breton Village. The time was September, 1934. Edir was highly nervous and was subject to attacks Mr. Joubert described as madness. He thus was a failure. Clap was stolen before he had a chance to prove himself.

That first year, ten Brittanys were registered, and the next year seven were. Thereafter, the breed began a slow increase before increasing at a pace few breeds have equaled. In 1950, 1,098 were registered, and in 1954, 2,425. These figures do not tell the whole story. In many cases, and probably more often than not, not all the puppies in the litter will be individually registered. Buyers may take puppies not considered of a quality to be used for breeding. Registration papers are lost. Puppies may go through several ownerships without proper endorsement of papers, and then cannot be registered. Also, and particularly in the beginning years, owners registered in the Field Dog Stud Book. Other pups were often sold to Canadians, and so were lost to American Kennel Club registry. The year 1976 will serve as an example. Brittany registrations reached an all-time high of 20,222. Yet only 5,942 litters were registered. This would mean that, if every pup in every litter was

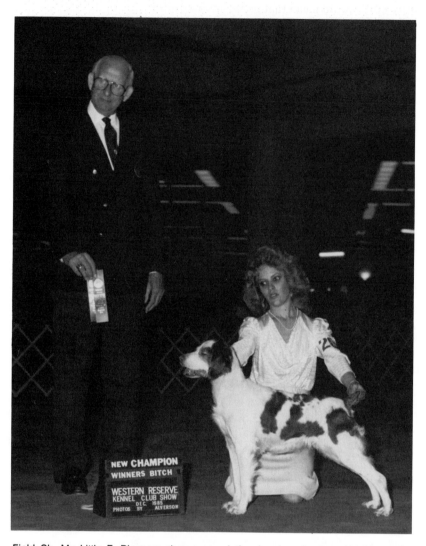

Field Ch. My Little F. Blossom shown completing her bench championship at the Western Reserve KC show, December 1985, handled by Bobbi Kinley under judge Edmund J. Kauffman, Jr. This win made her a dual champion at the remarkable age of almost 12 years. *Alverson photo.*

registered, it would mean that bitches averaged less than four pups per litter.

Given below are year-by-year Brittany registrations, as published by the American Kennel Club.

1934	10	1961	5,476
1935	7	1962	6,146
1936	39	1963	6,660
1937	51	1964	7,247
1938	46	1965	7,644
1940	56	1966	8,314
1941	56	1967	9,464
1942	90	1968	9,620
1943	91	1969	10,761
1944	129	1970	13,400
1945	316	1971	15,622
1946	622	1972	16,644
1947	723	1973	18,503
1948	918	1974	18,503
1949	985	1975	19,188
1950	1,098	1976	20,222
1951	1,319	1977	19,267
1952	1,579	1978	18,478
1953	1,937	1979	17,008
1954	2,425	1980	17,146
1955	2,719	1981	17,411
1956	3,313	1982	17,349
1957	3,614	1983	18,433
1958	3,946	1984	17,048
1959	4,777	1985	15,048
1960	5,000		

44

How to Name
Your Brittany

THE PROBLEM OF NAMING dogs is often extremely puzzling to newcomers to the dog game and has no simple answers. This is because no two dogs can have the same name unless sufficient time has passed so that the first dog is dead. At this writing, Brittanys are exceeding 15,000 registrations a year. Each of the 15,000 must have names not previously used, except as will be noted. Now, if you add up the registrations for 15 years, you will have an idea of the problem.

In general, people want simple names for their dogs. Often they try to insist that the dog's call name be used. Yet the chances that the American Kennel Club would allow such names as Prince, Duke, Joe, Princess, Duchess or Lady are zero. One Brittany was, somewhat miraculously, allowed to be registered as Della. But with rare exceptions such as that and those that follow, compound names must be used.

Because of their color, common Brittany names have been Rusty, Freckles, Ginger and Sandy. You might be able to use one of these names alone. But you would have to expect that the American Kennel Club would add a numeral after the name. Thus, there have been at least 14 Brittanys named Ginger—Ginger II to Ginger 14. And there is a Freckles VI. All these names, by the way, have been used for dogs of both sexes.

Popular names for female Brittanys have included Sue, Susie, Kate, Princess, Duchess, Bonnie, Lady, Queen, Penny and Nell. Most popular for males have been King, Prince, Duke, Joe, Buddy, Beau and Ranger. They are excellent for call names because they can be spoken in a "command" tone of voice. But they must be combined with other name parts. For example, Sweet Sue of Valley Britt, Speedy Lady of Hayhurst Farm and Dual Champion Doctor Joe of Kaymore.

The name combinations are worked out in many ways. Fred and Ann White developed the kennel name *Fredan.* Edward and Dorothy Borger combined their nicknames to make *Edandot.* Henry Holleyoak used *Holley Haven.* Dr. Frank McHugh, the nutritionist, used *UltraMend,* the name of the food supplement he had developed. The pioneer Walter B. Kleeman named his kennel *Klemanor.* And John W. Lee made his *Leeway.* John G. and Ellyn Lee made theirs *Joel.* Some have used their own names. Thomas Passamonte has used *Passamonte.* Elmer Flack used *Flack's Tip Top Kennels.* And E. and Gilda Lund use *Lund,* as in Dual Ch. Lund's Trooper. Kennels have used valleys, cities, states and even streets. Examples of the former are *Allamuchy Valley, Albedo Valley, Olentangy Valley, Vitchie Valley,* and *Fontaine Vallee.* There are *Spindle City Shorty, Jersey Jeff,* and *Kansas Kid.* The pioneer breeder Jack L. Whitworth used *Avono* because he lived at Avon Lake, Ohio.

Years ago, the American Kennel Club would grant—and register—a kennel name for the life of the breeder. The Club felt then, as it does now, that when a person applies for a kennel name, he or she is intent upon becoming a serious breeder. But studies have shown that only a small number of people remain in the breeding field for longer than five years. In one case, the AKC protected a name under the lifetime rule even though its owner had been in an insane asylum for six years. It will now register for a fee a kennel name for five years, with renewal privileges. If, however, the owner of the name does not use it for six years, renewal might be refused, or the name might be granted to another kennel.

Many people make up a kennel name and do not bother to register it. They can use these names so long as they are not registered by others. In one case, a man had used an unregistered kennel name for 20 years. Then he was notified that he could no longer use it. A person in another breed had registered the name. It could happen that even if you use your own name, it could be taken away from you by a person with the same name.

Half a century ago, if you imported a dog from another country, you could change the name in registering the dog with the American Kennel Club. This practice caused tremendous confusion in pedigree keeping, so the AKC banned the practice. If you have a kennel name, you can, under most circumstances, add this to the imported dog's name. For example, Premier De Callac of Pennbritt.

In naming your dog, several other factors should be observed. The first rule is to keep the name simple. Every dog is given a pet, or call, name. If this is a name that carries authority when spoken sharply, so much the better. The

Ch. Copper Jill of Edwards, owned and handled by
R. H. Edwards.

Ch. Cranbrook's Great Decision (Cranbrook's Copper-
clad ex Woodstock's Wild Ginger), bred by Donna M.
Cheek and Linda L. Dark and owned by Janet C. Stewart
and Mary Beth Stewart. *Alverson photo.*

authoritative voice and the sharply called name are major factors in dog control. If the call name fits into the full name, excellent. But remember, you are limited by the American Kennel Club to not more than 25 letters in the name.

Brittany names that fit these suggestions and rules are given here as examples: Gunners Mate of Cyrus, whose call name could be Gunner, Mate, or even Cy or Gun. Jig of Kaymore is an example. So is Meadow Wink Buzz, whose call name could be either Wink or Buzz. There is another reason for using a simple name—it is less likely to be misspelled. Many owners misspell names in registering their dogs. They then ask the AKC to correct this. But once registered, the name will not be changed by the AKC. You will have to use the misspelled name forever.

Newspaper writers unfamiliar with dog names often rebel at both their complexity and length. Newspapers have only limited space to give to reports of dog shows and field trials. Sometimes the complexity of the names has caused an entire field or bench report to be thrown into the wastebasket.

In the early days, Brittany progress was seriously held up because of the unpronounceable and difficult to spell Breton names. Some of the names that have been the despair of newspaper and magazine writers are MacEochaidh, Aotrou, l'Argoat, Enqueue and Ch. Count Guilliwime De Gwennec, C.D. Some of these names were, of course, given to the dogs in France. When imported, they had to be used here. They have survived in part in the names of some of their descendents for an important reason. If part of the name of a sire can be used in your dog's name, then the line from which it comes is readily recognized by all in the breed.

This brings up another point. If a kennel name is registered, you cannot use the name without permission from the owner. The owner of the registered name may grant permission to use the kennel name. This may be done if the breeder feels the dog has a championship in its future. Permission to use the name must be written in by the registered breeder on space provided on the registration application.

There is an axiom among breeders of Thoroughbreds that "No great horse has a bad name." This is only true most of the time. And many racing failures have great names. Yet the point is worth bearing in mind. In the names listed above, the dogs survived their names to become great. But, while Suzie Woozie may be a child's cute pet name for a pet, it is no name for a Brittany champion.

Because of their supreme worth as field dogs, Brittanys offer many opportunities for attractive and appropriate names. Some particularly successful ones follow: Betty Briarhopper, Lady of Quail, Grouse Feathers, Zipp's Feather Merchant, Pacolet's Bushmaster, Prairie Ranger, Ultra-Mend Birdy Biddy and Britt Afield Chummy. Thomas Melville used Fun Galore as a kennel name. It was a perfect title for promoting the breed.

Many a man registers his dogs in his wife's name. This is a courteous and gallant thing to do. But in one respect it is wrong. The report of a dog's victory in a magazine or local newspaper could mean the sale of both puppies and grown dogs. Often, however, the prospective buyer cannot reach the owner because the wife's name is not listed in the phone book. This is, of course, also the problem with registered kennel names. But there are two possible solutions to this. One is to list one's name after the kennel name in parenthesis. Thus: Homewood Kennels, Reg. (J. R. Holmes). The other is to list the wife's name in the telephone directory, or to list the kennel in the yellow pages of the phone book.

45

AKC Hunting Tests for Brittanys

BRITTANYS NOW HAVE A fourth sport in which they can compete. The first three of course are field trials, dog shows and obedience trials. Now there is an AKC licensed hunting test. It is designed for the average pointing dog who is just shy of the quality and training needed to compete in licensed field trials.

Dogs work in braces in a five-acre field that has enough cover to hold planted birds. Pheasants, chukar and quail can be used, also pigeons. The type of game must be listed in the entry forms. The dogs are allowed 15 minutes in which to find and point the game. Handlers are on foot, but the judges may use horses. The dogs are scored on hunting, bird-finding ability, pointing, trainability and retrieving. The latter does not apply to junior dogs.

All dogs must be registered with the American Kennel Club. Ribbons are awarded. They are of a different color from those used in the other three sports. The American Kennel Club has a printed booklet, *Regulations for AKC Hunting Tests for Pointing Breeds.* Single copies can be obtained free by writing to the AKC at 51 Madison Ave., New York, NY 10010. If ordered in quantity, the cost is 25 cents per copy.

June 19, 1944.

Mr. Jack L. Whitworth, Sec'y,
American Brittany Club,
Nagel Road,
Avon, Ohio.

Dear Mr. Whitworth:

        I am in receipt of your letter of
June 6th, with its enclosures.

        I am certainly glad to learn that
you have finally been able to accomplish the amalga-
mation of the two Brittany Spaniel clubs. It is a
real job to do a thing of this kind and the documentary
evidence shows that a real job was done in this case.

        I will bring the merger before the
Directors of the Kennel Club at their July meeting and
I have no fear that it will not be approved; the name
of the member club being changed from the Brittany
Spaniel Club of North America to that of the American
Brittany Club.

                    Very truly yours,

                    H. D. Bixby,
                    Executive Vice-President.

hdb:jb

July 14, 1944.

Mr. Jack L. Whitworth, Secretary,
American Brittany Club,
Nagel Road,
Avon, Ohio.

Dear Mr. Whitworth:

        The Board of Directors of the American
Kennel Club at their meeting on July 11 approved the change
in name of our member club from that of the Brittany Spaniel
Club of North America to the "American Brittany Club".

        There was no occasion for them to formally
approve the merger, but they asked me to write you and the
officials who had charge of working out the merger, complimenting
them on the very efficient and complete way in which the matter
was accomplished. It is a pleasure to see such careful work
done as was evident in this case, and I wish to compliment you
upon finally effecting the change, which I sincerely believe
will be for the betterment of the Brittany Spaniel.

                    Very truly yours,

                    H.D. Bixby,
                    Executive Vice-President.

HDB:PBE.

**These letters from the American Kennel Club are part of the correspondence
concerning the merger of the Brittany Spaniel Club of North America and
the American Brittany Club.**

Appendix

THE MATERIAL THAT FOLLOWS is taken directly from the files of the American Kennel Club. It is presented here through the courtesy of A. Hamilton Rowan Jr., former secretary of the American Kennel Club. These records give the organization date of the Brittany Spaniel Club, and the later change in its officers.

In a letter dated May 1, 1944, Laurence Richardson reported to Jack Whitworth that Miss Clara Perry had escaped from France on the last ship to leave before France fell to the Germans.

Mr. Richardson, an army officer, had just been placed on inactive duty for the duration of the war. Louis de la Fleche had returned to France. Apparently, he had taken the club's files with him, and he could not be reached by mail. We quote here from Mr. Richardson's letter.

> I have no list of the old club members. I find a letter dated May 10, 1939, from Mr. Stuyvesant which says: "Unfortunately we have not got M. de la Fleche's files. I don't know whether he took them away to Europe with him, but Mr. Thebaud, when he asked me to take over the reorganization of the club, was unable to find them."

Later, as will be seen, Mr. Whitworth was able to reach M. de la Fleche, and did get his approval for the merger of the two clubs.

BRITTANY SPANIEL

Admitted to the American Kennel Club Stud Book at the August 1934 Board Meeting. Standard of perfection received from the French Kennel Club in July 1934.

Translation of the Standard of Perfection sent in by Miss Clara G. Perry approved by the American Kennel Club—March 12, 1935.

Mr. Arthur F. Jones wrote the Article on the Brittany Spaniel which appeared in the 1935 edition of Pure-Bred Dogs.

Mr. Louis A. Thebaud was the person who brought up the question of recognizing this breed.

American Brittany Club

CLUB NAME — LICENSED ✓ — MEMBER ✓ — LOCATION

SHOW DATES	JUDGES APPROVED	PROOFS RETURNED	PREMIUM LIST CHECKED	FEE RECEIVED	DEPOSIT RETURNED	SUPT.	O.T.	REMARKS
Nov. 27, 1943	11-4	11-9	✓	$25 11-8-43.		Riddle		
" 11, 1944	8-15	10-4						
" 9+10, 1945	8-20	10-5	✓					
" 8, 1946	9-6	10-3	✓					Amherst Fined $10.
" 28, 1947	10-29	10-29	✓			S.S.		Fined $10
" 19, 1948	9-20	9-20	✓			S.S.		
May 16, 1949	3-1	3-29		$15 4-1-49?				
Nov. 11, 1949	9-1	9-22		$25 dep. } 9-25				
" 3, 1950				$25 dep. } 9-25 $15 fee				Ravenna, Ohio.
Dec. 1, 1950	8-16	8		$25 dep. 1/10 pd $50 rcd 3-15-51		S.S.		Carbondale, Ill.
Nov. 26, 1951	9-21	10/8		$25 dep. 1/10 $25 rcd 8-22		S.S.		
" 30, 1952	7-30			$15 8-13 1-28-53				
" 8, 1952		10-7						

SEE NEW CARD

11C-1M 6-49

JOINT RESOLUTION BY

The Board of Directors of the American Brittany Club, hereinafter referred to as the ABC, and the Board of Directors and/or properly authorized agents and/or highest available ranking officers of the Brittany Spaniel Club of North America, hereinafter referred to as the BSC of NA.

Whereas, the ABC and the BSC of NA have each held a meeting according to the constitution of their respective clubs, and

Whereas, the ABC and the BSC of NA have each independently considered their activities affecting themselves, their members, the other Brittany spaniel clubs and all other organizations having an interest in the Brittany spaniel, and

Whereas, the BSC of NA, a member club of the American Kennel Club, has not been active for several years and has not shown any interest in the promotion of Brittany spaniels, bench shows or field trials, and

Whereas, the BSC of NA is not in a position to fully discharge its duties to the Brittany spaniel breed, its members, owners and breeders, and

Whereas, the ABC, an active club of Brittany spaniel owners and breeders, and recognized by the American Field (F. D. S. B.), has been active and is able to continue to be actively helpful to owners and breeders of Brittany spaniels, its members and non-members; and

Whereas, the ABC is unable otherwise, at the present time, to obtain free action as the parent club, and fully discharge its duties to breeders and owners of Brittany spaniels and its members, and

Whereas, at the present time, neither the BSC of NA or the ABC are able to obtain complete recognition and become the approved authority of the breed in this country;

Be it Hereby Resolved, that

1. The ABC and BSC of NA are separately and jointly in favor of a merger of the two clubs.
2. Such merger should be dependent upon a majority vote of each qualified member of each club.
3. For the purpose of convenience, the vote shall be taken by closed ballot, jointly, for each club.
4. Each club shall count the ballots from their members independently from those of the other club.
5. A majority shall be required by each club to enable the ABC and BSC of NA to effect a merger.
6. A majority shall mean a majority of ballots returned, except when, due to conditions of war, a ballot unreturned from a member in the armed forces, if entitled to a vote, shall be construed to mean a vote against the merger.
7. Should the members of each club indicate, as above, that a merger is favored, such merger shall take effect not more than 60 days following the announcement to all voting members of the results.
8. Not less than 10 or more than 14 days shall be allowed from the time the ballots are mailed to the time the ballots are counted.
9. Ballots shall be numbered and each eligible voter assigned a number, a complete list of voters with their addresses and numbers shall be supplied to Mr. Frank L. Grant, 145 E. 209th St., Euclid, Ohio, who shall have the duty of checking and mailing the ballots and to whom the ballots must be returned. A notarized statement of the results shall be furnished the secretaries of each club by Mr. Grant, but the actual ballots shall be sealed and remain in his possession.
10. Ballots should be clearly printed to indicate their purpose, identical ballots being supplied to all eligible voters, by mail, of both clubs.
11. All records of above action are to be kept in a safety deposit box for a period of 7 years under the name of ballot supervisor, the expenses of which are to be carried by the ABC.
12. There shall be no contest of the ballots after 60 days following the merger.

Be it Further Resolved, that

1. The two clubs will become one.
2. The revised organization shall be known as the American Brittany Club and shall operate under the Constitution of the original American Brittany Club as of January 1, 1944.
3. No changes in the constitution, mentioned above, be made until after the next annual election, which shall be postponed to such date as to make it possible to hold a general meeting at the same time as the Bench Show and Field Trial of 1944 sponsored by the original American Brittany Club.

301

4. All offices of the revised American Brittany Club be held by the present officers of the original American Brittany Club as of this date until the 1944 general election.

5. All active members of the Brittany Spaniel Club of North America be automatically admitted to paid up membership of the revised ABC for the year, and entitled to all rights and privileges equal to those of the members of the original ABC.

6. All officers now holding office with the BSC of NA shall be considered as still holding such office jointly until next election with the present officers of the ABC, wherever there are similar offices in both organizations.

7. The function of the officers, until next election, shall be as follows:

   (a) President: The officer holding this office in the original ABC shall continue to retain all former duties and functions, and shall in all cases be the presiding officer. In case the president's power to vote is ever called upon, it shall be paired with that of his jointly holding officer from the BSC of NA before it is counted.

   (b) All other officers representing the two clubs hold the same relationship to each other as the two presidents.

   (c) The officers from the original ABC shall, in all cases, until election, be the functioning officers.

   (d) The officers from the BSC of NA shall hold what amounts to honorary office, whose assistance may be called upon by his ABC counterpart, but whose policy forming duties and powers, until next election, are purely veto in character, in which case they may pair off their votes against those of their ABC counterparts.

8. The new American Brittany Club shall apply for, and be empowered to. transfer, with the approval of the American Kennel Club, all parent membership rights and privileges of the AKC to itself from the Brittany Spaniel Club of North America.

9. Such AKC membership transfer shall not involve any transfer of funds, the AKC being empowered to credit the new ABC with the membership funds now held by AKC.

10. No act or action by any member or officer shall be construed as obligating or cancelling or transferring of obligations or funds of any member, officer or club to any other member, officer or club, except as mentioned above.

11. The transfer of ownership of the membership fee deposited with the AKC shall have no effect, past, present or future upon obligations to or by members of, officers of or the organizations of the ABC or the BSC of NA.

12. As soon as merger is effected, a commission of not more than 3 men be appointed by the original ABC president, and approved by the highest available ranking officer of the original BSC of NA, and instructed to clarify the standards of the Brittany spaniel, with explanatory notes, for adoption by the new ABC and the American Kennel Club, such work to be completed and ready for submission to the club one month before the next annual meeting.

NOTE: Original, used above, applies to status immediately before merger of either club.

Signed by

Jack L. Whitworth, Secretary
American Brittany Club

Louis N. de la Fleche, Secretary
Brittany Spaniel Club of N. America

Revised List of Members of the Brittany Spaniel Club of
North America and the American Brittany Club Now Merged
and Known as the

American Brittany Club
(January 1, 1944)

Adams, Mrs. Katherine
Ady, A. H.
Ady, Mildred
Alford, Mrs. S. E.
Ashworth, R. D.
Averill, Edgar W.
Baldridge, Raymond H.
Barcroft, Gladys
Barcroft, W. H.*
Batson, Dr. G. C.
Becht, William J.
Becker, Dr. R.
Benjamin, Donald L.
Blohm, Wallace
Bray, Dr. Harry A.
Britton, E. D.
Brown, Thomas M.
Burnham, Mike
Burnside D. R.
Busteed, Dr. Robert
Clements, Howard P.
Cline, Hal P.
Conover, H. B.
Conwell, Coy M.
Cooley, Dr. R. M.
Corbin, George A.
Cox, Thomas W.
Cullen, Jack
Danforth, R. E.
Dasher, Don E.
Dell, Kenneth
Denne, Walter
Detmold, G. W.
Doerr, J. Paul
Elliot, Dr. E. S.
Erhardt, George*
Evans, Scott
Feeley, James
Feeley, Mrs. Mildred
Ferguson, Sen. Homer
Felt, Harold B.
de la Fleche, Louis
Frank, C. E.
French, Lee I.
Fisher, H. J.
Fitzpatrick, Thomas C.
Floyd, L. B.
Forthofer, Dr. C. H.
Galloway, Edgar B.
Gayek, Bill
Gee, Joseph Sr.
Germain, U. E.
Gillen, J. J.
Gillen, Tommy*

Hacquoil, James A.
Haehnle, Casper
Halle, Jerome N.*
Hamill, James L. III
Hamill, Dorothy B.
Hanlon, Miss Ainslee
Heffner, A. D.
Higbie, Western
Hostetter, Harry B.
Hughes, Ralph E.
Joubert, Réne
Katterheinrich, V. E.
Kerr, S. H.
Keil, William E.
Keogh, Dr. Chester H.
Kern, Fred
Kleeman, Walter B.
Lankester, Stephen
Larson, Wallace*
Larson, Mrs. May*
Laughter, John
Lucas, Paul A.
Lynch, Dr. Charles C.
MacMichaels, Jack
Martin, William K.
Maul, Carl
McCurdy, R. B.
McWhorter, Thrumond
Moulton, Dr. Allen
Mowbray, Frank W.
Nothstine, Lloyd
Nothstine, R. M.
Oberlin, W. S.
Olson, Thorwald
Patterson, L. D.
Pease, H. Randall
Perry, George B.
Perry, Miss Clara
Peterson, Hilmer
Plank, Edward
Plyler, C. P.
Plyler, Lena B.*
Powers, Jack
Pringnitz, Louis A.
Reed, Fred T.
Richardson, Laurence E.
Riddle, Maxwell
Ritts, Elias E.
Ruskin, Dr. D. B.
Roush, J. R.
Savage, Terry
Schaufelberger, Hugo S.
Schmidt, William T.*
Scoonover, H. M.

Shepard, Ernest E.
Smiley, R. Z.
Spangler, Robert M.
Sprague, L. M.
Smith, Howard M.
Stafford, T. C.
Starke, James*
Stinchcomb, Keith V.
Stobie, George J.
Strobel, Lester A.
Stout, Lee H.
Stuit, Melvin R.
Stuyvesant, Allan R.
Tasche, Dr. Leslie W.
Todd, William V.
Ufford, Laurence J.
Ufford, Mrs. Laurence J.*
Ufford, Lucien H.
Ufford, Mrs. L. H.*

Van Buren, Robert S.
Vietto, John
Waller, Don
Wassau, Herb
Warren, D. M.
Wheeler, George C.
White, J. G.
Whitin, Paul Jr.
Whitworth, Jack L.
Whitworth, Genevieve
Williams, Charles L.
Williams, Mrs. Charles L.
Williams, Walden J.*
Wittig, Dorothy
Wood, E. L.
Yant, Dr. J. R.
Yoder, Ivan
Yoder, Paul

* Denotes Associate Member